D1503183

Quantitative Analysis for Health Services Administration

Quantitative Analysis for Health Services Administration

Charles J. Austin
Stuart B. Boxerman

with contributions by
Tee H. Hiett

AUPHA Press / Health Administration Press

Ann Arbor, Michigan 1995

04 03 02 01 00   6 5 4 3 2

Library of Congress Cataloging-in-Publication Data

Austin, Charles J., date.
   Quantitative analysis for health services administration / Charles J. Austin, Stuart B. Boxerman ; with contributions by Tee H. Hiett.
      p.   cm.
   This book is designed to be used with a basic computer software package in the field of quantitative decision analysis.
   ISBN 1-56793-032-8
   1. Health services administration—Mathematical models.   2. Health services administration—Statistical methods.   3. Operations research. I. Boxerman, Stuart B.   II. Hiett, Tee H.   III. Title.
   [DNLM: 1. Health Services—organization & administration—United States.   2. Decision Making, Organizational.   3. Management Information Systems. W 84 AA1 A9q 1995]
   RA394.8.A94   1995   362.1'068—dc20   95-9346

Health Administration Press
A division of the Foundation
   of the American College of
   Healthcare Executives
1021 East Huron Street
Ann Arbor, Michigan 48104
(313) 764-1380

Association of University Programs
   in Health Administration
1911 North Fort Myer Drive, Suite 503
Arlington, VA 22209
(703) 524-5500

To the memory of my late mother,
Catherine M. Austin,
whose love and support were with me
in all of my professional activities.
Charles J. Austin, Ph.D.

To my loving wife, Susan,
without whose support and understanding
this book would not have been possible.
Stuart B. Boxerman, D.Sc.

CONTENTS

Background and History: Operations
   Research/Management Science *5*
Management Problems of the 1990s *6*
A Framework for Quantitative Analysis
   in Decision Making *8*
Introduction to Models and Modeling *12*
Content and Format for the Remaining Chapters *14*

Part I Planning and Decision Making

Introduction of Case Problem *21*
An Overview of Break-Even Analysis *22*
Model Formulation, Quantification,
   and Data Requirements *24*
Solving the Case Problem *25*
Model Variations *26*
Description of Available Computer Software *27*

Part IV   Simulation: An Alternative Approach to Management Decisions

LIST OF TABLES

LIST OF FIGURES

LIST OF EXHIBITS

PREFACE AND ACKNOWLEDGMENTS

T HIS BOOK is intended to aid health services administrators in understanding principles and techniques of quantitative analysis and their application to management problems in health services organizations. The material is presented from a managerial perspective with emphasis on effective use of quantitative analysis in management decisions. Sufficient technical detail is included to enable the manager to become an intelligent consumer of these processes, one who can work comfortably with technical specialists in the organization.

The book is suitable as a textbook for a one-semester graduate or advanced undergraduate course in operations research/management science for students in health administration educational programs. It can also serve as a general reference book for health services administrators. Readers will require only a basic knowledge of college algebra and elementary probability and statistics.

The book is designed to be used with a basic computer software package in the field of quantitative decision analysis. Most examples and case problems are solved using *QuickQuant Decision Making and Production Management Software*. Health Administration Press has made special arrangements with the author and publisher of *QuickQuant* to provide the software manual and disk at a discount when ordered together with this book.

The authors are indebted to our friend and colleague, Dr. Tee Hiett, for contributing the excellent chapter on simulation (Chapter 11). Emily Sanford, a graduate student at the University of Alabama at Birmingham, provided invaluable assistance in library research and problem formulation. Particular thanks go to Carrie Harris for out-standing work on editing and manuscript preparation.

The support and encouragement of our faculty colleagues at the Medical University of South Carolina, the University of Alabama at Birmingham and Washington University are greatly appreciated.

The responsibility for any errors or oversights lies solely with the authors.

AN INTRODUCTION: MANAGERIAL PROBLEM SOLVING IN HEALTH SERVICES ORGANIZATIONS

D URING THE latter part of the twentieth century, the management of health services organizations has become a very demanding process. Health care executives face a complex set of competing pressures from a myriad array of stakeholders as they provide leadership for their institutions and for the communities they serve.

Facing a rate of escalation in the cost of health care that exceeds the general rate of inflation in the economy, health administrators have had to initiate programs of cost containment, productivity improvement, and prudent use of capital resources as an essential component of organizational strategy. Public and political concern about access to health care has grown with an increasing percentage of the population uninsured, underinsured, or concerned about the possible loss of coverage. At the same time, continuous quality improvement has become the battle cry of American industry, especially health services organizations. Consequently, health care executives and governing boards are faced with a delicate balancing act of simultaneously expanding access, improving quality, and reducing costs.

Outcomes measurement has become a second battle cry of health care policymakers and purchasers of care. Studies of the medical effectiveness of alternate treatment protocols are influencing reimbursement policies and purchase decisions. Health administrators must develop information systems and related analytical studies that demonstrate the quality and cost-effectiveness of services provided by their organizations.

Health care executives still face personnel shortages and maldistribution in selected clinical specialties and geographic areas. Many administrators in the 1990s face shortages of nurses and certain allied health professionals (physical therapists, clinical lab technologists). Rural hospitals and clinics still have problems attracting primary care physicians to serve their communities. Also, the rapid march of medical technology continues with new drugs, and expensive devices and procedures being developed at a rapid pace. Demands from physicians for access to the latest technology coupled with competitive pressure to have the most modern facilities available make programs of technology assessment essential but difficult to implement.

Major programs of health care reform are being debated at the national and state level as this book is being written. While the process of reform will likely be evolutionary rather than revolutionary, it seems certain that *changes* in the way health services are delivered and paid for will be continuous throughout the remainder of the 1990s and beyond. Whatever the shape of health care reform, government will play an increasing role in the regulation of the system, adding to the competing pressures faced by health care executives in managing their institutions and serving their communities.

In the face of these often competing pressures, health administrators must provide leadership while responding to the needs and demands of several stakeholder groups (see Figure 1.1). The needs of patients and the unmet needs of those in the community must be considered first. However, there are many other important stakeholders whom health care executives will ignore at their peril, including the governing board, the medical staff, employees of the organization, employers and purchasing cooperatives in the service area, third-party insurers, managed care organizations, political leaders, and consumer and community groups interested in health care for local citizens.

Stephen Shortell and his colleagues conducted an extensive study of strategic management in 370 hospitals that were components of eight health care corporations (not-for-profit and investor owned). In considering the strategic issues faced by these institutions and systems, the investigators determined that hospitals' executives required fundamental reorientation of their organizations, including

1. the need to move from a product orientation to a market orientation

Figure 1.1 Key Stakeholders

2. the need to move from a caretaking mentality to a risk-taking mentality
3. the need to move from operational management to strategic management (Shortell, Morrison, and Friedman 1990, 9)

In considering the competing pressures on health care organizations, the demands of many stakeholders, and the need for change and reorientation, certain management tasks take on critical importance. In broad categories, these include strategic and operational planning; optimum allocation of limited resources; managerial control to obtain appropriate quality, effectiveness, and efficiency in service delivery; and evaluation of the outcomes of services provided to the community.

These important managerial tasks can be carried out more effectively if information and quantitative analysis are used where appropriate in the decision-making process. Managers must, of course, recognize that there are costs and benefits associated with the use of quantitative analysis, and the projected benefits (tangible and intangible) should exceed the costs of analysis before studies are initiated or major systems developed. Not all problems lend themselves to quantitative analysis, and cultural or political factors may override a "rational" decision in some situations. However, the intelligent use of information and quantitative analysis will help to inform administrators and governing boards about the costs of suboptimal solutions in the face of political factors that influence major decisions:

> Even a decision that is heavily entrenched in political factors and special interests can likely be improved if the political actors involved are required to justify their respective positions in the face of certain fundamental facts about the costs and potential benefits of alternates available. Suboptimal decisions are often required in the face of reality, but a board of trustees and chief executive officer are still wise to keep as well informed as possible about the costs to the organization of suboptimization in the face of special interests or special problems. (Austin 1992, 6)

Quantitative analysis and the techniques described in this book can assist managers of health services at both the operational and strategic level. Some objectives served by quantitative analysis might include (but not be limited to) the following:

1. Improvement in the efficiency and effectiveness of operations within the health services organization
2. Support for strategic planning
3. Support for negotiations with external groups (e.g., managed care contracting)
4. Improvement in budgeting and allocation of resources
5. Helping to achieve an appropriate balance between competing goals and objectives (e.g., cost/quality trade-offs)
6. Evaluation of programs and services and their outcomes

This book is intended for use by students and practitioners who are, or aspire to be, generalist administrators. Consequently, the focus is on application of quantitative analysis to the managerial process rather than the detailed mathematical derivations of the techniques themselves. The goal of the book is to assist the generalist administrator in setting a tone within the organization and becoming an advocate for use of quantitative analysis where appropriate. We hope the material that follows will help the generalist administrator be an intelligent consumer of quantitative analysis, be comfortable in communicating and working with technical analysts in the organization, and be able to apply the results of analysis appropriately for decision making and control.

Background and History: Operations Research/Management Science

Quantitative analysis for managerial problem solving developed extensively during World War II when a group of scientists applied mathematical and statistical techniques to military planning, tactical problems, and weapons' utilization. Interdisciplinary teams of scientists worked on problems of this type in Britain and the United States and their work came to be known as "operational research":

> The techniques of operational research were developed during the late war for such purposes as improving the use of scarce resources, selecting routes and schedules for shipping, determining the best size for a convoy, and using bombs more efficiently. The basic features common to these studies were an analytical model of the problem; implementation of the model with statistical evidence; and the solution of the problem by finding the alternative policy which maximised or minimised the value of a particular equation in the model. (Feldstein 1963, 491)

Quantitative analysis for management problem solving expanded during the postwar period, and industrial organizations began using techniques that had been shown to be effective by the defense establishment. The term "operations research" came into general use, replacing its earlier counterpart, and in 1953 the Operations Research Society of America was formed. Professional and scholarly journals began to appear, and the term "management science" was coined to describe academic units in business and engineering schools where the principles and theories of this interdisciplinary science began to be codified and taught.

Operations research began to be applied to health care in the late 1950s and early 1960s. Charles D. Flagle of Johns Hopkins University was an early pioneer. In a classic paper published in 1962, Flagle describes four areas for application of operations research to management problems in health services delivery:

1. Demands for service—a set of problems related to demand for and utilization of facilities
2. Resource and logistics—the allocation, distribution, and utilization of personnel and materials to meet demands for service
3. Communications—the use of information in the patient care and management process
4. Organization and scope of services—improving the efficiency and quality of service delivery

After identifying problems faced by hospitals and other health services organizations, he concludes:

The interest of the health services in the potentials of operations research and management science is undoubtedly growing. . . . Those from operations research . . . will find in the health services a set of new colleagues, already familiar with the notion of multidisciplinary and broad system studies, alert and shrewd, and seeking solutions to old problems in new ways. (Flagle 1962, 627)

By the mid-1970s, the application of operations research to health care had expanded substantially (Shuman, Speas, and Young 1975; Fries 1976). However, much of the research was characterized as too theoretical and conducted by academicians whose "chief interests seem to be directed toward increasingly elegant . . . models and algorithms . . . rather than their possible application to real-world problems" (Shuman, Speas, and Young 1975, xii).

During the last twenty years, management engineers in health services organizations have applied principles of operations research and management science within their facilities, and the literature describing real-world applications has expanded. For example, Keller (1992) cites many studies published through 1991 in his bibliography on systems simulation.

Spurred by the "quality movement" in the U.S. industrial sector, programs of continuous quality improvement (CQI) were initiated by most health services organizations in the late 1980s and 1990s. CQI programs have revitalized the application of operations research techniques as tools for process improvement and quality management in the delivery of health services.

Over the years, national professional organizations such as the Operations Research Society of America (ORSA) and the Institute for Management Science (TIMS) developed active special interest groups on health care. These two organizations merged on January 1, 1995, to become INFORMS, the Institute for Operations Research and the Management Sciences. Management engineers and academicians involved in health care projects have their own speciality societies including the Society for Health Systems and the Healthcare Information and Management Systems Society (HIMSS).

Management Problems of the 1990s

There is no shortage of important areas for study and analysis in today's complex health care environment. Quantitative analysis can and will continue to be applied to improve the operations of patient service and administrative units of hospitals and other health services organizations. Managerial decisions related to resource allocation and utilization, scheduling of facilities and personnel, and other internal procedures will continue to be improved through simulation, modeling, and other tools of management science. Important areas of study for the 1990s and beyond will include the following:

1. *Clinical outcomes analysis.* A national program of research has been initiated to study the clinical effectiveness and costs of alternate treatment modalities for a number of high-volume medical procedures. These outcome studies will have a major impact on the way medical care is practiced and will directly influence purchase decisions and reimbursement policies by managed care organizations and other major purchasers of care. Health services organizations will need to carry out their own studies of clinical outcomes and have results available for accrediting agencies such as the Joint Commission on Accreditation of Healthcare Organizations (JCAHO) and for use in negotiations with managed care organizations, insurers, and other purchasers of health services.

2. *Case-mix analysis.* An increasing percentage of health services are being reimbursed on a prospective basis such as the fixed-payment reimbursement system by diagnosis-related groups (DRGs) employed by the Health Care Financing Administration for Medicare patients. Hospitals must be able to identify their costs and match resource consumption to units of service delivered if they are to survive financially. Quantitative analysis of an institution's case mix and simulation of the effects of changes in case mix or reimbursement rates (or both) can be important tools for management decisions in this environment (Hatcher and Connelly 1988).

3. *Managed care contracting.* Hospitals and other health service units increasingly face contract negotiations with managed care organizations, purchasing cooperatives, and large employers with self-insurance programs, all seeking deep discounts on the price of health services for their employees or subscribers. Quantitative analysis, simulation, and forecasting studies can provide critical management information on the financial effects of such contracts and their potential impact on demand for services.

4. *Continuous quality improvement.* As mentioned previously, quality improvement and management of quality have become the watchwords for most organizations in this country, particularly the providers of health care. Management engineers are assisting managers by conducting studies of quality, measuring patient satisfaction, and establishing systems for measuring and controlling service quality.

5. *Patient-focused care and process redesign.* With the increased emphasis on service quality, health care organizations are

reviewing the process by which services are delivered and redesigning internal procedures and processes to ensure that the primary focus is on the patient.

6. *Case management and resource scheduling.* With an increasing percentage of patient care reimbursed on a fixed-payment or discounted-price structure, health services organizations are seeking ways to reduce length of inpatient hospital stays and better coordinate services with other providers of care in their communities. Quantitative techniques are being used to coordinate and improve preadmission processing, scheduling of testing and treatments during an inpatient stay, and postdischarge planning.

These are only examples of the type of management problems and decisions that can be supported through quantitative analysis. Some of these problems are operational and others relate to important strategic decisions that must be made by the health care executive.

Operations research and management science studies have been criticized because of their focus on operational rather than strategic issues. Kirkwood disputes this criticism and states that "quantitative operations research methods can, in fact, bring more clarity and quality to the strategic decision making process" (1990, 748). He points out that strategic decisions often involve conflicting objectives, multiple stakeholders, alternatives that differ both qualitatively and quantitatively, longer time horizons, and higher degrees of uncertainty and risk. These are the types of decisions for which judicious investment in careful study and analysis can have the greatest payoff. However, before quantitative analysis has a major impact on strategic decision making in health services organizations, the chief executive officer and other senior managers must have sufficient knowledge and comfort with the use of these methods to champion their use and apply them to strategic planning and selection of strategic options.

A Framework for Quantitative Analysis in Decision Making

The procedures followed in quantitative analysis for managerial decision making parallel the scientific method used by investigators in basic and applied research. There are also close parallels to the process of systems analysis employed by management engineers in the study of organizational processes.

The general framework for analysis includes the following steps:

1. Preliminary observation
2. Problem definition

3. Model formulation
4. Determination of data requirements and availability
5. Preliminary examination of data
6. Selection of appropriate analytical techniques for solving the problem
7. Selection of computer software to be used in the analysis
8. Running the analysis
9. Analyzing and interpreting results (sensitivity analysis)
10. Application of results to management decisions
11. Postimplementation evaluation of decision

Step 1: Preliminary Observation

Organizational problems or decisions that may lend themselves to quantitative analysis must first be identified by managers involved in the decision process. If managers believe that analysis and modeling may be useful to the decision, they will consult with appropriate technical staff (management engineers and analysts) who will conduct preliminary observation and discussion with individuals in the organization to be studied. The purpose of this step is twofold: (1) to determine (in a preliminary way) the feasibility of the study and (2) to help establish the basic parameters for defining the problem to be solved.

Step 2: Problem Definition

This step involves establishment of objectives for the analysis stated in functional (managerial) terms. For example, objectives for a study of managed care contracting might be stated as follows:

> The purpose of this study is to estimate the financial impact of contracting with the Tri-County Health Maintenance Organization for the provision of inpatient services to members of the HMO for two years. Objectives of the analysis include (1) estimating incremental demand for inpatient services and additional revenue generated as a result; (2) estimating incremental costs associated with provision of these services; and (3) determination of the level of service required for net revenue from the contract to be positive.

During this step in the process, analysts should assist managers in stating clear *functional* objectives and should avoid the tendency to begin casting the problem in mathematical terms.

Step 3: Model Formulation

Working from a clearly stated set of functional objectives, the analysts assigned to the study should develop a model of the process to be studied. A model is a representation of some real-world process expressed in physical, graphical, or mathematical terms. For the managed care contracting example described in Step 2, the model might take the form of a set of mathematical equations expressing the relationship between incremental costs and incremental revenue resulting from the proposed new contract. A more detailed introduction to models and modeling is included later in this chapter.

Step 4: Determination of Data Requirements and Availability

Quantitative analysis requires data as basic input to the process. A critical step in the process (and one frequently ignored or minimized in many operations research textbooks) is the determination of (1) what data are required for the model or analytical process and (2) where these data can be obtained. In the previously cited example, data will be required on the direct and indirect costs of providing inpatient services from the internal information systems of the hospital considering the managed care contract. In addition, the hospital must have access to external data from the HMO on the number of members, basic demographic characteristics of the membership, and previous utilization history, if available. Ideally, much of the internal data required for analyses can be obtained from the organization's information systems, but unfortunately this is not always the case. Collection of data required for an analysis is possible but is often an expensive and time-consuming process. If extensive data collection is required, then management must determine if the costs involved will be worth the benefits to be obtained from conducting the study. Special attention is given in this book to the question of data availability and linkage to an organization's information systems to support modeling and analysis.

Step 5: Preliminary Examination of Data

Frequently in the conduct of a management study, much can be learned by preliminary examination of raw data before any models are constructed and solved. Simple grouping of information using descriptive statistics (e.g., means and frequency distributions) along with "eyeballing" of data may provide important insights into the problem to be solved and may result in reformulation of study objectives or model development. In the managed care contracting problem described above, if information on inpatient utilization of the HMO membership is inadequate or not available, then it may be necessary to obtain additional data from external sources on utilization of services by other populations with similar demographic characteristics (age, sex, income, etc.) to the HMO membership in order to develop estimates of probable utilization.

Step 6: Selection of Analytical Techniques

Given a problem definition, study objectives, model formulation, and preliminary examination of data, then those conducting the study will determine the appropriate techniques to be used for the analysis. For the managed care contracting example, the analysts might choose to use the mathematical technique of break-even analysis. What-if analysis might also be employed if the hospital wanted to forecast alternative cost/revenue break-even points using different assumptions about future utilization patterns by the HMO membership.

Step 7: Selection of Computer Software

Operations research relies heavily on the computational power of computer technology for modeling and problem solving. Most studies will involve computer processing of data. Although some analysis may require the development of special computer programs, most studies can be carried out using standard computer software available from commercial or nonprofit sources. Thus, one step in the process is determining and obtaining appropriate computer software for problem analysis and solution. References on available operations research software are included throughout this book.

Step 8: Running the Analysis

After obtaining data, completing the final model formulation, and selecting computer software, the next step in the process is running the model and obtaining a solution. This often involves multiple repetitions (iterations) of the process as preliminary results are obtained and modifications are made to the model.

Step 9: Analyzing and Interpreting Results

This step, often referred to as *sensitivity analysis*, should be carried out as a joint effort of the analysts and managers involved in the study. It involves careful examination of the results of the analysis in terms of its sensitivity to study design, quality of data, assumptions built into the model, and any compromises necessary in data collection and quantification (Warner, Holloway, and Grazier 1984, 40).

Step 10: Application of Results to Management Decisions

After managers and analysts are satisfied with the sensitivity of the results and alternative runs have been made if necessary, managers can use the information obtained from the analysis to support management decisions. For the managed care contracting example, information on cost/revenue break-even points under alternative assumptions about utilization should assist the hospital CEO and other executives in reaching a decision about whether or not to contract with the HMO. Data obtained in the analysis may also help the management team formulate its negotiating strategy with regard to prices and discounts to be included in the contract.

Step 11: Postimplementation Evaluation

The use of analytical studies should be evaluated at an appropriate point after the results have been applied to organizational decisions. For the example used in this section, management should evaluate its decisions regarding the managed care contract after the contract goes into effect to determine how well the break-even analysis has forecast actual financial experience in the provision of inpatient services under the contract.

Introduction to Models and Modeling

Models are important tools for operations research and management science projects, particularly decision support studies. As stated previously, a model is a representation of some real-world process expressed in physical, graphical, or mathematical terms. Models necessarily simplify the representation of an operation, process, or decision, and include only those aspects that are of primary importance to the problem under study.

Physical models often are used in construction or remodeling projects to aid in the design of functional work space for a building. Graphic models are used to display relationships among variables through charts, trend lines, histograms, and a variety of other graphic formats, aided by computer terminals with high-resolution color displays. Multimedia workstations add audio and video capabilities to the stationary display capabilities of computer monitors. Most operations research projects in health services organizations will employ mathematical models, a set of equations that relate significant variables in an operation to the outcome of the process or decision under study.

Mathematical models fall into two general categories: deterministic and probabilistic (or stochastic). Deterministic models are used in situations where chance plays a small or insignificant role and the effects of a given action will be closely determined by the values of the elements of the model. In using deterministic models and analytical techniques, the process or decision is treated as if there is no uncertainty involved. In a materials management system, medical supply items are automatically reordered when inventory levels reach a predetermined minimum quantity. A requisition for reordering is automatically generated and determined by the inventory quantity on hand. There is no uncertainty involved in the process. Certain types of resource allocation problems in health services organizations can be solved using deterministic models and analysis.

Most often, however, management decisions must be made under conditions of uncertainty, and stochastic (probabilistic) models are used for this type of analysis. With stochastic models, probabilities must be determined and assigned to the elements of the model, and the results are conditioned by statements of statistical limits and confidence. Forecasting demand for services in hospitals and health care organizations often involves stochastic models in which statistical data on previous utilization patterns for the same or a comparable population are used in a set of prediction equations. The forecasting model cannot determine exactly what the demand will be, but uncertainty can be reduced through appropriate use of sampling and statistical distributions for the elements of the model.

> Models cannot make management decisions. However when properly applied, they can play an important supporting role: In most cases, modeling makes available more information about the possible consequences of alternative actions. In some cases, its role lies in more precisely predicting such consequences. In a few cases, modeling may help the administrator choose that one or those few alternatives which best meet specified criteria. Modeling, however, should only be viewed as an aid to decision making (Warner, Holloway, and Grazier 1984, 20).

There are limitations to the modeling process. Some major constraints and caveats include the following:

1. Not all management decisions and operational problems lend themselves to quantitative modeling. Decisions may be concerned primarily with institutional politics and may not easily lend themselves to quantitative analysis. It is unwise to try to fit every management problem into an operations research framework.

2. Some models oversimplify the real-life problem and produce a questionable solution. Oversimplification usually results from complexity of the problem (large number of complex and interrelated variables), inability to quantify key elements of the

problem, or both. Use of no model may be preferable to use of an oversimplified one that produces misleading results.

3. In some cases, the costs of modeling could exceed the benefits obtained from the solution. Preliminary analysis of the problem should help identify the cost of data collection and analysis as well as the time required to carry out the study. Analysts should advise managers of situations where they believe the cost and time factors will be excessive.

4. Solutions to managerial problems through modeling may call for significant organizational change. Managers and analysts must take into consideration important human factors and elements of the organizational culture in evaluating how to implement such change in a labor-intensive service organization.

5. Some models may be too sophisticated for the organization's existing or potential databases. If a model requires accurate information on elements of cost for a given department but no cost-accounting system is in place, the organization must weigh the costs of a special, one-time cost-finding study against the benefits to be obtained from running the model. Lack of data availability is a major constraint for many health services organizations. Those who plan their information systems and decision support systems with the needs of operational and strategic management in mind will be far ahead in their ability to employ quantitative analysis effectively.

A final caveat is to avoid modeling for the sake of modeling. Managers should become active partners with technical staff in identifying appropriate applications and ensuring that results are implemented in the organization.

Content and Format for the Remaining Chapters

The remaining chapters of this book cover several major operations research techniques and models that have been applied to management problems in health services organizations. No attempt has been made to cover all types of models or control processes with potential application to health care. Problems involving direct application of statistical theory to health services (e.g., regression analysis for forecasting demand) have, with a few exceptions, not been included. Material of this type is generally covered in separate courses on statistics or epidemiology for students in health services administration.

As mentioned in the preface, this book is written from a managerial perspective and is intended for use by students and practitioners in the field of health services administration. Consequently, the emphasis is on problem identification and description, model formulation, data capture, solution using computer software packages, analysis, and application of results. No attempt is made to present detailed mathematical formulas for all the techniques described, particularly when good computer programs are available to carry out these computations. The emphasis is on the *application* of quantitative techniques rather than their mathematical derivations. Sufficient technical detail on model assumptions and limitations is included to enable the manager, working in conjunction with technical specialists in the organization, to become an intelligent consumer of these processes.

Specific quantitative techniques are categorized and covered in three major sections:

* Part I, "Planning and Decision Making"—problems involving strategic planning, operations improvement, and business planning
* Part II, "Resource Allocation"—problems involving allocation of resources and staffing
* Part III, "Control"—management control systems for project scheduling, continuous quality improvement, and materials management

Each chapter of the book employs a case example problem, introduced at the beginning of the chapter and used throughout for illustrative purposes. Some simplifications of the case problems have been made to facilitate classroom use of the material. Additional examples are used to illustrate special points and variations in the basic models presented. All of these case problems, examples, and end-of-chapter exercises are fictitious. However, each chapter includes one or more actual health care applications described in mini-case formats. A standard chapter format includes the following sections:

* Introduction of Case Problem
* An Overview of the Model
* Model Formulation, Quantification, and Data Requirements
* Solving the Case Problem
* Model Variations
* Description of Available Computer Software
* Analysis, Interpretation, and Application of Results to Management Decisions
* Case Studies from the Literature

Discussion questions and problems and a list of references and additional readings conclude each chapter.

This book is designed to be used with a basic computer software package in the area of quantitative decision analysis. Several good packages are available for both classroom and operational use, and many of these would be suitable as companion volumes to this text. A decision was made to use the package *QuickQuant Decision Making and Production Management Software* to illustrate the solution to most case problems and examples. Sample *QuickQuant* output will be found in most chapters, coded in color. Only text material directly related to *QuickQuant* is color-coded. Health Administration Press has made special arrangements with the author and publisher of *QuickQuant* to provide the software manual and disk at a discount when ordered together with this book.

Discussion Questions

1.1 Why has quantitative analysis in support of health services management increased in importance in the 1990s?

1.2 List five general types of health care management decisions that can be improved through judicious use of quantitative analysis.

1.3 Define "operations research." What are the origins of this interdisciplinary science?

1.4 Why should "generalist" administrators in health services organizations learn about operations research and management science? What role(s) should the generalist manager play in the conduct of an OR study?

1.5 Describe the general process followed in quantitative studies conducted to support management decision making.

1.6 Define the term "model" as used in operations research. What are some of the limitations of the modeling process in health care?

References

Austin, C. J. 1992. *Information Systems for Health Services Administration*, 4th Ed. Ann Arbor, MI: AUPHA Press/Health Administration Press.

Feldstein, M. S. 1963. "Operational Research and Efficiency in the Health Service." *The Lancet* (2 March): 491–93.

Flagle, C. D. 1962. "Operations Research in the Health Services." *Circulation Research* 11 (September): 621–28.

Fries, B. E. 1976. "Bibliography of Operations Research in Health-Care Systems." *Operations Research* 24 (March): 801–14.

Hatcher, M. E., and C. Connelly. 1988. "A Case Mix Simulation Decision Support System Model for Negotiating Hospital Rates." *Journal of Medical Systems* 12 (6): 341–63.

Keller, L. F. 1992. *Systems Simulation Bibliography*. Orem, UT: PROMODEL Corporation.

Kirkwood, C. W. 1990. "Does Operations Research Address Strategy?" *Operations Research*, 38 (5): 747–51.

Shortell, S. M., E. Morrison, and B. Friedman. 1990. *Strategic Choices for America's Hospitals*. San Francisco: Jossey-Bass Publishers.

Shuman, L. J., R. D. Speas, and J. P. Young. 1975. *Operations Research in Health Care: A Critical Analysis*. Baltimore: The Johns Hopkins University Press.

Warner, D. M., D. C. Holloway, and K. L. Grazier. 1984. *Decision Making and Control for Health Administration: The Management of Quantitative Analysis*. 2d ed. Ann Arbor, MI: Health Administration Press.

Additional Readings

Ackoff, R. L., and M. W. Sasieni. *Fundamentals of Operations Research*. New York: John Wiley & Sons, Inc., 1968.

Cook, T. M., and R. A. Russell. *Introduction to Management Science*. Englewood Cliffs, NJ: Prentice-Hall, Inc., 1977.

Gass, S. I. "The Many Faces of OR." *Journal of the Operational Research Society Ltd.* 42 (1991): 3–15.

Griffith, J. R. *Quantitative Techniques for Hospital Planning and Control*. Lexington, MA: D. C. Heath and Company, 1972.

Starr, M. K., and I. Stein. *The Practice of Management Science*. Englewood Cliffs, NJ: Prentice-Hall, Inc., 1976.

$$\boxed{\text{I}}$$

Planning and Decision Making

T HE QUANTITATIVE techniques described in Chapters 2, 3, and 4 have particular applicability to planning and managerial decisions in health services organizations. They have the potential to assist health care executives on strategic issues such as estimating the impact of service expansion or contraction in a competitive market place.

Break-even analysis, described in Chapter 2, is an important technique for financial forecasting. It is a planning tool used to estimate the point at which revenue will exceed the costs of providing services, given different estimates of demand for these services. It is particularly useful in estimating the impact of proposed managed care contracts. A recent survey of alumni of two graduate programs in health administration ranked break-even analysis in the top ten of topics of greatest importance for inclusion in the financial management curriculum (Clement and Gapenski 1994).

Decision theory (Chapters 3 and 4) helps the manager address the difficult problem of making complex decisions under uncertainty. Today's health care environment is marked by complexity and rapid change. The techniques described in these two chapters can assist decision makers in reducing the risks associated with their decisions through careful analysis of available data.

Some decision variables are under the manager's control, but many others are not (environmental and political factors, demographic changes, market response to new services, to mention just a few). Decision analysis provides a tool for choosing among alternative strategies, for making discrete choices among probabilistic events. Frequently, additional information can result in an improved decision, but information is not cost free. Decision analysis can be used to help determine the value of additional information given the uncertainties that surround the decision. This capability can be particularly important in periods of rapid change, when past history may no longer be a good predictor of future events.

Reference

Clement, J. P., and L. C. Gapenski. 1994. "Health Care Financial Management Curriculum Content: Views of Practitioners and Academics." *Journal of Health Administration Education* 12 (1): 39–50.

BREAK-EVEN ANALYSIS

W HETHER OPERATING as nonprofit organizations or as investor-owned facilities, health care organizations must generate revenue to pay for the costs of providing services. Matching revenue generated to the costs of providing specific services is an important element of prudent financial management if the organization is to remain solvent.

Break-even analysis is a useful and frequently employed technique for determining the volume of service needed to ensure that revenue generated will exceed costs. This chapter describes this quantitative technique and its application to financial planning and management in health services organizations.

Introduction of Case Problem

Jefferson Community Health Plan is a nonprofit, full-service health maintenance organization operating in a tri-county region of a midwestern state. Jefferson is considering the development of a new satellite health center to serve a growing suburban area in its service region.

Consideration of the new facility has been stimulated by discussions between Jefferson and ARGO Industries. ARGO is a growing electronics company with a new plant in the suburban area where the health center would be located. ARGO Industries has proposed contracting with the Jefferson Community Health Plan to offer comprehensive health services for its employees on an annual capitated payment basis. The capitated HMO plan would be offered as one of two health insurance options to ARGO's 2,500 employees.

Financial officers of Jefferson Community Health Plan have estimated the costs associated with the new health center as follows:

1. Construction costs (to be amortized over ten years) $1,800,000
2. Capital equipment (to be amortized over ten years) $500,000
3. Fixed annual operating expenses (utilities, maintenance, central administration, security, etc.) $370,000
4. Variable annual operating costs per 100 enrollees in a capitated plan (based on financial data from other Jefferson units):
   a. Supplies and materials $15,000
   b. Clinical staff $76,000
   c. Support services $18,000
   d. Contract services (inpatient care) $48,000

In preliminary negotiations, ARGO has proposed contracting with Jefferson at an annual capitated payment of $1,800 per enrollee in the HMO. ARGO's vice president for human resources has conducted an employee survey, and she estimates that initial annual enrollment would be 1,500 (employees and dependents).

1. Would the proposed new contract with ARGO cover the full costs for the new satellite health center?
2. If not, how many additional enrollees from the community would be required for the health center to break even financially?
3. To break even on the basis of the ARGO contract, what capitated payment should Jefferson negotiate?

An Overview of Break-Even Analysis

A preliminary examination of the requirements for this case suggests that break-even analysis may be an appropriate technique for Jefferson Community Health Plan managers to employ in answering the questions about the proposed new facility and contract with ARGO Industries.

Break-even analysis matches total revenues with total costs as the volume of service increases. Figure 2.1 is a generalized diagram of a break-even chart. Total revenue and total costs are plotted against volume of service. At point *A* on the diagram, volume of service is such that total revenue and total costs are exactly equal. This is the break-even point, below which the service would operate at a loss and above which the service would be provided at a profit (or with positive

Figure 2.1   Break-Even Chart

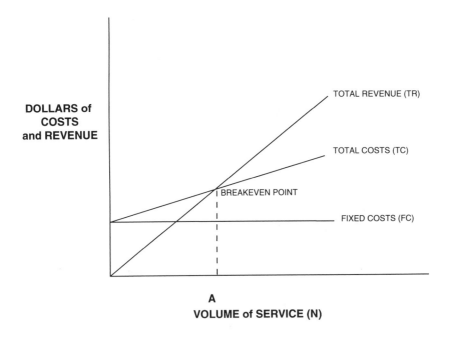

net revenue). Note that in this diagram, both costs and revenue are linear and are represented as straight lines. This means that costs and revenue increase by a fixed amount for each unit of service added. This is not always the case, and further discussion of nonlinear functions is included later in the chapter.

Costs associated with break-even analysis will fall into two categories: fixed costs and variable costs. *Fixed costs* are those that are incurred regardless of how much service is provided. They include items such as the capital costs of equipment and facilities, overhead items such as utilities and maintenance, and minimum personnel requirements to operate the facility. *Variable costs* are items of expense that relate to the direct cost of providing care and are expressed as costs per unit of service delivered. Note that in Figure 2.1, fixed costs are plotted as a horizontal line in which the dollar value remains the same regardless of the volume of service. *Total costs* are the sum of fixed costs and variable costs and are plotted as a straight line that increases as the volume of service increases.

The mathematical formulas involved (assuming straight-line cost and revenue functions) are as follows:

$$TR = REV \times N$$
$$VC = COST \times N$$
$$TC = VC + FC$$

where

TR	= total revenue
REV	= revenue generated for each unit of service
N	= the number of units of service provided
VC	= variable costs
$COST$	= the cost incurred for each unit of service
TC	= total cost
FC	= fixed costs

Model Formulation, Quantification, and Data Requirements

Jefferson Community Health Plan must be able to generate certain data sets in order to compute the break-even point for the proposed new satellite facility. Some of these data elements can be obtained from existing information systems, and others must be estimated or obtained through surveys. The available data include the following:

1. Data from existing information systems: variable costs for operating the new facility, obtained from the cost-accounting system for other units of the health plan:

Supplies and materials	$15,000 per 100 enrollees
Clinical staff costs	$76,000 per 100 enrollees
Support services	$18,000 per 100 enrollees
Contract services	$48,000 per 100 enrollees
Total variable costs	$157,000 per 100 enrollees or $1,570 per enrollee per year

2. Data obtained from estimates:
    a. Revenue per enrollee based upon preliminary discussions with ARGO $1,800 per enrollee per year.
    b. Fixed costs for the new satellite center:

(1) Construction	$1,800,000
(2) Equipment	$ 500,000
	$2,300,000 amortized for ten years = $230,000 per year
(3) Fixed operating costs	$370,000 per year
Total fixed costs	$600,000 per year

3. Data obtained from a survey of its employees by ARGO Industries: 1,500 employees are likely to enroll in the Jefferson Plan if the new facility is built.

Note that in this case problem, the data are readily available because the Jefferson Plan had cost-accounting systems in place and could draw on experience from existing units within the Plan. In some cases, health services organizations may not have reliable cost-accounting information systems, and special cost-finding studies might be required before the break-even analysis could be carried out.

Solving the Case Problem

Management analysts at Jefferson now have the necessary data and problem formulation. The solutions requested by management can be computed as follows.

Total revenue (TR) = $1,800 \times N$
Fixed costs (FC) = $600,000$
Variable costs (VC) = $1,570 \times N$
Total costs (TC) = $FC + VC = 600,000 + 1,570 \times N$

The break-even point will occur when total revenue equals total costs. This is computed by setting $TR = TC$ and solving the equation for N:

$$TR = TC$$
$$1,800N = 600,000 + 1,570N$$
$$N = 600,000/(1,800 - 1,570)$$
$$= 600,000/230 = 2,609 \text{ enrollees per year}$$
$$\text{required to break even}$$

Note that the general formula for computing the break-even point is

$$N = FC/(REV - COST)$$

A break-even chart for this case problem is shown in Figure 2.2.

Since ARGO estimates that 1,500 enrollees would sign up, the contract with ARGO alone (at $1,800 per enrollee) would not be sufficient to operate the facility at a profit. For 1,500 enrollees, the loss is computed as follows:

TR = $1,800 \times 1,500$ = $2,700,000$
TC = $600,000 + ($1,570 \times 1,500)$ = $2,955,000$
$LOSS$ at 1,500 enrollees = ($ 255,000)

To break even at the $1,800 price, Jefferson would have to attract additional enrollees from other sources in the community. The number

Figure 2.2   Case Problem—Break-Even Chart

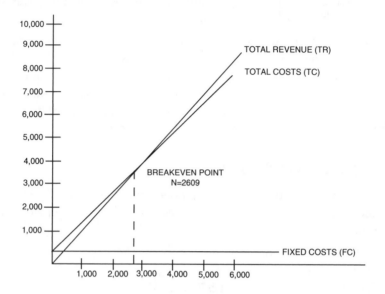

of additional enrollees required would equal the break-even quantity minus the number from ARGO:

$$2,609 - 1,500 = 1,109 \text{ additional enrollees required}$$

To break even on the basis of the proposed ARGO contract alone, Jefferson would have to negotiate a higher price per enrollee. The required price is computed as follows:

$$
\begin{aligned}
TC &= TR \\
VC + FC &= TR \\
(COST \times N) + FC &= REV \times N \\
(1,570 \times 1,500) + 600,000 &= REV \times 1,500 \\
2,955,000 &= REV \times 1,500 \\
REV &= 2,955,000/1,500 \\
&= \$1,970 \text{ per enrollee required for break-even with 1,500 enrollees}
\end{aligned}
$$

Model Variations

Total costs and total revenue are straight-line functions in this example problem. There are situations where this may not be the case. Figure 2.3 is a generalized break-even chart where total costs are linear, but total revenue is a nonlinear function in which revenues start to level off as volume increases. This situation might arise when the health care organization is pressed into offering deep discounts for services rendered in negotiations with a large purchasing cooperative representing multiple companies in its service area.

Note that in Figure 2.3 there are two break-even points, designated as *A* and *B* on the chart. Services would only be profitable on that part of the graph between points *A* and *B*.

Another common variation on the break-even chart is shown in Figure 2.4. In this situation, total costs follow a pattern known as a step function. This situation could occur when fixed costs remain the same for a certain volume of service and then jump upward when a new threshold level of service occurs.

This often is the case when additional personnel must be added to provide service at different threshold levels. Note that in Figure 2.4, there are five break-even points designated as *A*, *B*, *C*, *D*, and *E*. The organization will not reach a level of continuous profit until point *E* on the diagram is reached.

Description of Available Computer Software

Determination of break-even points requires simple algebraic computation as described in the previous section, "An Overview of Break-

Figure 2.3 Break-Even Chart with Nonlinear Functions

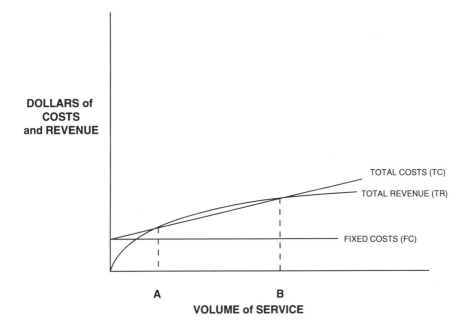

Figure 2.4 Break-Even Chart with Cost Step Function

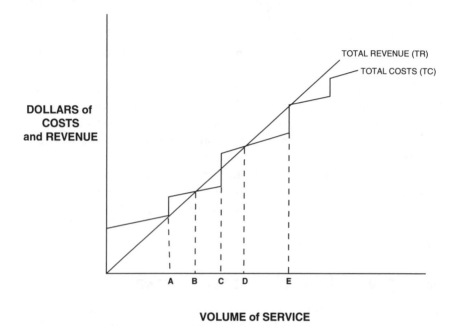

VOLUME of SERVICE

Even Analysis." No special computer software is needed for carrying out these calculations. However, spreadsheet software packages may be useful in specific applications of break-even techniques as described below.

What-If Analysis

In using break-even analysis to estimate the financial impact of proposed new services or expansion of existing services, managers of health care organizations may wish to use multiple estimates of key variables, including the price to be charged in generating revenue (REV), the variable cost per unit of service $(COST)$, the fixed cost for providing service (FC), or some combination of these.

Spreadsheet software can be a helpful tool in developing a matrix of assumptions and estimates, and comparing the impact of these alternatives on total costs, total revenue, and break-even points. Exhibit 2.1 is a sample spreadsheet showing this type of analysis for the case problem used in this chapter.

Some commonly used spreadsheet and statistical software packages include Lotus 1-2-3, Excel, and @Risk. The names and addresses of software vendors referenced in the text are included in Appendix B.

Exhibit 2.1   Case Problem—Spreadsheet

	A	B	C	D	E	F	G
Notes	**Revenue**	**Cost**	**Fixed Costs**	**Break-Even N**	**Variable Costs**	**Total Costs**	**Total Revenue**
1	1,800	1,570	600,000	2,608.696	4,095,652	4,695,652	4,695,652
2	2,000	1,570	600,000	1,395.349	2,190,698	2,790,698	2,790,698
3	1,800	1,500	600,000	2,000.000	3,000,000	3,600,000	3,600,000
4	1,800	1,570	500,000	2,173.913	3,413,043	3,913,043	3,913,043

Notes: 1 = Original case problem
2 = Change price to $2,000 per enrollee
3 = Reduce variable costs to $1,500 per enrollee
4 = Reduce fixed costs to $500,000

Spread Sheet Formulas: Column D $= \dfrac{C}{A-B}$
Column E $= B \times D$
Column F $= C + E$
Column G $= A \times D$

Analysis, Interpretation, and Application of Results to Management Decisions

As a result of the analysis described above, managers of the Jefferson Community Health Plan have improved information to apply to decisions about the proposed new satellite facility and potential contract with ARGO Industries.

At an initial negotiated capitation rate of $1,800 per enrollee, revenue from a contract with ARGO would not, by itself, meet the fixed and variable costs of the new satellite center. Jefferson must evaluate the potential ability to attract 1,109 additional enrollees during the first year to break even. Or, as an alternative, Jefferson could attempt to negotiate a higher capitation amount from ARGO, with $1,970 per enrollee required to break even on the basis of the ARGO contract alone.

Management can now consider several options for additional action:

1. Conduct market research in the community to estimate the potential for additional enrollees if the satellite center is built.
2. Further discussions with ARGO about the potential to increase the capitation amount for employees who would enroll in the Plan.

3. Consideration of the possibility of operating with an initial loss during the first year of operation with a subsidy to come from other sources of revenue or from operating reserves (if any).
4. Combinations of the above three options.

Management could also carry out what-if analysis, as illustrated in Exhibit 2.1, to simulate the impact of potential cost-reducing actions.

Without break-even analysis and consideration of alternative courses of action, as described in this case, Jefferson Community Health Plan would be in the difficult position of making an important strategic decision with inadequate management information.

Case Studies from the Literature

Pharmaceutical Services (Caselnova et al. 1985)

R. E. Thompson General Hospital in El Paso, Texas, is a 335-bed county hospital. The Texas Tech University Regional Academic Health Center is located adjacent to it. Ten years ago, a full-time faculty oncologist was hired by the academic health center to implement a clinical pharmacy service in the health center's outpatient oncology clinic with the director of pharmacy at R. E. Thompson.

The pharmacists' role in the program was designed to go beyond the traditional dispensing one. Pharmacists were to have direct involvement in the administration of IV therapies in the oncology clinic on a biweekly basis. The clinics were staffed by a team consisting of two pharmacists, three nurses, two faculty physicians, and a rotating resident physician. The pharmacists provided an array of clinical and distributive services, including patient monitoring and medication storage, preparation of antineoplastic agents, and administration of the clinic.

After a one-year trial period, principles of break-even analysis were used to justify the costs of the program with pharmacy participation. The new service would break even when sales equal expenses, or when there is a no-profit, no-loss operation. When determining the fixed costs of the model, the existing facilities such as building space, clinic fixtures, and examining rooms were excluded. It was assumed that personnel and equipment costs incurred by the academic medical center would have been required regardless of the involvement of the pharmacy department; thus, they too were excluded as fixed costs. Only the fixed and variable costs associated with providing pharmaceutical services were included in the break-even analysis. Because the pharmacy department used existing facilities, expenses for fixed costs were reduced. Bid prices and invoices were used to determine supply costs.

Break-even analysis showed that the pharmaceutical services in the outpatient oncology clinic would break even at 1,153 patient visits. An annual revenue of $64,308 would have to be generated to break even. The clinic treated 1,162 oncology patients during the one-year trial period. The pharmacy generated annual revenue of $64,793 and profit of $485. The program would remain an integral part of R. E. Thompson's pharmaceutical services.

Clearly, the two institutions benefited financially from implementing the new program. The hospital received a cost-effective program believed to reduce liability because of the increased professional handling of neoplastics. Moreover, the involvement of trained hospital pharmacists was beneficial to both outpatients and the clinic staff. The patients benefited from the convenience of receiving chemotherapy on an ambulatory basis and from the health care expertise of a multidisciplinary team of physicians, nurses, and pharmacists.

Nursing Home Occupancy (Goggans 1981)

The Sooner Nursing Home is a 100-bed, long-term care facility operating in the Southwest region of the United States. At the time of this study (1981), the facility operated at 100 percent occupancy. The patient mix was 80 percent Medicaid and 20 percent private pay with a $24.66 per day revenue charge for both classes of patients. Accordingly, there was a "lid" on the revenue per patient, and the organization was limited to increasing net income through either reducing costs or increasing the number of patients served in the facility.

Break-even analysis was employed to determine the profitability of the facility at different occupancy levels and to examine the financial feasibility of expanding the institution. Most out-of-pocket costs, such as professional salaries, food, and linen, were considered variable since they are a function of activity or patient census. Fixed costs included salaries and wages for full-time personnel, taxes, rent, interest, and depreciation.

The model suggested that the facility needed to generate $720,000 gross revenue to break even. This could be achieved at an 80 percent occupancy rate. If the owners expanded the facility by 50 percent (to 150 beds), fixed expenses would increase by approximately 40 percent. Variable expenses would decrease about 5 percent as a percentage of revenue, because of economies of scale due to increased capacity. At this level, the facility would need to generate a revenue of $896,000 at a 66 percent occupancy rate to break even. A net income of $204,000 would be achieved if the nursing home operated at 100 percent occupancy.

The results of the model provided information to assist management in evaluating options. Management must also consider the time that it may take to achieve the 100 percent occupancy and resultant net income upon expansion. Managerial implications are multifaceted, and a balance between time constraints and financial gains must be achieved.

Additional Reports from the Literature

Logical expansion of a dental practice typically involves the addition of equipment and personnel. However, an analytic assessment of practice needs is necessary before embarking upon any expansion. Caplan (1988) describes the use of break-even analysis to estimate the potential level of profitability derived from the addition of a hygienist and associated profit centers to a dental practice.

Break-even analysis was used to study home- and community-based long-term care services offered in more than two dozen controlled experiments conducted over the last 30 years (Weissert and Cready 1989). The authors found that health care costs for the treatment group averaged only 14 percent more than for the control group across all studies. Because patient benefits were found to be so minimal, they would have to be valued at an exceedingly high rate to break even from a social perspective. However, improved operating efficiency might make cost-accounting break-even an achievable goal. Needed improvements included better targeting of high-risk patients and better utilization controls on home and community care services.

Owens and Neubecker (1992) examined methods of implementing stress thallium cardiac imaging services at a group physicians' office. The hospital involved had three alternatives from which to choose in order to provide the office with an imaging camera: (1) purchasing a new camera, (2) purchasing used equipment, or (3) leasing a new camera. Break-even analysis was used to determine the most financially feasible method without sacrificing the quality of services. Using budgeted income statements, net present value, and the internal rate of return for each method, it was determined that the method of choice, without sacrificing quality of service delivery, was to purchase a used camera.

Carney et al. (1989) employed break-even analysis to examine the adequacy of Medicare reimbursement in covering hospice costs. Hospice costs are high during the first few days after enrollment; therefore, a long period of enrollment is required for per diem reimbursement to cover costs. It was determined that the length of stay for the hospice to break even is greater than the median length of stay. Generally, the length of time prior to break-even is longer for Medicare recipients than for the total patient population. The authors proposed two changes to alleviate this problem: supplement the per diem rate with an additional fixed amount of reimbursement for each hospice enrollee, or seek higher reimbursement for the first few days of hospice care.

Gapenski (1989) describes a hypothetical situation in which a hospital's single-standing ambulatory clinic has failed to generate the patient volume that it is capable of handling. A break-even analysis may be employed to determine the profitability of three scenarios: (1) expand the clinic's marketing program, (2) extend the clinic's service hours, or (3) extend the clinic's service hours and expand the clinic's marketing program. Analysis of patient revenue per visit, variable costs, and fixed costs reveals that the expanded marketing plan offers the lowest fixed costs and takes the most advantage of excess capacity. Thus, it is the most profitable at any given level of incremental visits.

Discussion Questions

2.1 Define *break-even analysis*. When would it be appropriate to use?

2.2 Define *fixed costs* and *variable costs*. Give examples of each. How are the two related?

2.3 When is a break-even point reached?

2.4 Are total costs and total revenue always linear functions? If not, give an example.

2.5 What is a *step function*? When does it occur?

Problems

2.1 A regional clinical laboratory is considering offering a new test to its clients. The test can be offered in one of two ways. Plan A would use existing equipment but would require more personnel time per test. Plan B would have higher fixed costs because of the need to purchase new capital equipment, but personnel requirements would be lower. Cost and revenue data are as follows:

	Plan A	Plan B
Fixed costs	$10,000 per year	$50,000 per year
Variable costs	$15 per test	$7 per test
Price (based upon competitor data)	$30 per test	$30 per test

Requirement: Prepare a break-even chart and compute the break-even points for both plans. At what volume of service (if any) would Plan B become more profitable?

2.2 A community hospital is considering offering executive physical examinations to local companies as part of its occupational health program. Initial cost and revenue estimates for the new services are as follows:

Fixed costs per year	$12,000
Variable costs per exam	$ 140
Price per exam	$ 250

Requirement: Use a computer spreadsheet program to build a what-if table that computes and displays the answers to the following questions:

a. How many exams would be required for the proposed new service to break even?

b. If the price were reduced to $220 to better meet competition in the area, what would be the new break-even point?

c. If the hospital were to provide the service to only one large company and that company was willing to guarantee 100 exams per year through a contract, what price per exam would the hospital need to charge to break even on the contract?

2.3 A regional medical center is considering the expansion of the emergency room to accommodate an expected increase in patient loads. Cost and revenue estimates for the first year of the project are as follows:

Fixed costs (includes five-year amortization of construction costs)	$250,000
Variable costs per ER visit	$ 55
Average revenue per ER visit	$ 165

The medical center estimates that the volume of emergency room activity will increase by 2,000 visits the first year, and this number will grow by 20 percent per year thereafter. The chief financial officer estimates that fixed and variable costs will increase by 5 percent per year due to inflation. However, because of growing regulatory pressure and managed care contracting, average revenue per visit is not expected to increase for the next five years.

Requirement: Use a computer spreadsheet program to build a five-year table of costs and revenue.

a. In which year will the facility break even?

b. Compute total profits for the five-year period.

2.4 As director of a home health agency, you are in the process of evaluating the possible addition of physical therapy services for your clients. Two options are under consideration. Option A would be to contract with an independent practitioner at a contract rate of $60 per home visit. Option B would involve hiring a staff physical therapist with costs estimated as follows:

Automobile lease	$ 400 per month
Salary and fringe benefits	Range of $4,000–$5,000 per month
Medical supplies and gasoline	Range of $7–$10 per home visit

Using Medicare reimbursement rates, the average payment for a physical therapy home visit would be $75 per visit.

Requirement:

a. Compute the break-even point for Option B with the most optimistic cost estimates, and with the most pessimistic cost estimates.

b. Your best estimate of demand for this service is 90 visits per month. At this level of service, would you choose Option A or B? Why?

References

Caplan, C. M. 1988. "Practice Expansion: The Decision-Making Process and Related Strategies." *Dental Clinics of North America* 32 (January): 85–97.

Carney, K., N. Burns, and B. Brobst. 1989. "Hospice Costs and Medicare Reimbursement: An Application of Break Even Analysis." *Nursing Economics* 7 (January–February): 41–60.

Caselnova III, D. A., S. H. Dziebra, M. S. O'Neill, K. R. Dillon, and P. C. Farley. 1985. "Implementing Clinical Pharmacy Services in an Outpatient Oncology Clinic." *American Journal of Hospital Pharmacy* 42 (June): 1348–52.

Gapenski, L. C. 1989. "Analysis Provides Test for Profitability of New Services." *Healthcare Financial Management* 43 (11): 48, 52–54, 58.

Goggans, T. P. 1981. "The Use of Break Even Analysis in Long-Term Care Facilities." *The Journal of Long-Term Care Administration* 9 (Fall): 1–9.

Owens, R. G., and J. S. Neubecker. 1992. "Starting Up Stress Thallium Cardiac Imaging Services." *Radiology Management* 14 (Winter): 33–39.

Weissert, W. G., and C. M. Cready. 1989. "A Prospective Budgeting Model for Home-Community-Based Long-Term Care." *Inquiry* 26 (Spring): 116–29.

Additional Readings

Starr, M. K., and I. Stein. *The Practice of Management Science.* Englewood Cliffs, NJ: Prentice-Hall, Inc., 1976. Note particularly Unit 3, "Break Even Analysis."

Warner, D. M., D. C. Holloway, and K. L. Grazier. *Decision Making and Control for Health Administration: The Management of Quantitative Analysis.* 2nd Ed. Ann Arbor, MI: Health Administration Press, 1984. Note particularly Chapter 3, "Simple Deterministic Analysis."

3

DECISION ANALYSIS WITH PAYOFF TABLES

HEALTH CARE executives and managers spend a great deal of their time making decisions. The complexity and significance of these decisions range from the relatively simple question of which of three food service contractors will be chosen to provide meals for patients and employees, to the much more difficult question of whether an institution should merge with two other local hospitals.

Regardless of their level of complexity, all decisions share certain attributes. First, they all involve two or more alternatives available to the decision maker. In fact, the number of alternatives may be either finite or infinite. Second, the decision problem typically involves uncertainty. For example, deciding whether to implement a new program is made complicated by the uncertainty of demand for this program. Finally, the consequences of a particular decision can be specified in combination with each of the possible realizations of uncertainty. Thus, for example, a knowledge is assumed of the consequences of implementing a new rehabilitation program just weeks before development of a technique for regenerating spinal cord tissue in paraplegics.

Skeptics will argue that seasoned executives have the experience and intuitive sense to make appropriate decisions using a "seat of the pants" technique. Furthermore, they would say, politics and policy often drive the decision-making process. These assertions are not lacking in truth. Nevertheless, it can be argued that quantitative models do provide useful *support* tools that can be beneficial to the decision maker. These models are discussed in detail in a number of decision theory texts (see, for example, Clemen 1991). The purpose of this chapter, along with the next one, is to provide an introduction to the quantitative decision-making process. This chapter presents algebraic models, while graphical models are discussed in Chapter 4.

Introduction of Case Problem

As a case problem, consider once again Problem 2.4 from the previous chapter. Assume now that the home health agency is considering *three* options for adding physical therapy services for their clients:

Option A: The home health agency would contract with an independent practitioner to provide PT services on a fee-for-service basis.

Costs: The PT will be paid $60 per home visit.

Option B: The home health agency would hire a staff physical therapist, provide the therapist with an automobile, and cover medical supplies and gasoline.

Costs: • Monthly PT salary of $4,000
• Monthly automobile lease payment of $400
• Medical supplies and gasoline allowance of $7 per visit

Option C: The home health agency would utilize an independent contractor to provide PT services, provide the contractor with an automobile and fringe benefits, and pay a medical supply and gasoline allowance.

Costs: • PT services of $35 per visit
• Monthly automobile lease payment of $400
• Fringe benefits (including insurance) of $200 per month
• Medical supplies and gasoline allowance of $7 per visit

Under all three alternatives the average payment for a PT home visit is $75 per visit.

The home health agency is trying to decide for which of these three options the maximum profit would be realized. In searching for the best option, the agency realizes that the demand for services influences the optimum choice. The agency would like to better understand the relationship between demand and optimum choice. Specific questions that the agency has posed include the following:

1. With no knowledge of demand for PT services, which option should be chosen?
2. For a given probability distribution of demand for PT services, which option provides maximum profit?
3. How sensitive is the choice of best option to the probability distribution of demand?

4. How much value should be placed on a system that can forecast future demand for PT services?

An Overview of Decision Analysis

It has been indicated that quantitative models provide useful support tools that assist executives in their role as decision maker. Decision analysis provides a logical framework for constructing these models, particularly when there is uncertainty associated with the decisions. For convenience, the discussion can be separated into two parts— single-stage decision-analysis problems and multistage decision-analysis problems.

Single-Stage Decision Analysis

In a single-stage decision-analysis problem, the executive has a number of alternatives available from which one must be chosen. In the simplest case, the number of alternatives available is finite and the choice is a discrete one. More complicated is the case in which an infinite number of choices is available from which one must be chosen. An example is a staffing decision in the clinical laboratory. Possible staffing might range continuously from 4 staff hours (0.5 full-time equivalent) to 24 staff hours (3 full-time equivalents). In this case, the optimum choice is really one of setting a *level* of service. While such problems are common in health care applications, the focus in this discussion is on the discrete case.

Once an alternative has been chosen, the executive knows that Nature—a powerful force beyond the executive's control—will cause one of several alternative events to take place. The executive does not know specifically which event Nature will choose, but it is assumed that the number of such possible events is also discrete. Typically this collection of possible events is referred to as the **alternative states of Nature**. For some decision makers, the sequence of Nature's selecting a particular state in response to the decision maker's having chosen a given alternative is viewed as a "two-person game" between the decision maker and Nature.

Each "decision alternative/state of Nature" combination has an economic consequence, or "payoff," associated with it. Depending on the particular problem, this payoff might be a profit or a loss, and it might be expressed in dollars or some other resource measure. Sometimes these payoff values are transformed into units that express the value or **utility** that is placed on the particular "decision alternative/state of Nature" combination. Whether viewed as outcomes of a game or parameters of the decision-making model, these "payoff" values provide a guide for searching for the optimum decision to choose.

Finally, decision-analysis problems can be further characterized according to one's knowledge of the probability values associated with the occurrence of the states of Nature. If one has no knowledge of these probabilities, the problem is known as **decision making under uncertainty**. If, on the other hand, the probability value for each state of Nature is known (or can be approximated in some way), the problem is known as **decision making under risk**. Both of these problem categories will be considered in the forthcoming discussions.

Multistage Decision Analysis

In a multistage decision-analysis problem, once Nature "chooses" a particular state in response to the executive's choice of a decision alternative, the executive is then called on to make at least one more decision. Each of the executive's subsequent decisions could be followed by additional "choices" by Nature. For example, the case problem could be expanded to include the executive's choosing from among several alternative marketing strategies after deciding on the method for providing PT services. The subsequent alternative states of Nature would then be the range of possible demands for service that each marketing strategy might create.

Multistage decision-analysis problems are usually more easily modeled with graphical techniques than with algebraic approaches. Therefore, a discussion of these models is deferred to the next chapter.

Model Formulation, Quantification, and Data Requirements

The discussion now turns to formulating a model for the single-stage decision-analysis case problem. The approach is to use a **payoff matrix** in order to display the components of the problem. This matrix is a rectangular array of numbers, c_{ij}, that represent the consequence or "payoff" resulting when the decision maker chooses a particular alternative, a_i, and Nature adopts a particular state, s_j. The alternatives available to the decision maker correspond to the rows of the matrix, and the states of Nature correspond to the columns. The general form of such a payoff matrix is presented in Table 3.1.

For the case problem, the payoff matrix will have three rows since the executive has three possible ways of providing PT services. The columns, or states of Nature, relate to possible values of demand. The number of columns in the matrix depends on the number of

Table 3.1 General Form of Payoff Matrix

Decision Alternative	States of Nature			
	s_1	s_2	$\ldots$	s_n
a_1	$c_{1,1}$	$c_{1,2}$	$\ldots$	$c_{1,n}$
a_2	$c_{2,1}$	$c_{2,2}$	$\ldots$	$c_{2,n}$
$\vdots$	$\vdots$	$\vdots$	$\vdots$	$\vdots$
a_m	$c_{m,1}$	$c_{m,2}$	$\ldots$	$c_{m,n}$

possible values assumed for demand. Obtaining this number is not always straightforward, and often one must make assumptions. Perhaps the best source is historical data. If the service under consideration is a new service, however, such historical data might not be available. In this case a marketing study could be beneficial. It is not unusual for intelligent guesswork to play an important role, too, in this part of the analysis.

Assume that, using a combination of marketing analysis, analysis of competitors' volume data, and some careful assumptions, it has been determined that there are only four possible values of monthly demand for PT services: 30, 90, 140, or 150 visits. Assume further that the relative frequency with which each of these demands occurs is also available from health facilities utilization data compiled in a recent statewide study. These relative frequencies provide reasonable estimates of the probabilities associated with each value of monthly demand, which for the case problem are assumed to equal 0.1, 0.4, 0.2, and 0.3, respectively. The discussion below will look at appropriate solution techniques for cases when these probabilities are *not* known (decision making under uncertainty) as well as those in which the probabilities *are* known (decision making under risk).

For the case problem, the cell values or "payoffs" will denote the **net** profit associated with each alternative method for providing PT services corresponding to each possible demand for PT services. A total of 12 such values of net profit (3 alternatives × 4 possible values of demand) must be computed. Denote the value of **monthly** demand by d.

For the first alternative—contracting with an independent practitioner at a contract rate of $60 per visit—the net profit per month is

$$\text{net profit/month} = (\$75 - \$60) \times d$$
$$= \$15 \times d$$

When demand, for example, is 30, net profit/month = $450.

For the second alternative—a monthly salary of $4,000, monthly car allowance of $400, and gasoline and medical supply payment of $7 per visit—the net profit per month is

$$\text{net profit/month} = -(\$4{,}000 + \$400) + (\$75 - \$7) \times d$$
$$= -\$4{,}400 + \$68 \times d$$

Again, when demand is 30, the net profit/month is equal to $-\$4{,}400 + \$68(30)$ or $-\$2{,}360$.

Finally, for the third alternative—monthly car allowance of $400, monthly fringe benefits (including insurance) of $200, a contract rate of $35 per visit, and gasoline and medical supply payment of $7 per visit—the net profit per month is

$$\text{net profit/month} = -(\$400 + \$200) + (\$75 - \$35 - \$7) \times d$$
$$= -\$600 + \$33 \times d$$

In this case, when demand is 30, the net profit/month is equal to $-\$600 + \$33(30)$, or $390.

These formulas can be evaluated for the remaining values of demand, and the results can be tabulated in a "payoff matrix," as shown in Table 3.2. This payoff matrix serves as the model for the home health agency to use in determining which payment option is best when they add physical therapy services for their clients. (When the problem is viewed under risk, the assumed probability values associated with the states of Nature are added to the model.)

Solving the Case Problem

The payment option that is best for the home health agency depends on the "criterion of goodness" it uses to evaluate alternative options. These criteria, in turn, can be divided into two groups—a group that does not require knowledge of the probabilities associated with each state of Nature, and a group that does require this knowledge. As

Table 3.2 Case Problem Payoff Matrix

Decision Alternative	States of Nature (monthy demand)			
	30	90	140	150
A	$ 450	$1,350	$2,100	$2,250
B	−2,360	1,720	5,120	5,800
C	390	2,370	4,020	4,350

was mentioned earlier, these two groups give rise, respectively, to decisions made under uncertainty and decisions made under risk. The case problem will be solved based on each of these goodness criteria.

Decisions under Uncertainty

Decision makers face a decision under uncertainty when they are unwilling or unable to specify the probabilities associated with the states of Nature. In such a case, a number of approaches are available. They tend to span the spectrum from extreme optimism to extreme pessimism on the part of the decision maker.

The **maximax criterion** represents a very optimistic approach to decision making. Under this criterion, each decision alternative is evaluated according to the profit that will be realized under the most optimistic conditions. The decision with the highest profit under such conditions is deemed optimum. For the case problem, a column of values is constructed corresponding to the maximum profit that could result for each decision alternative (Table 3.3).

According to the maximax criterion, then, Alternative B would be the optimum choice since it has the largest maximum profit ($5,800). A decision maker adopting this criterion is surely an optimist who feels that generally things "will go his way." It should be noted that, for problems formulated in terms of costs rather than profits, the procedure involves tabulating a column of minimum costs and choosing the decision alternative with the lowest minimum. In such a case, the criterion is known as the **minimin criterion.**

For the decision maker convinced that Nature deals with a vengeance, an appropriate criterion might be the **maximin criterion.** For each decision, the lowest profit is determined. The optimum choice is the decision that has the largest minimum profit. Again, for the case problem the computations would proceed as shown in the "Min. Profit" column in Table 3.3. The optimum decision alternative would

Table 3.3 Case Problem Payoff Matrix with Maximum and Minimum Profit Values

Decision Alternative	States of Nature (monthy demand)				Max. Profit	Min. Profit
	30	90	140	150		
A	$ 450	$1,350	$2,100	$2,250	$2,250	$ 450
B	−2,360	1,720	5,120	5,800	5,800	−2,360
C	390	2,370	4,020	4,350	4,350	390

be Alternative A since it has the largest minimum profit ($450). The decision maker who adopts this strategy is generally a pessimist who is certain that whatever alternative he or she chooses, Nature will choose a state most detrimental to the decision maker.

For problems formulated in terms of costs, the corresponding criterion is known as the **minimax criterion**. The procedure is to identify the largest cost associated with each alternative and to choose as the optimum decision the one with the smallest maximum cost. It is this minimax criterion that provides justification for the purchase of insurance policies or extended warranties since the maximum repair expenditure with the policy is considerably lower than the maximum possible repair expense without the warranty coverage. (This approach totally ignores the fact that these expensive repairs might be very rare. When the chance of such expensive repairs is added to the problem, the result is a problem involving decision making under risk. Such problems are considered shortly.)

The **minimax regret** criterion represents a third approach available to the home health agency. For payoff tables containing profit values, "regret" represents the amount of profit lost by choosing a nonoptimal alternative for a given state of Nature. That is, for each cell within a given column of a payoff matrix (column j, for example), values of regret, $r_{i,j}$, are obtained from

$$r_{i,j} = [\text{largest profit in column } j] - c_{i,j}$$

For example, the maximum profit that is obtainable when Nature "chooses" State 1 is $450. If, when Nature "chooses" State 1, one were to choose Alternative C, the result would be a profit of only $390, or $60 less than the maximum possible. Therefore, $r_{3,1} = \$60$.

Proceeding in this way, the decision maker can compute the regret table shown in Table 3.4. Each regret value is analogous to an opportunity cost associated with not making an optimal decision for a given state of Nature. In fact, some authors refer to regret as "opportunity loss."

The goal now is to minimize regret, but unfortunately the exact state that Nature is going to choose is not known. The common procedure is to assume the worst. To that end, the decision maker identifies the maximum regret that is incurred for each decision alternative. These values are included in Table 3.4. The solution is to choose the alternative that has the minimum value of maximum regret. For the case problem, the optimum alternative using the minimax regret criterion, then, is Alternative C since it has the smallest maximum regret value ($1,450).

Table 3.4 Case Problem Table of Regret Values

Decision Alternative	States of Nature (monthy demand)				Max. Regret
	30	90	140	150	
A	$ 0	$1,020	$3,020	$3,550	$3,550
B	2,810	650	0	0	2,810
C	60	0	1,100	1,450	1,450

Decisions under Risk

The discussion now turns to those problems for which the probability distribution of the states of Nature is either known or can be assumed. In this case it is possible to compute an expected profit for each alternative decision. The criterion, then, will be to choose the action that has the largest expected profit. (For problems involving costs, of course, the decision with the lowest expected cost would be chosen).

Recall in the model formulation that the probabilities associated with the states of Nature were assumed to have values of 0.1, 0.4, 0.2, and 0.3, respectively. The expected profit for Alternative A is then given by

$$\$450 \times 0.1 + \$1,350 \times 0.4 + \$2,100 \times 0.2 + \$2,250 \times 0.3$$

or $1,680. The expected profit values for the remaining decision alternatives are similarly computed, and the results are now summarized:

Decision Alternative	Expected Profits
A	$1,680
B	$3,216
C	$3,096

Alternative B—hiring a staff physical therapist at a monthly salary of $4,000 and providing an automobile, medical supplies, and gasoline— yields the highest expected monthly profit. For the assumed demand distribution, this would be the optimum choice.

Rather than looking at expected profits, the home health agency decision makers could focus their attention on expected regrets. Referring to Table 3.4 (and recalling the probabilities associated with the states of Nature), observe that the expected regret associated with Alternative A would be computed as

$$\$0 \times 0.1 + \$1,020 \times 0.4 + \$3,020 \times 0.2 + \$3,550 \times 0.3$$

which equals $2,077. The expected regret values for the three decision alternatives are presented below:

Decision Alternative	Expected Regret
A	$2,077
B	$541
C	$661

The goal of the decision maker is to minimize the expected regret. Notice that Alternative B, which yields the maximum expected profit, also provides the minimum expected regret of $541. The fact that the same alternative maximizes expected profit *and* minimizes expected regret is not accidental! This will always be the case. In addition, the minimum expected regret value, $541 in the case problem, has special significance, as will be seen later in the chapter.

Although the analysis of payoff tables involves only basic algebra, decision makers often find it convenient to use a computer package to perform the computations. Exhibit 3.1 displays the *QuickQuant* solution to the case problem. Notice that this program has adopted a convention of equating the rows of a matrix to the possible states of Nature (referred to as "Events") and the columns to the alternatives available to the decision maker (known as the "Acts"). The values that have been obtained thus far "by hand" can be found in the printout.

For each "Act" (alternative) *QuickQuant* displays the expected payoff, expected opportunity loss (regret), minimum payoff, and maximum opportunity loss. In the overall summary, the optimum strategies based upon the decision criteria discussed above are also shown. Observe that these solutions match those obtained with a hand solution.

One quantity in the printout has not yet been discussed. *QuickQuant* reports the maximum likelihood act—the alternative that maximizes profit when the state of Nature with the highest probability occurs. State 2 (demand = 90) has the highest probability (0.4). For this state, Alternative C yields the highest profit ($2,370).

Having determined that Alternative B yields the highest expected profit (and minimum expected regret), the home health agency is now interested in learning how sensitive the optimum alternative is to the assumed probability distribution of demand for PT services. When there are only two possible states of Nature, studying the relationship between the state of Nature probabilities and the optimum decision alternative is relatively straightforward and unambiguous. Expected profit can be plotted against the probability of the first state of Nature for each decision alternative. (With only two states of Nature, the

Exhibit 3.1   Case Problem—*QuickQuant* Solution

```
                        Problem Data

---------------------------------------------------------
             |            | Act 1    Act 2    Act 3
   Events    |Probability | Alt. A   Alt. B   Alt. C
-------------+------------+-------------------------------
1 Dem =  30  |    .1      |   450    -2360     390
2 Dem =  90  |    .4      |  1350     1720    2370
3 Dem = 140  |    .2      |  2100     5120    4020
4 Dem = 150  |    .3      |  2250     5800    4350
---------------------------------------------------------


                     Act Summary

                   Act 1      Act 2      Act 3
                   Alt. A     Alt. B     Alt. C
-----------------------------------------------------
Expected Payoff     1680       3216       3096
Exp. Oppor. Loss    2077        541        661
Minimum Payoff       450      -2360        390
Max. Oppor. Loss    3550       2810       1450


                   Overall Summary

Maximum Expected Payoff:  3216 (Act 2--Alt. B)
Minimum Expected Opportunity Loss:  541 (Act 2--Alt. B)
Maximin Payoff:   450 (Act 1--Alt. A)
Minimax Opportunity Loss:  1450 (Act 3--Alt. C)
Maximum Likelihood Act: 3 (Alt. C)    Most Likely Event: 2 (Dem = 90)
Expected Value of Perfect Information: EVPI = 541
```

probability of the second state is just one minus the probability of the first).

Assume that the home health agency is fairly confident that a monthly demand of 90 and 140 will occur with probability 0.4 and 0.2, respectively. However, they are less certain about the probabilities associated with a monthly demand of 30 and 150. To that end, they are interested in performing a sensitivity analysis for these probabilities. Observe that since their analysis involves only two probability values, the procedure outlined above can be followed.

Notice that the probabilities of a demand of 90 and 140 sum to 0.6 (0.4 plus 0.2). Since the four demand probabilities must sum to 1, then the sum of the probabilities of a demand of 30 and 150 will equal 0.4 (1 minus 0.6). If the probability that monthly demand equals 150 is denoted by the symbol p_{150}, then the probability that monthly demand equals 30 will equal 0.4 minus p_{150}. It is possible, then, to compute the expected monthly profit for each alternative as a function of p_{150}. For Alternative A this expected profit is given by

$$\$450 \times (0.4 - p_{150}) + \$1,350 \times 0.4 + \$2,100 \times 0.2$$
$$+ \$2,250 \times p_{150} = \$1,140 + \$1,800 \times p_{150}$$

Expressions for the expected profit with the other two alternatives can be obtained in a similar manner. A graph of the results appears in Figure 3.1.

From the graph it is obvious that Alternative A is never favored since one of the other alternatives always yields a higher value of expected profit. In fact, the expected profit with Alternative C is higher than that obtained with Alternative A for all values of p_{150}. As a result, Alternative A is said to be *dominated* by Alternative C. In a given analysis, a strategy that has been shown to be dominated can be dismissed from further consideration.

The sensitivity analysis focuses, then, on Alternatives B and C. Notice that Alternative C is optimum for values of p_{150} that are less than 0.27143. When p_{150} is greater than this value (as it is in the case problem), Alternative B is preferred. Thus, if the value of p_{150} were to drop slightly from its original 0.3, Alternative B would no longer yield the largest expected monthly profit. The home health agency would find it worthwhile to verify that their probability assignments are appropriate.

Figure 3.1 Expected Profit vs. P(Demand = 150)

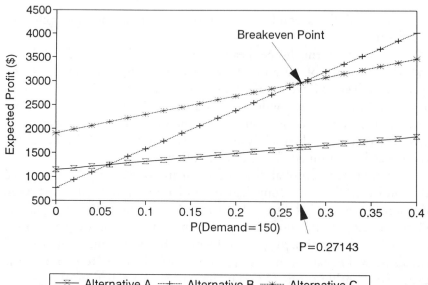

A general sensitivity analysis of the case problem would involve four states of Nature. While several analyses could be performed, based upon a different pair of monthly demand values, the format of an appropriate graph that looks at all four demand values simultaneously is not so immediately clear. Possible approaches to the general problem of sensitivity analysis are discussed in decision-analysis texts (see, for example, Clemen 1991, Chapter 5).

Having decided upon the optimal alternative based upon **maximum expected profit** (or minimum expected regret), the home health agency begins to explore the possibility of utilizing some type of forecasting to help identify the demand for the following month. The question arises whether the availability of such information could improve upon the expected monthly profit. The answer follows from a discussion of the notion of **information**.

Assume for the purposes of discussion and further model elaboration that the home health agency has the ability to vary their choice of options for providing PT services to their clients from month to month. (In practice such variations might only be feasible for longer time intervals.) Assume further that at the beginning of each month they are able to perfectly identify the demand for PT services for the coming month (that is, they have **perfect knowledge** of the upcoming state of Nature). Then, their optimum strategy would be to choose the decision alternative having the highest profit (or minimum regret) for the given state of Nature that is about to occur.

For example, if they knew that demand would equal 30 in the coming month, they would choose Alternative A, thereby achieving a profit of $450. A demand of 90 would lead to their choosing Alternative C and a subsequent profit of $2,370. Likewise, demands of 140 and 150, respectively, both result in a choice of Alternative B, and profits of $5,120 and $5,800, respectively. Since the states of Nature occur according to their probability distribution, the availability of this forecast information produces an expected monthly profit of

$$\$450 \times 0.1 + \$2,370 \times 0.4 + \$5,120 \times 0.2 + \$5,800 \times 0.3$$

or $3,757. This quantity is known as the **expected value under perfect information**. It represents the expected monthly profit with a **perfect forecasting device**.

The home health agency can now address its final concern—how much value it should place on a forecasting system. Without the system, the agency would simply adopt Alternative B and earn an expected monthly profit of $3,216. With a perfect forecasting device (and the flexibility to alter its contractual arrangement with its supplier of PT services on a month-to-month basis), the agency can earn an expected monthly profit of $3,757. The difference, $541, is known as the **expected value of perfect information**. It represents the maximum that the agency should pay for a perfect forecasting system. Of course, a forecasting system that is not perfect would be worth less. Notice that *QuickQuant* also reports this value of $541, which it designates by EVPI (see Exhibit 3.1).

Recall that Alternative B had the minimum value of expected regret, which was equal to $541. The fact that the expected value of perfect information equals the minimum expected regret is no coincidence. This will always be the case.

The home health agency has now answered its four original questions. A discussion of how to apply these answers to its proposed PT services is presented later in this chapter. First, however, an alternative perspective on the case problem will be considered.

Model Variations

The decision-making criteria considered thus far have all been applied to a payoff matrix containing cell entries expressed in units of net **dollar** profit. In many cases the relative value that a decision maker places upon a given quantity of dollars is not equal to the face value of the currency. A decision maker's relative value or preference for money is known as **utility**. Suppose that the home health agency decides to replace the net dollar profits in their payoff matrix with utility values in order to observe the impact on choice of optimum alternative for providing PT services to their home health clients.

In order to obtain specific utility values for each cell of their payoff matrix, the home health agency must quantify its preference for money. This preference is expressed in the form of a **utility function**, which provides a relationship between dollars and utility. Without any loss of generality, the lowest dollar value of interest can be assigned a utility value of 0 and the largest dollar value can be assigned a value of 100. Intermediate dollar values have a corresponding utility value reflective of the decision maker's attitude toward risk. The process of obtaining these intermediate values is quite subjective and is known as **utility function assessment**.

Detailed descriptions of methods for assessing utility functions can be found in numerous texts on decision analysis (see, for example, Clemen 1991). A brief overview of three approaches will be presented here.

In the **certainty-equivalent** approach, the decision maker is offered two alternatives: (1) win X dollars with certainty, or (2) win Y_1 dollars with probability 0.5 or Y_0 dollars with probability 0.5. To be useful for utility function assessment, Y_1 and Y_0 must have known utility equivalents. They are initially set equal, respectively, to the largest and smallest dollar values of interest (since their corresponding utilities have been defined), and the decision maker is asked to identify the "minimum value of X for which he or she is indifferent between the two alternatives." Because of this indifference, the utility associated with alternative 1 can be equated to the expected utility of alternative 2, that is,

$$U(X) = 0.5 \times U(Y_1) + 0.5 \times U(Y_0).$$

In this way a third point on the utility curve can be obtained, the utility associated with X. Additional points on the curve can be found by successive applications of this methodology.

In the **probability-equivalent** approach, the decision maker is once again presented with two choices: (1) win X dollars with certainty, or (2) win Y_1 dollars with probability p or Y_0 dollars with probability $(1 - p)$. Again, to be useful for utility function assessment, Y_1 and Y_0 must have known utility equivalents. In this case the value of X is specified, and the decision maker is asked to indicate the value of p that makes him or her indifferent between the two choices. The utility associated with X can then be obtained from

$$U(X) = p \times U(Y_1) + (1 - p) \times U(Y_0)$$

By considering different values of X, the decision maker can obtain additional points on the utility curve.

A third approach utilizes a particular mathematical function as the basis for the utility assessment. One common choice is an exponential model in which one of the parameters is used to represent the degree to which the decision maker is risk-averse. Of course, other functional relationships can be chosen. It must only be demonstrated that the model reflects the decision maker's attitudes about risks well enough to support the analysis of a particular decision under consideration.

If utility is a linear function of dollars, the graph of the utility function will be a straight line. The decision maker favoring such a utility function is said to be a "risk-neutral" decision maker, and such an individual is advised to choose a decision alternative strictly on the basis of dollar values. A decision maker is said to be "risk-averse" if he or she favors a utility function having a graph that always lies *above* the risk-neutral line. This utility function has the property that utility values are increasing but at a diminishing rate of increase. Risk-averse decision makers are typically conservative individuals. Finally, a decision maker whose utility function lies *below* the risk-neutral line is said to be "risk-seeking." In this case, utility increases at an increasing rate.

Examples of these three types of utility functions derived for the case problem are shown in Figure 3.2. The risk-averse function was chosen first so that the utility associated with −$2,360, $U(-2,360)$, equals 0; $U(5,800)$ equals 100; and the curve lies above the risk-neutral line. Many functions would satisfy these criteria. For the present discussion, an arbitrary but reasonable choice is

$$U(dollars) = \sqrt{dollars + 2,360} \times \frac{100}{\sqrt{8,160}} \qquad \text{(E 3.1)}$$

This curve has been chosen for illustrative purposes only. No claims are made about the decision maker's underlying risk attitude other than the fact that the decision maker is risk-averse. The risk-neutral line is simply that straight line that connects the points (−2,360, 0) and (5,800, 100). Finally, the risk-seeking curve was chosen to have these same two points as endpoints and to lie below the risk-neutral line. From the many possible analytical curves, the following was chosen for the case problem:

$$U(dollars) = 1.2332 \times 10^{-6} \times dollars^2 + 0.008013 \qquad \text{(E 3.2)} \\ \times dollars + 12.04176$$

Again, this is an arbitrary choice for illustrative purposes only. When the risk-averse utility function (Equation 3.1) is applied to the net

Figure 3.2 Case Problem—Utility vs. Dollars

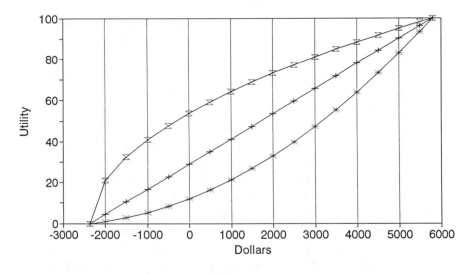

profit figures in the case problem payoff matrix (Table 3.2), the matrix of utility values displayed in Table 3.5 is obtained. Note that Alternative C has the largest expected utility and would be considered the optimum choice using a criterion of maximum expected utility.

On the other hand, applying the risk-seeking utility function to the case problem payoff matrix (Table 3.2) yields the matrix of utility values displayed in Table 3.6. Now, Alternative B has the largest expected utility and would be the optimum choice.

The best strategy for the home health agency to employ in order to add physical therapy services to their service offerings appears to depend on the decision criterion employed in performing their decision analyses. This point is discussed further later in the chapter.

Description of Available Computer Software

The analysis of payoff tables can be performed with QSB+, STORM, *QuickQuant*, or AB:QM. In addition, as seen in this chapter, the algebraic equations involved in the analyses can easily be programmed in a spreadsheet environment.

Table 3.5 Case Problem—Matrix of Utility Values: Risk-Averse Utility Function

Decision Alternative	States of Nature (monthy demand)				Expected Utility
	30 $p = 0.1$	90 $p = 0.4$	140 $p = 0.2$	150 $p = 0.3$	
A	58.68	67.43	73.93	75.16	70.17
B	0.00	70.71	95.74	100.00	77.43
C	58.05	76.14	88.42	90.68	81.15

Table 3.6 Case Problem—Matrix of Utility Values: Risk-Seeking Utility Function

Decision Alternative	States of Nature (monthy demand)				Expected Utility
	30 $p = 0.1$	90 $p = 0.4$	140 $p = 0.2$	150 $p = 0.3$	
A	15.90	25.11	34.31	36.31	29.39
B	0.00	29.47	85.40	100.00	58.87
C	15.35	37.96	64.18	70.23	50.63

For more complex decision-making problems, a number of decision-support systems are available in a variety of application areas. The *Hospital Software Sourcebook* (McKenzie 1993) lists a number of such systems.

Analysis, Interpretation, and Application of Results to Management Decisions

The home health agency now realizes that deciding which of three options to adopt for adding PT services is not a simple issue. In fact, depending upon the criterion of goodness employed in the analysis, different answers result. Adding to the complication is the question of whether to assume knowledge of the demand probabilities.

By way of summary, when demand probabilities were not assumed (decisions under uncertainty), three criteria were considered: maximax, maximin, and minimax regret. It is interesting to note that each criterion resulted in a different "optimum" decision choice:

Criterion	"Optimum" Decision
Maximax	B
Maximin	A
Minimax Regret	C

The agency then assumed a reasonable set of probabilities for the four demand levels. Using these probabilities and the criterion of maximum expected profit (or equivalently minimum expected regret), Alternative B was found to be optimum. However, when the notion of utility was introduced, a risk-averse preference for money shifted the optimum alternative to C, while a risk-seeking preference maintains the optimality of Alternative B.

The home health agency will now naturally ask, Which is the right answer? In fact, all of them are correct. The concept of an optimum decision depends upon the criterion of goodness used to compare the alternative decisions. Perhaps the agency should really ask, Which criterion should we apply? This depends quite a bit on how conservative the home health agency staff is (or perhaps more importantly, how conservative the agency's board of directors is).

A conservative posture would suggest applying the maximin criterion. No assumptions about demand probabilities would be needed. In this case the optimum option for adding PT services would be defined as Alternative A—contracting with an independent practitioner at a rate of $60 per home visit.

A more aggressive home health agency, however, would make an effort to determine appropriate probabilities for the demands for PT services. With such knowledge, the optimum alternative would be Alternative B—hiring a staff physical therapist at a monthly salary of $4,000 and covering the PT's automobile, medical supplies, and gasoline. This option yields an expected monthly profit of $3,216. It is interesting to note that Alternative A, the "best" choice under uncertainty, has the lowest expected monthly profit, $1,680. Frequently the optimum choice using the maximin criterion will have the lowest expected value. This emphasizes the fact that the maximin criterion is a very conservative approach.

In applying the criterion of maximum expected profit (or maximum expected utility), the home health agency must be aware that the optimum solution may be relatively sensitive to the assumed probability distribution of demand. If, for example, the probability of a demand for 150 PT visits were to drop below 0.27143 while the probability of a demand for 30 visits increased correspondingly, the agency would need to shift to Alternative C—contracting with a contractor at $35 per visit, and covering medical supplies, gasoline, fringe benefits, and automobile lease—in order to continue operating optimally. This result is based on the specific assumption that the demand probabilities for 90 and 140 visits remain unchanged. The home health agency would need to perform additional sensitivity analyses if it felt that other probability distributions of demand were possible.

Finally, the analysis of this case problem has indicated that forecasts of future demand for PT services could possibly lead to higher expected profits. When perfect forecasts are available, the expected monthly profit could be increased by $541, to $3,757. Forecasting systems that are less than perfect would, of course, have less value.

Assuming that reasonable estimates of demand probabilities are available, then the home health agency would typically employ a criterion of maximum expected profit. The availability of a forecasting system appropriately priced could potentially assist management in increasing its profit. Finally, the management's (and board's) relative value for money may lead to their defining a utility function, in which case their decision would be based upon maximum expected utility. For the risk-averse utility function illustrated in the analysis, Alternative C would be the optimum choice.

It is important that the home health agency realize that this is not a static problem. The probability distribution for demand can change, new alternatives could become available for providing PT services, the revenue for PT visits could change, and new forecasting technology might become available. As a result, the agency should certainly periodically review its choice of option for providing PT services in order to determine if that choice remains the optimum one.

Case Studies from the Literature

A number of applications of decision analysis appear in the medical literature. These studies are frequently presented in the context of a decision tree, although they tend to be single-stage problems that could be described with a payoff matrix model. Although these cases have a strong clinical focus, the managerial issues of cost, quality, and pricing should be of interest to health administrators.

Cost-Effectiveness of Routine Testing for Gonococcal Infection of the Cervix (Phillips et al. 1989)

Phillips et al. used decision analysis to calculate the economic implications of routine testing for *Neisseria gonorrhoeae* of the cervix. Their model compared performing endocervical cultures in all women seeking routine gynecologic care to a no-test strategy. Costs associated with the culture strategy included the cost of the test, cost of treatment, and costs related to undetected infections. The only cost associated with the no-test strategy was that of undetected infection.

The researchers concluded that routine testing for gonorrhea will result in cost savings, given the prevalence of infection typically found in office practices. Specifically, testing reduces overall costs if the prevalence of infection exceeded 1.5 percent. Direct medical costs would be reduced by routine testing if the prevalence of infection exceeded 2.5 percent.

Quality Assurance (Carter et al. 1992)

Carter et al. conducted a pilot study to examine whether decision analysis could be applied to a clinical quality assurance program. The setting for the study was a family practice residency clinical practice. A computerized decision-analysis model was developed that would select the initial drug therapy for hypertension.

Medical records for 52 resident-managed patients with hypertension were reviewed. The residents' drug prescribing was evaluated by faculty reviewers as well as by the decision-analysis model. There was good agreement between the faculty reviewers and the computerized decision-analysis model. The results of the study demonstrate that computerized decision-analysis techniques provide a useful adjunct to other clinical quality assurance procedures in residency training programs.

Case-Mix Analysis (Hatcher and Connelly 1988)

Under a prospective payment system, hospital administrators must pay increased attention to case-based financial planning. The linking of hospital revenues to patient diagnoses calls for increased awareness of the financial implications of different case mixes. Hatcher and Connelly developed a case-based financial planning model that assists managerial decision making in the strategic areas of case-mix planning and pricing.

In the model, hospitals are characterized as product manufacturers, and the product is defined as discharged patients. Diagnoses are grouped by payer and similar treatment cost experiences in order to create a limited set of managerially meaningful case types. The model projects the number of patients of each case type and total patient volume. In addition, the model projects prices and contribution margins for each case type, as well as the total contribution to the hospital's overhead.

The researchers tested the model using a hypothetical example of a hospital strategic planning problem. The model's potential as a decision-making aid in case-mix planning and case-type pricing was demonstrated.

Additional Reports from the Literature

Arevalo and Washington (1988) have constructed a decision model in order to assess the cost-effectiveness of routine screening of all pregnant women in the United States for the presence of hepatitis B surface antigen (HBsAG). Neonates of mothers who test positive for this antigen would then receive hepatitis B vaccine and hepatitis B immune globulin at birth, and repeated hepatitis B vaccine at ages 1 and 6 months.

The decision analysis demonstrated that a national program that identifies mothers with hepatitis B virus markers in their blood and immunizes their neonates immediately after birth is economically justified. This conclusion, like most results of decision analyses, depends heavily on the data assumptions.

O'Meara et al. (1994) have used decision analysis to study whether patients with proximal deep-vein thrombosis should be treated with streptokinase followed by intravenous heparin or with intravenous heparin alone. These treatments result in a variety of outcomes—bleeding, pulmonary embolism, postphlebitic syndrome, and death.

A survey of patients helped define values attached to these outcomes. Using these values and published estimates of the probabilities of these outcomes, the researchers constructed a decision model. The model indicated a preference for the use of heparin alone over the combined use of streptokinase and heparin.

Glotzer et al. (1994) used decision analysis to compare the costs of three screening strategies for childhood lead poisoning—venipuncture, capillary sample with venipuncture confirmation if the blood level is elevated, and stratification by risk. Venipuncture was found to be the least expensive option.

Sun (1991) applied decision analysis and clinical data from the medical literature to identify the preferred anaesthesia for dental surgeries. Drugs and acupuncture were compared, and it was found that the optimum choice depends on the patient's physical or mental state, or both. In general, drugs are preferred, but acupuncture analgesia is best for dental patients with myocardial infarction.

Problems

3.1 As part of our analysis of three alternative capital investments, we have constructed the following payoff matrix of profits (expressed in millions of dollars) for each of four possible improvements in the economy:

	Improvement in the Economy			
Investment	None	Small	Moderate	Strong
A	20	24	27	30
B	24	27	23	26
C	22	25	25	28

The probability distribution of the improvement in the economy is as follows:

Improvement in the Economy	Probability
None	0.1
Small	0.4
Moderate	0.3
Strong	0.2

a. You know for sure that there will be a moderate improvement in the economy. Which investment should you choose?

b. You know for sure that there will be a strong improvement in the economy. You have chosen Investment B. What is the amount of your regret?

c. Which investment would a pessimistic decision maker choose?

d. Which investment would an optimistic decision maker choose?

e. Which investment is optimum if you wish to maximize expected profit?

f. Suppose you have access to perfect information about the changes in the economy. Compute the expected profit when you use this perfect information.

3.2 You must decide whether to buy a certain item now in anticipation of a price change or wait to purchase it until later. You have determined that there will be a moderate decrease, small decrease, small increase, or moderate increase in the price. You have also determined the cost associated with each of these four possibilities if you purchase now or if you purchase later. These costs are displayed in the following table:

**Table of Costs for Two Strategies
and Four Possible Price Changes**

Strategy	Moderate Decrease	Small Decrease	Moderate Increase	Small Increase
Buy Now	$900	$900	$900	$900
Buy Later	$700	$800	$1,100	$1,050

a. Assume that no information about the probabilities associated with these possible price changes is available. Should you buy now or buy later? (Show your thought process *clearly*!)

b. Suppose that the possible price changes are assumed to have equal likelihood of occurring. Would you buy now or later?

c. Now assume that you are quite confident that the probability of a small decrease and the probability of a moderate increase are each equal to 25 percent. What must the probability of a moderate decrease equal in order for you to be indifferent between buying now and buying later?

3.3 Three strategies are under consideration for staffing a new program: small in-house staff with overtime as needed (Strategy A); large in-house staff with no need for overtime (Strategy B); and outside contract personnel (Strategy C). The staffing costs for each strategy depend upon which of four possible demand levels for the new program actually occurs. The payoff matrix displaying the weekly costs (in thousands) is shown below:

Staffing Strategy	Demand Level			
	Low	Moderate	High	Very High
A	5	7	12	15
B	10	10	10	10
C	4	8	11	12

The probability distribution of demand level is as follows:

Demand Level	Probability
Low	0.1
Moderate	0.3
High	0.5
Very High	0.1

a. Which staffing strategy is optimal using a minimax criterion?

b. Which staffing strategy results in the minimum expected cost?

c. Suppose we have the flexibility to vary the staffing strategy every week. We are offered a system that is able to provide us with perfect information about the upcoming demand level in sufficient time for us to vary our staffing strategy accordingly. Using such a system, what is our expected cost?

d. What is the most you would pay for the system described in Part c?

3.4 A certain portable monitoring device costs your clinic the equivalent of $20 per day to own and operate. You are able to rent these devices to patients for $100 per day. If the demand on a given day for these units exceeds the number you own, you *must* satisfy your patients' needs by obtaining the required additional units from a supplier at a cost of $150 per day (your revenue for the device, unfortunately, is still only $100 per day). You must decide how many of these units to own. Your marketing department estimates that daily demand for these devices will have the following probability distribution:

Daily Demand (Units)	Probability
0	0.05
1	0.10
2	0.20
3	0.35
4	0.20
5	0.10

a. Construct the payoff matrix that models this decision problem.

b. How many units would a pessimistic decision maker own?

c. How many units would an optimistic decision maker own?

d. How many units should we own if we wish to maximize expected profit?

3.5 The Regional Medical Center is considering contracting (at discounted rates) with a major manufacturing plant in its service area. Plan A is based upon a discount of 5 percent, and Plan B is based upon a discount of 10 percent. Offering the discount is expected to increase net revenue through additional volume, but this can be affected by the state of the economy, which will determine total employment levels at the plant. The chief financial officer for Regional Medical Center projects the following changes in net revenue under the two alternatives:

	Plan A	Plan B
Economy Improves	0	100
Economy Declines	25	−50

The estimated probability that the economy will improve is 0.4.

a. What is the optimal action?

b. How much would you be willing to pay for perfect information about the upcoming change in the economy?

3.6 Reconsider Problem 3.1. Suppose you are a decision maker who has the utility function shown below:

Dollars (in millions)	Utility
20	0
22	36
23	51
25	75
26	84
27	91
28	96
30	100

a. Sketch the graph of this utility function. Are you a risk-averse, risk-neutral, or risk-seeking decision maker?

b. You are offered a choice between $24 million dollars for sure or a lottery where you can win $30 million with probability p or $20 million with probability $(1 - p)$. You are indifferent between these two choices if $p = 0.64$. What utility do you assign to $24 million?

c. Which investment is optimum if you wish to maximize expected utility? Does this answer agree with the answer to Part e of Problem 3.1? Explain.

References

Arevalo, J. A., and A. E. Washington. 1988. "Cost Effectiveness of Prenatal Screening and Immunization for Hepatitis B Virus." *Journal of the American Medical Association* 259 (3): 365–69.

Carter, B. L., C. D. Butler, F. Bakht, and J. W. Miller. 1992. "Decision Analysis as a Quality-Assurance Screening Tool." *Family Medicine* 24 (5): 362–67.

Clemen, R. T. 1991. *Making Hard Decisions: An Introduction to Decision Analysis.* Boston: PWS-Kent Publishing Co.

Glotzer, D. E., H. Bauchner, K. A. Freedberg, and S. Palfrey. 1994. "Screening For Childhood Lead Poisoning: A Cost Minimization Analysis." *American Journal of Public Health* 84 (1): 110–12.

Hatcher, M. E., and C. Connelly. 1988. "A Case Mix Simulation Decision Support System Model for Negotiating Hospital Rates." *Journal of Medical Systems* 12 (6): 341–63.

McKenzie, J. R. (ed.). 1993. *Hospital Software Sourcebook.* Gaithersburg, MD: Aspen Publishers, Inc.

O'Meara III, J. J., R. A. McNutt, A. T. Evans, S. W. Moore, and S. M. Downs. 1994. "A Decision Analysis of Streptokinase plus Heparin as Compared with Heparin Alone for Deep-Vein Thrombosis." *The New England Journal of Medicine* 330 (26): 1864–69.

Phillips, R. S., C. Safran, M. D. Aronson, and W. C. Taylor. 1989. "Should Women Be Tested for Gonococcal Infection of the Cervix During Routine Gynecologic Visits? An Economic Appraisal." *The American Journal of Medicine* 86 (3): 297–302.

Sun, S. 1991. "Choice of Anaesthesia in Dental Operations." *Medical Informatics* 16 (1): 15–24.

Additional Readings

Corner, J. L., and C. W. Kirkwood. "Decision Analysis in the Operations Research Literature, 1970–1989." *Operations Research* 39, no. 2 (1991): 206–19.

Gafni, A. "The Standard Gamble Method: What Is Being Measured and How It Is Interpreted." *Health Services Research* 29, no. 2 (1994): 207–24.

Hogan, A. "Capital Expenditure Planning: The Value of Information to Hospitals." *Hospital and Health Services Administration* 32 (1987): 21–37.

Koenig, H. G., S. M. Ford, and D. G. Blazer. "Should Physicians Screen for Depression in Elderly Medical Inpatients? Results of a Decision Analysis." *International Journal of Psychiatry in Medicine* 23, no. 3 (1993): 239–63.

Mushlin, A. I., and B. Littenberg. "Diagnosing Pedal Osteomyelitis: Testing Choices and Their Consequences." *Journal of General Internal Medicine* 9, no. 1 (1994): 1–7.

Nettleman, M. D. "Practical Applications of Decision Analysis." *Infection Control and Hospital Epidemiology* 9, no. 5 (1988): 214–18.

Pauker, S. G., and J. P. Kassirer. "Decision Analysis." *The New England Journal of Medicine* 316, no. 5 (1987): 250–58.

Sekita, Y., and M. Omichi. "A Decision Support Model and Analysis for Hospital Administrators When Choosing Future Strategies of Their Hospitals." *Japan Hospitals* 9 (1990): 31–36.

Weinstein, M. C., H. V. Fineberg, A. S. Elstein, H. S. Frazier, D. Neuhauser, R. R. Neutra, and B. J. McNeil. *Clinical Decision Analysis.* Philadelphia: W. B. Saunders Co., 1980.

4

DECISION ANALYSIS WITH DECISION TREES

T HE PAYOFF matrix, introduced in Chapter 3, provides a suitable model for single-stage decision analysis problems in which Nature "selects" a single state after the decision maker has chosen from among a set of alternatives. The consequence of each combination of decision maker's choice of alternative and Nature's choice of state results in a "payoff," which constitutes one of the cell values in the matrix.

The challenges and decisions facing today's health care executive are typically more complex than these single-stage decision problems. For example, the question of how physical therapy services are best offered to the clients of the home health agency will typically involve several interrelated decisions: Should market research about demand for these services be performed? What advertising medium is most cost-effective in promoting these new services? And what pricing scheme will offer maximum profit?

When these additional decisions are added to the problem, the home health agency must perform a multistage decision analysis. Payoff matrices are generally not convenient for modeling these problems. Rather, what is required is an approach that facilitates a display of every possible action that the decision maker can take as well as every possible outcome resulting from these actions. A convenient approach for doing just this is a graphical technique known as **decision tree models**. The construction, analysis, and interpretation of these models are discussed in this chapter.

Introduction of Case Problem

Consider once again the home health agency introduced in Chapter 3. The agency has been in operation for more than a year and is now reassessing its performance and staffing. In reviewing demand data compiled in its information system, the agency learns that monthly demand has actually been slightly different from what had originally been anticipated. In fact, the agency now feels that monthly demand is more realistically modeled by the following probability distribution:

Monthly Demand	Probability
30	0.10
90	0.27
140	0.33
150	0.30

The home health agency now has several things to consider as it plans how it will provide physical therapy services for its clients in the coming year. First of all, a new independent contractor has approached the agency offering to provide PT services for a flat rate of $55 per visit. No fringe benefits or other costs would be incurred.

In addition, this contractor has also developed a new marketing program that it has successfully applied in a number of other cities. This program consists of an intensive month-long campaign to recruit additional clients followed by a brief market research study to determine the success of the effort. The agency has the option of purchasing this marketing program whether or not it hires the contractor to provide PT services.

The agency has surveyed a number of organizations that have utilized this marketing program. The results of this survey indicate that the contractor has a 72 percent success rate in increasing demand for PT services. However, in the remaining 28 percent of the cases there was actually a decrease in demand for PT services because of the negative reaction by potential clients to the contractor's hard-sell marketing approach.

The home health agency carefully analyzes the results of this quick but methodical survey and derives two additional probability distributions for demand for PT services—one that is expected to hold if the marketing campaign to recruit additional clients is successful, and a second distribution applicable if the marketing campaign is a failure. The distribution of demand created by a successful marketing campaign is given below:

Monthly Demand	Probability
140	0.5
150	0.5

On the other hand, when the marketing campaign is not successful, the demand is expected to be described by the following distribution:

Monthly Demand	Probability
30	0.5
90	0.5

The home health agency now has several decisions to make. First of all, it must decide whether to negotiate with the new independent contractor to perform the marketing campaign and follow-up market research study. The cost of this program is $300 per month (for the 12-month planning period currently under study).

If the home health agency decides not to contract for the marketing program, then it must decide whether to continue utilizing its salaried PT (at a monthly salary of $4,000, monthly car lease of $400, and medical supplies and gasoline allowance of $7 per visit) or to utilize the contractor to provide PT services at a cost of $55 per visit with no additional fixed costs.

If the home health agency does decide to contract for the marketing program, then it will receive a marketing research report indicating whether the marketing program was a success or a failure. The agency must decide for each reported outcome whether it will continue utilizing its salaried PT or utilize the contractor to provide the PT services. The costs associated with these two options are the same as those outlined above. In all cases, the average payment for a PT home visit is $75 per visit, and the agency is trying to maximize expected net profit.

The home health agency realizes that the optimum approach is dependent upon the cost of the marketing program (currently set at $300 per month), so another objective is to investigate the sensitivity of the solution to this cost. Upon realizing that they must perform a multistage decision analysis, the agency staff turns their attention to the details of constructing an appropriate decision tree model.

An Overview of Decision Trees

The objective of a decision tree is to graphically display every possible sequence of decisions and random outcomes that can occur within a given decision making problem. The graphical model comprising the decision tree consists of points, called **nodes**, that are connected by lines, called **arcs** or **branches**. These arcs are **directed**, which means that the logical flow of decision making and chance events moves from left to right through the tree.

The logical flow through the tree begins at a single node, known as the **initial node**, and proceeds through the various possible paths until reaching one of several possible endpoints, known as **terminal nodes**. The point at which the decision maker must choose from several alternatives is known as a *decision node*. It is represented graphically by a square. Similarly, the juncture at which Nature "chooses" one of several stochastic outcomes is known as a *chance node*. It is customary to depict such a node with a circle. The terminal nodes are also drawn as circles.

The general form of a decision tree is shown in Figure 4.1. Node 1, which in this illustration is a decision node, represents the initial node. Nodes 2 and 3 are chance nodes, while nodes 4 through 8 represent terminal nodes. The arcs or branches correspond to the straight lines drawn between adjacent nodes. Decision tree analysis begins with the construction of the tree. Careful attention is given to identifying the decision nodes, chance nodes, and terminal nodes. Each is carefully labeled to indicate the corresponding action, stochastic event, or final outcome.

Before the more complicated tree diagram for the case problem is developed, it is instructive to consider a simpler illustration consisting of an investor who is trying to choose between two alternative strategies. Under Strategy A the investor must choose between two investments—one with a sure return of a specified amount and a second with two possible yields that occur with specified probabilities. Under Strategy B pure chance will determine whether the investor realizes a specified return or is given the opportunity to choose between two alternative returns. The goal is to determine the sequence of decisions that yields a maximum expected return and to determine the value of this maximum.

The first step in achieving this goal is to construct a tree diagram that displays all possible sequences of decisions and chance events that can occur. This is most easily accomplished by beginning with the first decision or chance occurrence and then following individual paths to completion. As the paths are drawn they are labeled in order to indicate clearly what decision or event in the problem is being modeled. The structure of the investor's decision tree is shown in Figure 4.2.

Since the investor's problem begins with his choosing between two strategies, the initial node is drawn as a decision node (node 1 in Figure 4.2). Two arcs leave this node, corresponding to the two strategies, A and B, that the decision maker can choose.

Figure 4.1 General Form of a Decision Tree

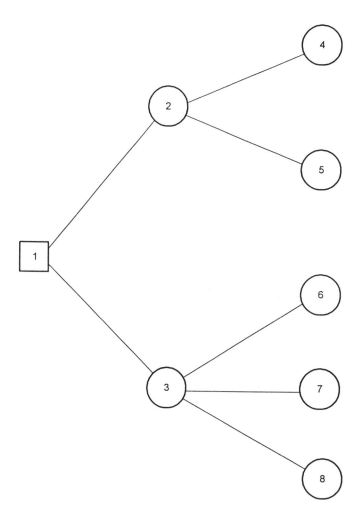

If Strategy A is chosen, then a second decision must be made. This is represented by a second decision node (node 2). The two arcs leaving this decision node correspond to the two choices available at this point to the decision maker. One choice (Choice C) leads to a chance node (node 4) that has two possible outcomes associated with it (the two terminal nodes, 6 and 7). The second choice (Choice D) leads to a "sure" outcome (terminal node 8).

If Strategy B is chosen, then a chance event will occur. This is depicted with a chance node (node 3). One of two chance outcomes

Figure 4.2 Structure of Investor's Decision Tree

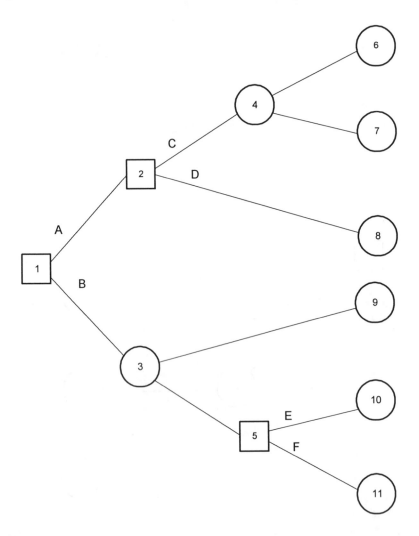

will result. The first is a specified return depicted with a terminal node (node 9). The second chance outcome provides the decision maker with the chance to make a second choice. This decision is shown as a decision node (node 5). The decision maker now has two choices (E and F), which lead, respectively, to specified outcomes (terminal nodes 10 and 11).

Once the tree has been drawn, the next step is to quantify the model. This quantification involves assigning probability values to the branches leaving chance nodes as well as indicating the outcome measure, usually a profit or loss figure, corresponding to each terminal node. Note that the probability values associated with the branches leaving each chance node must of course sum to 1. Assume that the branches leaving chance node 4 have probabilities 0.3 and 0.7, respectively. Similarly, assume that the branches leaving chance node 3 have probabilities 0.4 and 0.6, respectively. Finally, assume that the investor chooses as his outcome measure values of profit. The profit associated with each terminal node would now be determined and entered on the tree diagram adjacent to the node. The quantified decision tree for the investor is shown in Figure 4.3.

Once the tree diagram is completed, the investor is ready to proceed with the solution phase. Recall that the goal is to obtain the optimum expected payoff—maximum expected profit in this case—as well as the path through the decision tree that yields this optimum value. In this way the investor will be able to identify the optimum sequence of decisions that should be made. For problems that have been quantified in terms of costs, the goal would be to obtain the minimum expected cost.

The solution (shown in Figure 4.4) is obtained by working backwards through the tree, "averaging out" each chance node that is encountered and "folding back" each decision node. The "averaged out" value assigned to a chance node is defined as the expected value of the payoffs associated with the branches leaving that node. For example, the averaged-out value for node 4 is found by taking the expected value of +6 and +5. The probabilities used in the calculation are the branch probabilities, 0.3 and 0.7. The averaged-out value is thus

$$(6) \times (0.3) + (5) \times (0.7) = 5.3$$

For convenience, this value is often written inside a rectangle adjacent to the chance node, as shown in Figure 4.4.

A decision node, on the other hand, is "folded back," which consists of determining the largest payoff associated with the branches leaving the decision node. This largest value becomes the "folded back" value for this decision node. (In a minimization problem, one would look for the smallest cost.) Again, this value is customarily written inside a rectangle adjacent to the decision node as shown in Figure 4.4. Node 5 provides an example. The branches leaving this node have payoffs of 8 and 6. Since 8 is larger (and the problem is a maximization problem), 8 becomes the folded-back value associated with node 5. In addition, two small lines are often placed through each of the branches leaving a decision node that do not lead to the "optimum" destination. This makes it easier to trace through the tree after all nodes have

Figure 4.3 Investor's Quantified Decision Tree

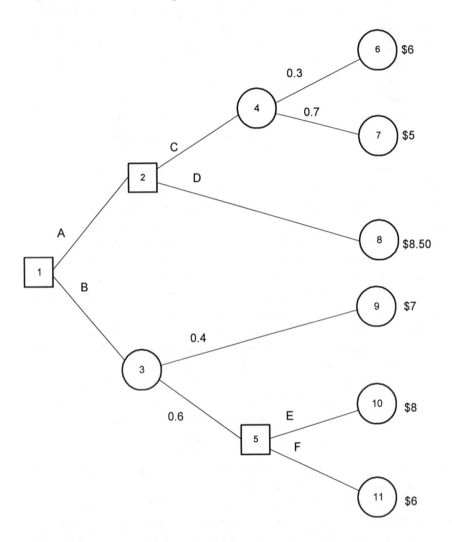

been averaged out or folded back in order to determine the optimum sequence of decisions.

The investor can now continue the averaging-out and folding-back procedures. For example, node 2 is folded back by choosing between 8.5 and 5.3. (Notice that 5.3 was itself obtained when node 4 was averaged out). Since 8.5 is higher, it becomes the folded-back value for node 2. Node 3 is a chance node, which needs to be averaged out. This averaged-out value is obtained from

$$(7) \times (0.4) + (8) \times (0.6) = 7.6$$

Figure 4.4   Investor's Solved Decision Tree

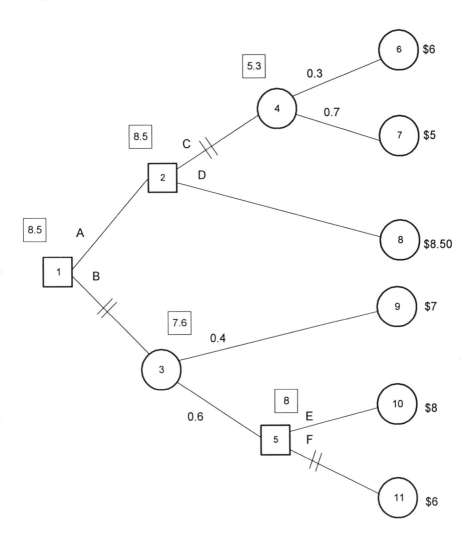

Again, observe that in the above expression, 8 is itself a folded-back value. Finally, node 1 is folded back by choosing between 8.5 and 7.6. Since 8.5 is larger, it becomes the value assigned to node 1, and two small marks are placed on the branch between node 1 and node 3.

The computations are now complete, and the solution can be read from the tree. The maximum expected profit is simply equal to the folded-back value of node 1, 8.5. (When the initial node in a tree is a chance node, the averaged-out value of that node yields the optimum expected value.) The sequence of decisions that will yield this optimum profit can be found by simply tracing through the tree along the paths which have not been blocked with small cross-marks. For the investor's tree the optimum sequence of decisions is to choose Strategy A and then to choose the sure outcome with a payoff of 8.5.

It is interesting to note that by choosing Strategy A and proceeding optimally, the decision maker obtains an expected profit that is $0.90 higher than the profit resulting from choosing Strategy B and continuing in an optimal manner. Thus, it is possible to perform sensitivity analyses to determine the impact that changing one or more problem parameters would have on the solution. For example, one might ask what profit associated with terminal node 9 would make a decision maker indifferent between choosing Strategy A and B. Denoting this profit by X, note that this break-even point occurs when

$$(0.4) \times X + (0.6) \times 8 = 8.5, \text{ or}$$
$$X = [8.5 - (0.6) \times 8]/0.4 = 9.25$$

Similar sensitivity analyses can be performed with other parameters in the problem.

Model Formulation, Quantification, and Data Requirements

The decision tree for the case problem can now be constructed. The structure of the tree appears in Figure 4.5. Recall that the home health agency must first make a decision about whether to hire the contractor to perform a marketing campaign. Thus, the initial node (node 1) of the decision tree is a decision node with two branches leaving the node.

If the home health agency decides not to contract for a marketing campaign, a decision must be made whether to continue utilizing its salaried PT or to purchase PT services from the contractor. This gives rise to a second decision node (node 2). In either case the monthly demand for PT services will be at one of four possible values. Thus, each of the two branches leaving node 2 goes to a chance node (nodes 4 and 5). Four branches leave each of these chance nodes (corresponding to the four possible levels of demand) and connect to terminal nodes (nodes 8 through 15).

If the home health agency decides to sign a contract for the marketing campaign, the resulting marketing report will show the campaign to have been either a success or a failure. This is represented by a chance node (node 3) having two departing branches corresponding to the two possible outcomes of the campaign. For each of these two possible outcomes, the agency must decide how it will provide PT

Figure 4.5 Structure of Case Problem Decision Tree

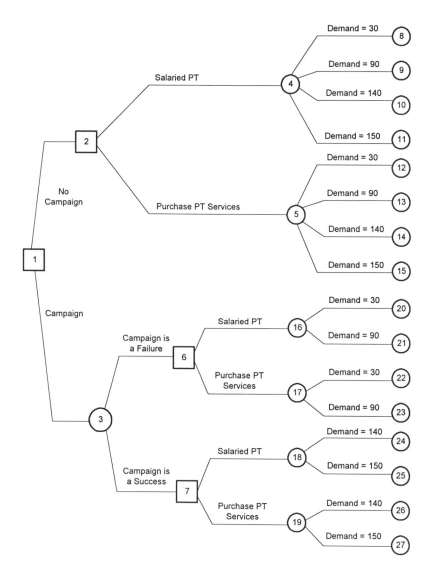

services. Two decision nodes (node 6 and node 7) model these two situations. Once the decision is made, Nature "chooses" a monthly demand level (represented by chance nodes 16, 17, 18, and 19). Each of these chance nodes has two departing branches corresponding to the respective possible values of monthly demand. These branches connect to terminal nodes (nodes 20 through 27).

In practice it is quite beneficial at this point to review the logic of the tree that has been constructed in order to make sure that the decisions and chance occurrences have been modeled correctly. When the decision maker has verified the tree's structure, the quantification of the model can begin. Recall that this quantification involves defining an outcome measure for each terminal node and assigning probability values to the branches that depart from a chance node.

Consider first the problem of obtaining an outcome measure—profit in this case—for each terminal node. When the agency does not contract for the marketing campaign and continues to use its salaried PT, the only cost is $4,400 per month (salary and expenses of the PT) plus $7 per visit. Since the revenue for each visit is $75, the net profit for this option, then, is

$$(75 - 7) \times X - 4,400 = 68 \times X - 4,400$$

where X is the number of monthly visits. Thus, for 30 monthly visits, the profit is equal to $68 \times 30 - 4,400$, or $-\$2,360$. This becomes the outcome measure for node 8. (The quantified decision tree for the case problem appears in Figure 4.6). The values for nodes 9 through 11 are obtained in similar fashion.

If the marketing campaign is launched, an additional cost of $300 per month is incurred. As a result, the net profit using the current salaried PT is given by

$$(75 - 7) \times X - 4,400 - 300 = 68 \times X - 4,700$$

where, again, X is the number of monthly visits. Now if there are 30 monthly visits, the profit will equal $68 \times 30 - 4,700$, or $-\$2,660$. This becomes the outcome measure for node 20. The values for nodes 21, 24, and 25 are obtained using this same formula.

A decision by the home health agency to utilize the contractor to provide PT services at a cost of $55 per visit will result in a profit of

$$(75 - 55) \times X \qquad \text{(E 4.1)}$$
$$\text{or } 20 \times X$$

when no marketing campaign is implemented and

$$(75 - 55) \times X - 300 \qquad \text{(E 4.2)}$$
$$\text{or } 20 \times X - 300$$

when the marketing campaign is purchased. Again, X denotes the number of monthly visits. Using these formulas, the outcome measures for the remaining terminal nodes can be computed (nodes 12 through 15 use Equation 4.1, while nodes 22, 23, 26, and 27 use Equation 4.2). Again, refer to Figure 4.6.

Figure 4.6 Case Problem—Quantified Decision Tree

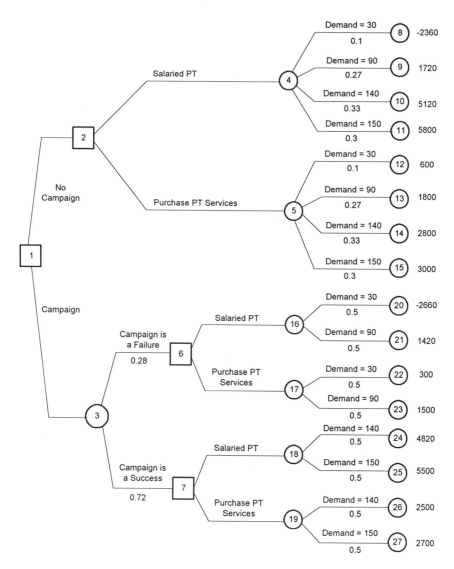

Next probabilities must be assigned to the branches flowing out of the chance nodes. Two branches leave node 3, corresponding to the two chance outcomes of the marketing campaign. It was indicated earlier that this campaign has been found to be successful in about 72 percent of the cases. Therefore, "Campaign Is a Failure" and "Campaign Is a Success" are assigned probabilities of 0.28 and 0.72, respectively. The remaining chance nodes represent the probability distribution of demand for PT services when no marketing campaign is conducted (nodes 4 and 5), when a marketing campaign is conducted and is not successful (nodes 16 and 17), and when a marketing campaign is conducted and is successful (nodes 18 and 19). These probability distributions were defined previously in the case problem introduction, and the appropriate outcome labels and probability values have been assigned to the branches leaving these chance nodes (see Figure 4.6).

The ease with which outcome measures can be computed for a decision tree analysis varies from problem to problem. In some cases, such as medical decision making, the outcomes are often most naturally described qualitatively—"patient's health improves," "surgery can be delayed for awhile," etc. The quantification of these outcomes is frequently difficult. In the case problem, on the other hand, it is obvious that monetary profit values are most appropriate, and any difficulty that might be encountered is related to cost-accounting issues or forecasts of future fee structures.

The probabilities can often present more difficulty. Estimating the probabilities of demand for PT services under various assumed conditions—no marketing campaign, a successful marketing campaign, or an unsuccessful campaign—is often quite challenging. Historical data from the organization's information system, experiences of other providers who are willing to share such data, or sheer guesswork are the most likely sources of such probability estimates.

Solving the Case Problem

Once the tree diagram for the case problem is completed, the solution proceeds by appropriately applying the techniques of averaging out and folding back. Recall that the procedure is to start at the terminal nodes and move to the left through all paths in the tree until the initial node is reached. At each stage of the process the computed value—folded-back or averaged-out value, as appropriate—is attached to the corresponding node.

The goal is to find the optimum expected outcome measure—maximum expected net profit for the case problem—as well as the sequence of decisions that will yield this optimum. Since the initial node in the case problem is a decision node, its folded-back value will equal the maximum expected net profit. It is then possible to trace through the tree to determine the optimum sequence of decisions.

While this solution can, of course, be obtained by hand, the use of computer software greatly facilitates the process. The *QuickQuant* program has a decision tree module that allows the user to sequentially "grow" the tree on the screen. Once the structure of the tree has been specified, along with the appropriate quantification, the program produces a graphical output, as shown in Exhibit 4.1.

In the *QuickQuant* output, chance nodes are represented with the letter "E" (event), while decision nodes are denoted with an "A" (action). Rather than assign outcome measures to terminal nodes, *Quick-*

Exhibit 4.1   Case Problem—*QuickQuant* Solution

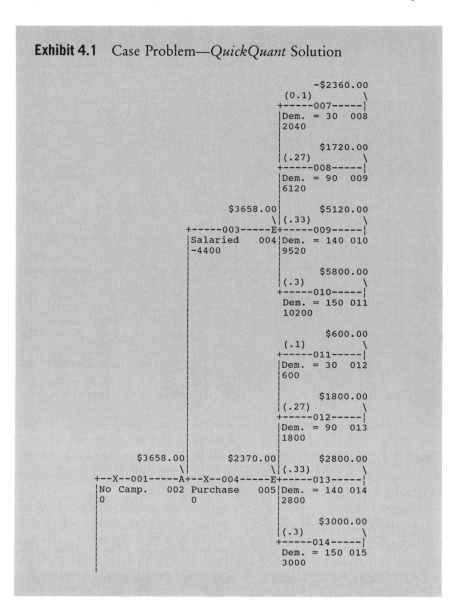

Exhibit 4.1   Continued

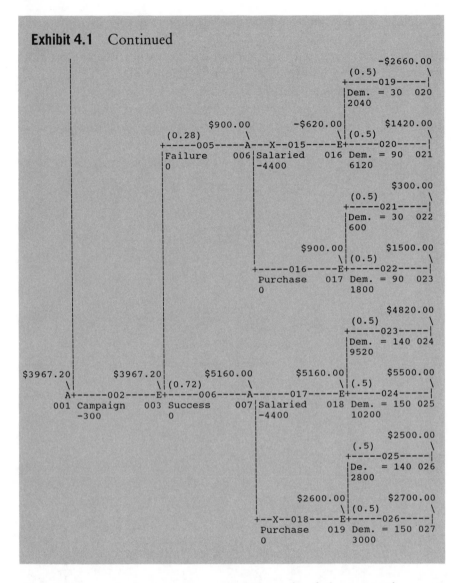

```
                                                         -$2660.00
                                               (0.5)            \
                                             +-----019-----|
                                             |Dem. = 30   020
                                             |2040

                           $900.00       -$620.00|      $1420.00
               (0.28)           \              \|(0.5)        \
             +-----005-----A---X--015-----E+-----020-----|
             |Failure    006|Salaried     016 Dem. = 90   021
             |0              -4400             6120

                                                          $300.00
                                               (0.5)            \
                                             +-----021-----|
                                             |Dem. = 30   022
                                             |600

                                 $900.00|      $1500.00
                                       \|(0.5)        \
                             +-----016-----E+-----022-----|
                             Purchase    017 Dem. = 90   023
                             0               1800

                                                         $4820.00
                                               (0.5)            \
                                             +-----023-----|
                                             |Dem. = 140 024
                                             |9520

$3967.20|       $3967.20|     $5160.00       $5160.00|      $5500.00
       \|              \|(0.72)      \             \|(.5)         \
    A+-----002-----E+-----006-----A------017-----E+-----024-----|
    001 Campaign   003 Success    007|Salaried    018 Dem. = 150 025
        -300           0              -4400            10200

                                                         $2500.00
                                               (.5)            \
                                             +-----025-----|
                                             |De.  = 140 026
                                             |2800

                                 $2600.00|      $2700.00
                                       \|(0.5)        \
                             +--X--018-----E+-----026-----|
                             Purchase    019 Dem. = 150 027
                             0               3000
```

Quant users assign a measure to each branch of the network, as applicable, while the tree is being grown. Likewise, probability values are assigned to those branches leaving chance nodes.

Computed quantities are attached to the nodes in *QuickQuant* using a backward slash (\). For example, *QuickQuant* has computed the outcome measure for terminal node 008 as −$2,360.00 and has attached this value to the node as shown in Exhibit 4.1. Similarly, since node 004 is a chance node, it is represented by a symbol "E" and a folded-back value of $3,658.00 has been attached to this node.

Observe that the averaged-out value associated with the initial node (node 001) is equal to $3,967.20. Thus, if the home health agency follows the optimal strategy, it will realize an expected monthly profit equal to this amount. In order to determine the sequence of decisions that constitutes this optimal strategy, one has only to trace through the tree, following those paths that have not been blocked. *QuickQuant* uses an "X" to block inappropriate paths.

Specifically, then, the home health agency should contract for the marketing campaign. If the market research following this campaign indicates that the effort was a failure, then the agency should purchase the PT services from the contractor. If, however, the market research reveals that the marketing campaign was a success, then the agency should continue utilizing its salaried PT to provide PT services.

Model Variations

The case problem assumed that the market research report provided perfect information about the success of the marketing effort. In other words, once the market research report indicated whether the marketing effort had been successful, it was known for sure that this information was 100 percent accurate and the appropriate demand distribution could be immediately applied.

Frequently, information is not perfect. Consider now a variation on the case problem that includes imperfect information. Assume that it is possible for the market research report to indicate "success" or "failure" for both the case where the marketing campaign was indeed a success as well as the case in which the marketing campaign is a failure. Thus, the content of the report does not provide the decision maker with certain knowledge about the true outcome of the campaign.

Despite this uncertainty, the decision maker must decide between using a salaried PT or purchasing PT services from the contractor on the basis of the contents of the marketing research report. Once this decision is made, Nature effectively "chooses" the actual state of the campaign outcome, failure or success, and then finally a monthly demand figure is generated. By way of summary, the sequence of events that has occurred here can be summarized as follows:

1. The decision maker receives imperfect information.
2. The decision maker chooses a course of action based upon this imperfect information.
3. Nature "chooses" a particular state (about which the information was actually providing imperfect information).

Figure 4.7 Modified Case Problem—Decision Tree

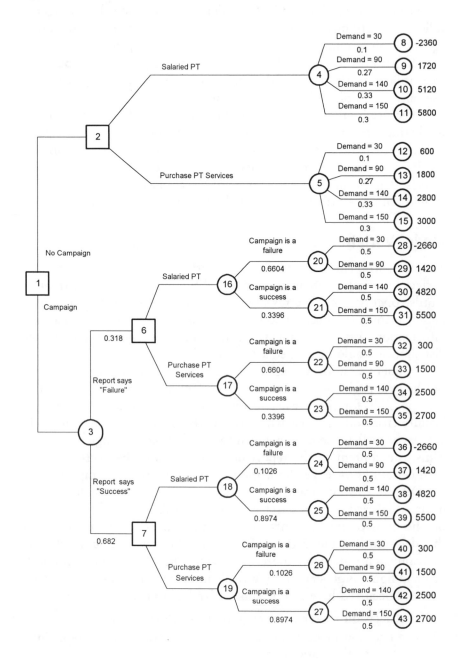

4. The decision maker incurs a payoff as a result of his or her decision and Nature's choice of state.

This sequence typifies decision making problems involving imperfect information.

To see this structure more clearly, refer to the tree diagram for this modified case problem in Figure 4.7. The branch of this tree diagram corresponding to the decision not to utilize a marketing campaign is identical to the case problem tree diagram in Figure 4.5. However, for the portion of the tree diagram depicting the decision to wage a marketing campaign, a major difference is evident.

The first chance node (node 3) corresponds to the chance outcome of the marketing research report. For each outcome, there is a decision node (nodes 6 and 7) that represents the decision of how to provide PT services (salaried PT or purchased services). The result of this decision moves the decision maker to one of four chance nodes (nodes 16, 17, 18, or 19). These chance nodes represent the actual outcome of the marketing campaign. Finally, based upon the result of the campaign, the number of PT visits demanded per month is "selected" by Nature (utilizing the appropriate demand distribution), and a profit figure is generated.

By averaging out the chance nodes and folding back the decision nodes, the decision maker can identify the strategy that maximizes the expected monthly profit. However, several probability values must first be quantified. In particular, the decision maker must identify the probability associated with each outcome of the marketing research report as well as the probability of the actual result of the marketing campaign given the outcome of the marketing research report.

The computation of these probabilities follows a procedure that is common to all problems involving decision making with imperfect information. The first step is to identify, typically from past history, a set of conditional probabilities defining the likelihood of each report outcome under each possible marketing campaign result. For example, consider the probabilities in the table below:

Outcome of Marketing Research Report	Marketing Campaign Result	
	Success	Failure
Report says "success"	0.85	0.25
Report says "failure"	0.15	0.75

Four probability values are displayed (the vertical line in the following notation denotes a conditional probability and is read "given"):

P(report says "success" | campaign is a success) = 0.85
P(report says "failure" | campaign is a success) = 0.15
P(report says "success" | campaign is a failure) = 0.25
P(report says "failure" | campaign is a failure) = 0.75

Recall also that the unconditional probabilities associated with the outcomes of the marketing campaign are as follows:

P(campaign is a success) = .72
P(campaign is a failure) = .28

The probabilities needed to complete the quantification of the tree diagram for this modified problem can now be computed using Bayes' rule, a topic discussed in detail in basic statistics texts (see, for example, Berenson and Levine 1992, 206–209). For example, define the following events:

F = {marketing campaign is a failure}
S = {marketing campaign is a success}
RF = {marketing report says "failure"}
RS = {marketing report says "success"}

Then according to Bayes' rule,

$$P(F|RF) = \frac{P(RF|F) \times P(F)}{P(RF|F) \times P(F) + P(RF|S) \times P(S)}$$

When the numerical values for these probability terms are substituted into this equation, the result is as follows:

$$P(F|RF) = \frac{(0.75) \times (0.28)}{(0.75) \times (0.28) + (0.15) \times (0.72)}$$

$$= \frac{0.21}{0.21 + 0.108}$$

$$= 0.6604$$

Bayes' rule can be used to solve for the remaining three conditional probabilities with the following results:

$$P(S|RF) = 0.3396$$
$$P(F|RS) = 0.1026$$
$$P(S|RS) = 0.8974$$

Finally, the probabilities associated with the marketing report indicating "success" or "failure" must also be determined. This computation will always involve a summation of product terms. In each product term a conditional probability—specific marketing report outcome given a particular campaign result—is multiplied by the probability of that particular campaign result.

For example, the probability that the marketing report says "failure" is computed as

$$P(RF) = P(RF|F) \times P(F) + P(RF|S) \times P(S)$$
$$= (0.75) \times (0.28) + (0.15) \times (0.72)$$
$$= 0.318$$

Similarly, the probability that the marketing report says "success" turns out to have a value of 0.682. (This value can be obtained either by applying a formula like the one above, or by subtracting $P(RF)$ from 1.

All of the values needed to complete the quantification of the decision tree for the modified case problem have now been computed. The solved tree is shown in Figure 4.8. Observe that with this imperfect information the optimum strategy is to not run the marketing campaign and to utilize a salaried PT. The result will be an expected monthly profit of $3,658.

An interesting question is what improvement in expected profit one can achieve if information that is "somewhat less imperfect" were available. To that end, consider an information source having the conditional probabilities displayed below:

Outcome of Marketing Research Report	Marketing Campaign Result	
	Success	Failure
Report says "success"	0.90	0.15
Report says "failure"	0.10	0.85

Notice that this source of information reflects the true outcome of the marketing campaign more frequently than did the information source in the previous example: P(report says "success"|campaign is a success) = 0.9 compared to 0.85, and P(report says "failure"|campaign is a failure) = 0.85 compared to 0.75).

The application of Bayes' rule yields the four conditional probabilities needed for the decision tree model of this problem (recall that F and S denote the events that the marketing campaign is a failure and success, respectively, and RF and RS correspond to the events that the marketing report says "failure" and "success," respectively):

$$P(F|RF) = 0.7677$$
$$P(S|RF) = 0.2323$$
$$P(F|RS) = 0.0609$$
$$P(S|RS) = 0.9391$$

Proceeding as in the previous example, one can obtain the probabilities associated with the outcome of the report:

$$P(RF) = P(RF|F) \times P(F) + P(RF|S) \times P(S)$$
$$= 0.85 \times 0.28 + 0.1 \times 0.72 = 0.31$$

and

$$P(RS) = P(RS|F) \times P(F) + P(RF|S) \times P(S)$$
$$= 0.15 \times 0.28 + 0.9 \times 0.72 = 0.69$$

The solved decision tree for this model appears in Figure 4.9. With this improved information the optimum strategy now calls for utilizing the marketing campaign. If the report says "failure," then PT services should be purchased, while a "successful" report would indicate that a salaried PT should be used. The expected monthly profit is $3,719.

Finally, it is interesting to consider the case where *no* information is available. That is, once the home health agency decides to employ a marketing campaign, no information about its success is available prior to the decision whether to utilize a salaried PT or purchase the PT services. One might expect, without information, an expected profit for the campaign alternative that is lower than that obtained when imperfect information is available. Indeed such is the case.

Consider Figure 4.10, which displays the tree diagram for the "no information" case. Observe that now the expected value of monthly profit using the campaign has dropped to $3,542 and that, of course, the optimum decision is not to utilize the marketing campaign.

Description of Available Computer Software

Decision tree analysis modules are contained within a number of micro-computer-based operations research software packages. For example *QuickQuant*, QSB+, STORM, and AB:QM all support the solution of decision tree problems. One difficulty with all of these packages is their lack of support for the computation of Bayesian probability revisions within the decision tree module itself. In the case of AB:QM and QSB+ these Bayesian calculations can be performed in a separate module. The results must then be manually entered into the decision tree program along with all of the other input data.

More sophisticated decision tree software is available. DATA (Tree-Age Software 1994) is a Windows-based software system designed to implement the techniques of decision analysis in an intuitive and easy-to-use manner. Its features include easy construction of the tree diagram, Bayes' revision, Markov analysis, Monte Carlo analysis, sensitivity analysis, and dynamic links among trees or between a tree and another application.

DPL (ADA Decision Systems 1995) is also a Windows-based software system that is a complete modeling environment. Its features

Figure 4.8 Modified Case Problem—Decision Tree Solution

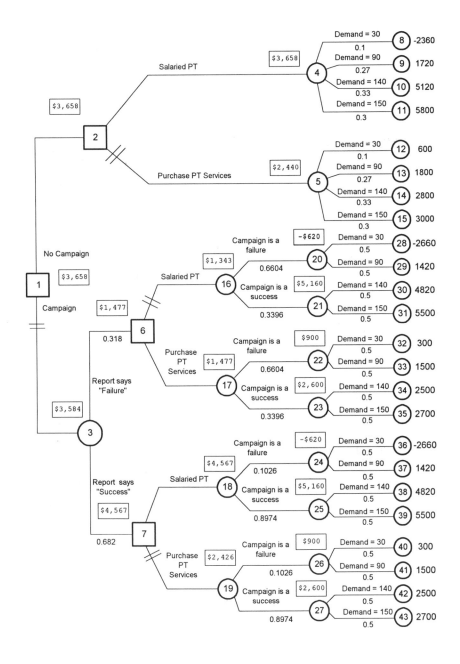

Figure 4.9 Modified Case Problem—Less Imperfect Information Decision Tree Solution

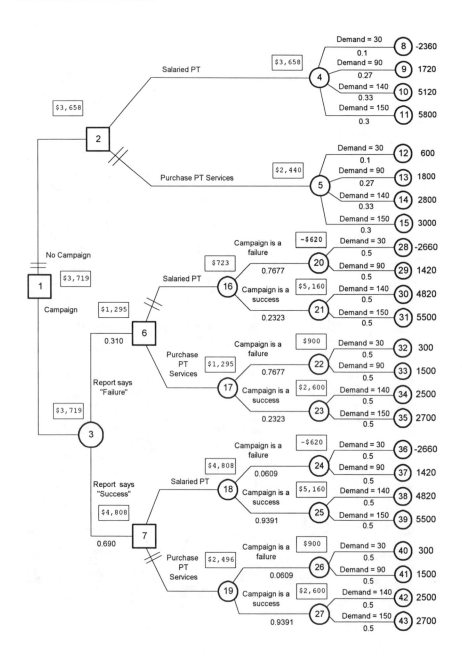

Figure 4.10 Modified Case Problem with No Information

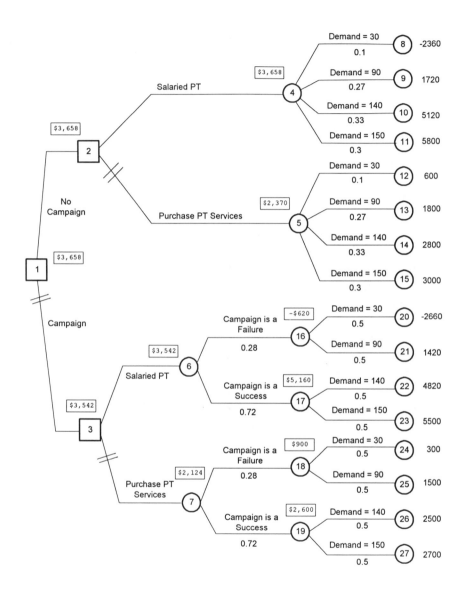

include linkage to spreadsheet models, sensitivity analysis, Bayes' revision (if the tree has been defined in terms of an influence diagram), and linkage to external programs.

Analysis, Interpretation, and Application of Results to Management Decisions

The home health agency continues to search for the optimum approach to providing PT services for its patient population. The use of decision trees has allowed the agency to examine alternatives that include multiple stages of decisions.

Four cases have been considered by the agency—no information, two levels of imperfect information, and perfect information. The results of these four analyses are summarized in Table 4.1. Several important implications for management emerge from this table.

First of all, when no information about the outcome of a marketing campaign is available (and the cost of the campaign is set at $300 per month), the optimum strategy for management is no campaign and the use of a salaried PT. This results in $116 per month more profit than the campaign alternative. Of course, if the monthly cost of the campaign were lowered by this amount, then management would be indifferent between the two alternatives.

Second, when information about the campaign outcome becomes available (and the cost of the campaign and this information remains at $300 per month), then the monthly profit with the campaign strategy begins to rise. However, only when this information becomes increasingly accurate will its value be sufficient for management to choose the campaign alternative. In fact, one could solve for the required degree of accuracy of the information in order to achieve a break-even monthly profit compared to the no-campaign alternative. For example, with information that accurately reports the success of successful campaigns

Table 4.1   Summary of Four Variations of Case Problem

Model Variation	Expected Profits		Value of Information	Optimum Strategy
	No Campaign	With Campaign		
No information	$3,658	$3,542	N/A	No Campaign
Imperfect information $P(RS|S) = 0.85$ $P(RF|F) = 0.75$	3,658	3,584	None	No Campaign
Imperfect information $P(RS|S) = 0.90$ $P(RF|F) = 0.85$	3,658	3,719	$61	Campaign
Perfect information	3,658	3,967	$309	Campaign

with probability 0.85 and the failure of nonsuccessful campaigns with probability 0.75, the expected monthly profit of the campaign strategy is only $3,584. Management in this case is well advised to reject the marketing campaign.

On the other hand, when the accuracy of the information increases so that successful campaigns are correctly identified with probability 0.90 and nonsuccessful campaigns are correctly identified with probability 0.85, the expected monthly profit of the campaign strategy increases to $3,719, so that this option is preferred. Thus, management must become a wise consumer of information as they evaluate available marketing campaigns and follow-up market research reports.

Finally, there is an upper limit to the expected monthly profit that can be generated with the campaign option. This limit is the expected profit with perfect information, which in this example is $3,967, or $309 more than the no-campaign alternative. Considering that the marketing campaign is currently costing management $300 per month and the marketing research report is offered at no cost, the combination of the two, with perfect information, has a maximum value of $609.

Decision tree analysis, then, offers the home health agency management a framework in which to evaluate multistage decisions such as the case problem presented here. The modeling process provides a structure for management to think about the important components of the decision and to obtain appropriate quantitative values for the significant components of the problem. The solution guides the agency in its choice of strategies and should help management to provide appropriate services in the most cost-effective manner possible.

Case Studies from the Literature

Evaluating a Proposed Drug-Testing Program (Feinstein 1990)

The Athletic Board of Governance at Santa Clara University was faced with a decision of whether to recommend implementing a drug-testing program for the university's intercollegiate athletes. The athletic director's proposal to the board argued in favor of the program. The arguments were supported by such notions as the need to comply with NCAA directives and the deterrent effects that testing offers.

One of the board members was a decision scientist who felt that this issue called for a simple analytical decision model that treats the question of whether or not to test a single individual for the presence of drugs. Such a model, the board member felt, was preferable to alternative, more aggregate, approaches because it highlighted the two essential issues in question—the reliability of the testing procedure and the benefits of identifying a drug user compared to the costs of errors (false accusations of usage and nonidentification of users). Since the NCAA does not require drug testing for all athletes, it was felt that compliance with NCAA guidelines was not an important issue when modeling the decision of whether to test an individual athlete.

Using a decision tree model, the decision scientist provided the board with the framework needed to debate the costs and benefits of a policy of mandatory testing. He showed that if the prior probability of drug use for a given individual is assumed to equal .05, and the reliability of the test (reliability = sensitivity = specificity) is equal to .95, then a positive test result indicates a 50 percent probability that the individual is a drug user. That is, the test had as much predictive power as the toss of a coin in a population of approximately 5 percent drug users.

The board felt that the cost of false accusation was considerably higher than the cost of failing to identify a drug user and that the prior probability that an athlete uses drugs is low—certainly less than 10 percent and perhaps closer to 5 percent. The model showed clearly that for this case a test that is 95 percent reliable is simply not accurate enough to justify the risk entailed in testing. That is, the expected cost of not testing is lower than the expected cost of testing.

The president of the university adopted the board's recommendation of not implementing a drug testing program. The board chairman acknowledged that the decision tree model heavily influenced the decision.

Deciding Whether to Join a PPO (Alemi and Agliato 1989)

The authors describe a study they performed for a bank that was trying to decide whether to contract with a preferred provider organization (PPO). Under their current health plan, employees were covered by a traditional indemnity plan, and care could be obtained from any physician. The plan offered partial reimbursement after an annual deductible was satisfied. Monthly premiums were less than 15 percent of the cost of the insurance plan.

The new plan under study offered employees lower out-of-pocket costs in the form of a 10 percent lower copayment. They were required, however, to switch their primary physician to one of the preferred providers. In both plans the bank was self-insured and thus paid for the actual expenses of its employees rather than a fixed premium per employee.

The decision facing the bank—join the PPO or continue with the current plan—can be modeled by a decision tree that is very easy to construct. The difficulty lies in the quantification of the tree. In particular, the bank needed to anticipate the employees' reactions to the new plan, how utilization would change, what would be the frequency of hospitalizations, and what would be the charge characteristics of the PPO and other providers of care.

By using a combination of actual utilization data as well as a variety of sources in the literature, the researchers were able to estimate the parameters of the decision tree. In addition, they looked at the impact of case mix, hospitalization rate, and outpatient charges on their decision about which health care plan to adopt.

As a result of the study, the bank decided to adopt the PPO plan. While the model was relatively straightforward, the study offered several advantages. It helped to increase the trust between the health care provider and the bank; it helped a benefit manager negotiate appropriate contract terms; it created an organizational climate that was receptive to the implementation of the PPO; and it made it easier to defend the decision to the bank's board of directors.

Additional Reports from the Literature

Phillips et al. (1994) have developed a decision tree model to evaluate the cost-effectiveness of alternative policies for human immunodeficiency (HIV) testing of physicians and dentists. Three major policy options were tested: (1) mandatory testing of all physicians and dentists or those performing invasive procedures; (2) increased voluntary testing; and (3) continued voluntary testing with no change in policies. In addition, three consequences of a positive test were examined: (1) mandate exclusion from patient care; (2) restrict performance of invasive procedures; and (3) require informing patients of their serostatus. Data were obtained from extensive literature review and consultation with experts.

Only one-time testing was considered. The results indicate that the cost-effectiveness of testing policies is highly sensitive to several data inputs including seroprevalence and transmission risk. The cost-effectiveness of mandatory testing decreases as seroprevalence decreases. While the analysis neither justifies nor precludes mandatory testing policies, it does provide new information and an analytic framework that can be used to evaluate alternative policies.

The cost-effectiveness of a routine varicella vaccination program for U.S. children has been studied with a decision tree model by Lieu et al. (1994). The researchers compared the costs, outcomes, and cost-effectiveness of a routine vaccination program with a policy of no intervention. They determined that 94 percent of all potential cases of chicken pox would be prevented, provided that the vaccination coverage rate is 97 percent at school entry. Including work-loss costs as well as medical costs, the program would save $5 for every dollar invested in vaccination. However, from the health care payer's perspective, the program would cost approximately $2 per chicken pox case prevented.

The authors conclude that a routine varicella vaccination program for healthy children would result in net savings from the societal perspective. In addition, compared with other prevention programs, it would also be cost-effective from the health care payer's perspective.

Bloom et al. (1993) used decision tree models to determine the clinical and economic consequences of alternative vaccination strategies for preventing hepatitis B virus infection (HBV). Three alternative strategies were considered—no vaccination, universal vaccination, and "screen and vaccinate"—in four populations (newborns, 10-year-old adolescents, a high-risk adult population, and the general adult U.S. population). Incremental cost-effectiveness was computed from the perspective of the payer of medical care and was subjected to sensitivity analysis.

The analysis suggests that the strategy of screening newborns should be combined with routine administration of HBV vaccine to 10-year-old children. This will result in a cost-effective improvement in the health of the public.

Problems

4.1 Consider the decision tree shown on the next page. The figures adjacent to the terminal nodes represent profits. Our goal is to maximize profit. Determine whether strategy A or B is optimum, and how much more profitable it is than the other strategy.

4.2 A patient suffering with a given condition must choose between having an operation now or waiting one year to see how the condition changes. Surgery now results in a good outcome (with probability 0.6), a fair outcome (with probability 0.2), or a poor outcome (with probability 0.2).

If the patient waits one year, the condition will get worse (with probability 0.2), stay the same (with probability 0.3), or get better (with probability 0.5). If the condition gets worse, the patient must have surgery. The outcome of this surgery will be good (with probability 0.3), fair (with probability 0.3), or poor (with probability 0.4). If the condition stays the same, the patient has a choice of either electing surgery or not electing

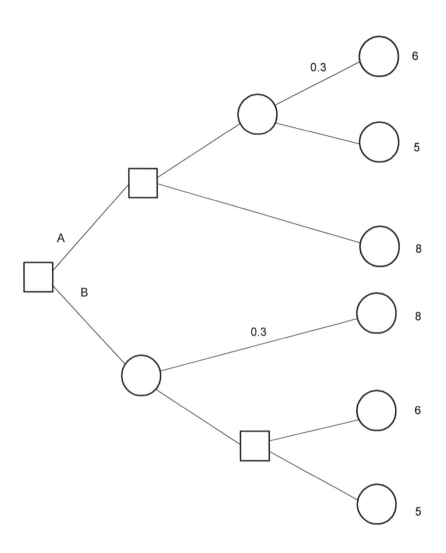

surgery. If the patient elects surgery, the outcome will be good (with probability 0.6), fair (with probability 0.1), or poor (with probability 0.3). On the other hand, if the patient does not elect surgery, the outcome will be good (with probability 0.5), fair (with probability 0.2), or poor (with probability 0.3). But, if the condition gets better, surgery is never performed, and the outcome is always good. Assume that the measure of goodness for good, fair, and poor is 10, 6, and 2, respectively.

a. Draw a decision tree to model the patient's decision problem.

b. Find the optimum strategy for the patient to follow in order to maximize the patient's expected measure of goodness.

4.3 Among your responsibilities at Kudley Memorial Hospital for Children is setting the staffing level in the patient transport unit. The personnel manager has said that you can have either three or four full-time positions. Each full-time person works eight hours per day. The number of patients that need to be transported each day follows the following distribution:

Number of Patients	Probability
15	0.2
20	0.5
25	0.3

The number of hours of transport time required per day is random and has a probability distribution that depends upon the number of patients as follows:

Number of Hours per Day	Probability If Number of Patients Is		
	15	**20**	**25**
24	0.7	0.4	0.1
28	0.2	0.3	0.2
32	0.1	0.3	0.7

If your patient transport unit can't handle the workload on a given day, overtime personnel are used at $7.50 per hour. You must tell the personnel manager whether to hire 3 or 4 people at a salary of $40 per day per person (ignore the cost of fringe benefits).

a. Construct a decision tree to model this decision problem.

b. Will you tell the personnel manager to hire 3 or 4 full-time people?

c. Find the hourly overtime that reverses your decision.

4.4 You are trying to decide between two management contract opportunities, A and B. Their economic payoff (profit) depends upon whether the economy for the next year is good or bad. Current conventional wisdom estimates that the probability of a good economy is 0.6 (so that the probability of a bad economy is, of course, 0.4). The payoffs for each contract opportunity, under each economic condition, are as follows:

Table of Payoffs (Profits)
(in thousands of dollars)

Contract Opportunity	Economic Condition	
	Good	Bad
A	800	500
B	600	700

An economic forecasting consultant has offered her services to help you predict what the economic condition will be. Her proposed fee is $35,000. After checking with some of her past clients, you are able to quantify her rate of accuracy in forecasting. This accuracy can be summarized as follows:

Probabilities of a Specific Forecast for Each Actual Economic Condition

Forecast Says	Actual Economic Condition	
	Good	Bad
Good	0.8	0.1
Bad	0.2	0.9

a. Draw a decision tree to model this decision problem.

b. Derive the optimum strategy.

c. What is the maximum fee you would pay to the forecasting consultant in order to be indifferent about using her consulting services?

d. Suppose that the consultant's forecast were perfect. What is the maximum fee you would pay her for her forecasting services?

References

ADA Decision Systems. 1995. *DPL*. Menlo Park, CA: ADA Decision Systems, 2710 Sand Hill Road.

Alemi, F., and J. Agliato. 1989. "Restricting Patients' Choices of Physicians: A Decision Analytic Evaluation of Costs." *Interfaces* 19 (2): 20–28.

Berenson, M. L., and D. M. Levine. 1992. *Basic Business Statistics: Concepts and Applications*. 5th Ed. Englewood Cliffs, NJ: Prentice-Hall, Inc.

Bloom, B. S., A. L. Hillman, A. M. Fendrick, and J. S. Schwartz. 1993. "A Reappraisal of Hepatitis B Virus Vaccination Strategies Using Cost-Effectiveness Analysis." *Annals of Internal Medicine* 118 (4): 298–306.

Feinstein, C. D. 1990. "Deciding Whether to Test Student Athletes for Drug Use." *Interfaces* 20 (3): 80–87.

Lieu, T. A., S. L. Cochi, S. B. Black, E. Halloran, H. R. Shinefield, S. J. Holmes, M. Wharton, A. E. Washington. 1994. "Cost-Effectiveness of a Routine Varicella Vaccination Program for US Children." *Journal of the American Medical Association* 271 (5): 375–81.

Phillips, K. A., R. A. Lowe, J. G. Kahn, P. Lurie, A. L. Avins, and D. Ciccarone. 1994. "The Cost-Effectiveness of HIV Testing of Physicians and Dentists in the United States." *Journal of the American Medical Association* 271 (11): 851–58.

TreeAge Software. 1994. *DATA for Windows*. Boston: TreeAge Software, Inc., PO Box 329.

Additional Readings

Brown, J. "Screening Infants for Hearing Loss—An Economic Evaluation." *Journal of Epidemiology and Community Health* 46, 4 (1992): 350–56.

Coleman, R. L. "The Use of Decision Analysis in Quality Assessment." *Quality Review Bulletin* 15, 12 (1989): 383–91.

Gluckman, J., and T. Michaelis. "Measuring Marketing Effectiveness." *Health Progress* 68, 7 (1987): 47–50.

Krieg, A. F., T. W. Abendroth, and M. B. Bongiovanni. "When Is a Diagnostic Test Result Positive? Decision Tree Models Based on Utility and Threshold." *Archives of Pathology and Laboratory Medicine* 110, 9 (1986): 787–91.

Meeker, T. "Decision Tree: A Process for Determining When to Withdraw or Continue Life-Sustaining Medical Treatment." *Health Progress* 74, 2 (1993): 48–51.

Milsum, J. H. "Determining Optimal Screening Policies Using Decision Trees and Spreadsheets." *Computers in Biology and Medicine* 19, 4 (1989): 231–43.

Resource Allocation

H EALTH CARE organizations face ever increasing pressures to control costs and operate efficiently. Proper allocation of resources is essential to cost containment and efficiency. Resource allocation is important for continuous improvement of service quality as well. Chapters 5, 6, and 7 describe quantitative techniques that can assist managers in resource planning and utilization. These techniques have application at both the strategic and operational management levels.

Chapters 5 and 6 describe processes for optimizing resource utilization within the constraints imposed by the organization and its environment (linear programming, and transportation and assignment models). At the strategic management level, these tools can be used to examine alternative use of funds and human resources in pursuit of institutional goals and objectives. Examples include portfolio analysis, financial mix strategies, and human resource planning. At the operational level, resource allocation models can assist in budgeting, assignment of staff, procuring supplies and materials, and scheduling of patient services.

Queueing models (Chapter 7) support facility and service planning. They can help managers balance the two important objectives of efficient use of resources and provision of timely service to patients.

Management's goal is to minimize two kinds of costs associated with patient care delivery—the costs of providing service and the costs associated with waiting times.

The models described in Part II can be used to analyze and improve current operations. They can also be employed in a what-if mode to analyze the impact of potential changes in resource allocation on the quantity and quality of services offered.

LINEAR PROGRAMMING

LINEAR PROGRAMMING is a useful technique for solving management problems that involve optimizing an organizational objective within the resources available to the manager. The management objective to be accomplished often includes one of the following:

1. Provide the largest quantity of service with the staff and other resources available for delivering the service.
2. Provide service at the lowest possible cost.
3. Provide service in a way that the staff are employed in the most efficient manner.
4. Provide service in a way that the organization receives the largest amount of net revenue (profit).

In health services organizations, linear programming has been applied to problems involving the most efficient allocation of resources and to problems involving the assignment and scheduling of staff in the delivery of patient care.

This chapter describes this technique and its application to planning and management in health services organizations.

Introduction of Case Problem

The administrator of a surgical specialty division of Northpark University Hospital and Medical Center is studying the potential impact of a planned marketing program on two high-volume, short-stay inpatient procedures offered by the division to its Medicare patient population.

These procedures are labeled DRG-1 and DRG-2 in the Hospital's case-mix coding system.

The division's hospital service unit has excess capacity for additional inpatients, with capacity expressed in terms of inpatient days, nursing service hours, and diagnostic procedures available per month on the unit. The administrator knows the amount of reimbursement from the Medicare agency for each DRG.

Working with a management engineer from the Hospital, the administrator wants to

1. compute the optimum mix of the two DRGs that would maximize net revenue within the excess capacity available on the division's nursing unit

2. determine where to place the emphasis in the planned marketing campaign

An Overview of Linear Programming

Linear programming models require formulation of the following functions in mathematical terms:

1. An **objective function** that expresses the variable to be optimized (maximized or minimized) in the form of a linear equation.

2. A set of **constraints**, linear inequalities and/or equations that determine the range or "solution space" of feasible solutions from which the optimum solution will be chosen. Constraints are of two types: binding and nonbinding. Nonbinding constraints have no effect on the solution to the linear programming problem.

The objective function and constraints are expressed in terms of a set of **decision variables** whose values are determined when the model is solved. Since all of these functions are expressed as linear equations, the model is called "linear" programming. Integer programming is a special case of linear programming in which whole number, or integer, solutions are required. Linear programming is a special case of mathematical programming. Nonlinear problems require more complex techniques for their solution. These model variations are discussed in a later section of this chapter.

For a simple example, assume that a clinical laboratory provides two types of screening tests and wishes to maximize the number of tests run each day. The objective function would be stated as follows:

$$\text{Maximize: } SVC = X_1 + X_2$$

where SVC represents the total number of tests performed per day, X_1 represents the number of type one tests performed per day, and X_2

represents the number of type two tests performed per day. X_1 and X_2 are the decision variables. Assume further that the number of tests that can be carried out is limited (or constrained) by the hours available from two categories of personnel working in the lab, professional and technician level. Test one requires two hours of professional staff time and one hour of technician time. Test two requires one hour of professional staff time and two hours of technician time. At present staffing levels, there are 10 hours of professional staff time and 8 hours of technician time available to work on these two tests each day. Staff time thus becomes a resource limitation or constraint on the optimum solution, expressed mathematically as follows:

$$2X_1 + X_2 \leq 10 \, (Professional\ staff\ time\ constraint)$$
$$X_1 + 2X_2 \leq 8 \, (Technician\ staff\ time\ constraint)$$

Note that there are two additional constraints,

$$X_1 \geq 0$$
$$X_2 \geq 0,$$

indicating that there cannot be a negative number for tests performed.

Figure 5.1 demonstrates the graphic formulation and solution of this simple problem. The constraint inequalities are plotted as straight-line equations. The shaded area below these equations determines the solution space where the optimum solution will lie. It can be proved that the optimum solution will only be found at one of the points of intersection of the constraints designated as points A, B, C on Figure 5.1. The point of intersection where the objective function has the highest value will determine the maximum number of tests that can be carried out within the resources available. In this example, point B is the point of maximization with an objective function value of six tests per day, four type one and two type two. At point A, a total of four tests (all type two) would be completed; and at point C, a total of five tests (all type one) would be completed.

Note that this graphic solution can be used only for very simple problems involving two variables. More detailed descriptions of linear programming model formulation and solutions using standard computer software are included later in this chapter.

Model Formulation, Quantification, and Data Requirements

The Northpark University Hospital and Medical Center case problem appears to be a candidate for analysis using linear programming techniques. The objective function is to maximize net revenue from service

Figure 5.1 Linear Programming—Graphic Formulation

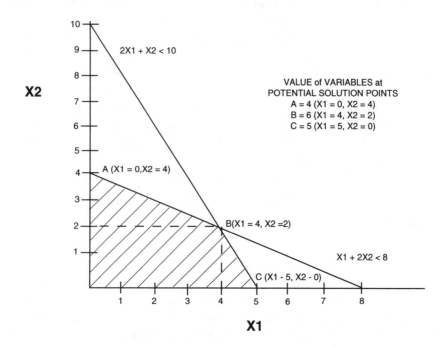

expansion involving two procedures, DRG-1 and DRG-2. To compute net revenue, the division administrator must be able to determine the margin of profit (or loss) for each of the two DRGs. The margin is the difference between the Medicare fixed reimbursement amount and the cost of providing service.

The constraints on maximizing net revenue are the limits of available capacity on the surgical specialty unit: inpatient days, nursing service hours, and number of diagnostic procedures available.

The administrator and management engineer working on the problem must now seek out sources of data to formulate the linear programming model.

The Hospital's accounting system provides the Medicare reimbursement amounts as follows:

DRG-1	$ 2,125
DRG-2	$ 2,500

Northpark University Hospital and Medical Center has developed a cost-accounting information system that provides the following information on unit costs:

Inpatient days	$600 per day
Nursing service	$ 40 per hour
Diagnostic procedures	$ 75 per procedure

The Hospital's management engineering staff has also carried out a cost-finding study on high-volume DRGs for use in the case-mix analysis management information system. The study provides information on resources consumed for each of the two DRGs under review:

	DRG-1	DRG-2
Average length of stay	2 days	1 day
Nursing hours	10	30
Diagnostic procedures	3	4

Excess service capacity on the surgical specialty unit is as follows:

Inpatient days	120 per month
Nursing service hours	900 per month
Diagnostic procedures	360 per month

Note that if the Hospital did not have cost-accounting and case-mix analysis systems in place, the management engineering staff would have to carry out a special study to obtain these data for use in the model.

The objective function can now be expressed in mathematical terms as follows:

Maximize: *Net Revenue* = *Margin* × DRG-1 + *Margin* × DRG-2

The margin for each DRG is the difference between the Medicare reimbursement amount and the cost for service.

For DRG-1:

Cost = (2 inpatient days × $600/day)
+ (10 nursing hours × $40/hour)
+ (3 diagnostic procedures × $75/procedure)
= $1,825

Margin = Reimbursement − Cost
= $2,125 − $1,825 = $300

For DRG-2:

Cost = (1 inpatient day × $600/day)
+ (30 nursing hours × $40/hour)
+ (4 diagnostic procedures × $75/procedure)
= $2,100

Margin = Reimbursement − Cost
= $2,500 − $2,100 = $400

Thus, the objective function becomes:

Maximize: $NREV = 300D_1 + 400D_2$

where

$NREV$ = net revenue
D_1 = number of DRG-1 patients
D_2 = number of DRG-2 patients

Constraint inequalities must be expressed in terms of the decision variables included in the objective function. There will be one inequality for each resource consumed in providing service, formulated mathematically as follows:

$2D_1 + D_2 \leq 120$ (Inpatient days constraint)
$10D_1 + 30D_2 \leq 900$ (Nursing hours constraint)
$3D_1 + 4D_2 \leq 360$ (Diagnostic procedures constraint)

Data have been obtained to provide necessary quantification and the linear programming model has been formulated.

Solving the Case Problem

For the Northpark University Hospital and Medical Center case-mix problem, we wish to

Maximize: $NREV = 300D_1 + 400D_2$
Subject to: $2D_1 + D_2 \leq 120$
$10D_1 + 30D_2 \leq 900$
$3D_1 + 4D_2 \leq 360$

Since this problem is two-dimensional, it can be solved graphically (see Figure 5.2). In examining the graphic formulation of the linear programming model, note that the constraint inequality for diagnostic procedures (labeled as C on the graph) is completely outside the solution space and does not affect the feasible solution point; that is, it is a nonbinding constraint. The optimum solution point is S_2 on the graph, indicating that 54 patients of DRG-1 and 12 patients of DRG-2 will yield the largest amount of net revenue within the resources available. The graphic method is useful for illustrating the process of solving a linear programming problem, but is not a practical solution method for most problems.

Linear programming models can be solved mathematically using a technique called the *simplex method* (Cook 1977). The simplex method is a specialized technique for solving a system of linear equations that also optimizes an objective function. The simplex process is iterative; an

Figure 5.2 Case Problem—Graphic Solution

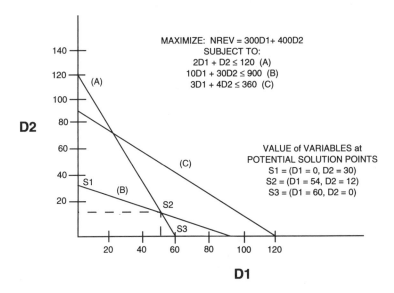

MAXIMIZE: NREV = 300D1 + 400D2
SUBJECT TO:
2D1 + D2 ≤ 120 (A)
10D1 + 30D2 ≤ 900 (B)
3D1 + 4D2 ≤ 360 (C)

VALUE of VARIABLES at
POTENTIAL SOLUTION POINTS
S1 = (D1 = 0, D2 = 30)
S2 = (D1 = 54, D2 = 12)
S3 = (D1 = 60, D2 = 0)

initial feasible solution is found and successive improvements are made repetitively until an optimum solution is found. The process, if performed manually, is very cumbersome for problems involving multiple variables and large systems of equations. Fortunately, good computer software is available for carrying out these calculations. Results of the computer formulation and solution of the problem using the *Quick-Quant* Version 4.0 software (Lapin 1994) are shown in Exhibit 5.1. (Note that all problems in this chapter are solved using *QuickQuant*.) The optimum solution point is

$D_1 = 54$, $D_2 = 12$ for net revenue of $21,000 per month

Note that the computer printout provides additional information useful in analyzing the solution. For each constraint, a slack (or surplus) number is included. Note that for constraint number 3 (diagnostic procedures), there is a surplus of 150 procedures still available for other purposes. The value of the dual variable for each constraint describes the size of the improvement in the objective function that would be generated by a unit increase in the resource. Thus, the addition of one available inpatient day would increase net revenue by $100. Adding one nursing hour would increase net revenue by $10. The dual value of 0 for diagnostic procedures indicates that this is a slack or nonbinding constraint with a potential surplus available. These values (also referred to as **shadow prices**) are useful in carrying out what-if analysis by

Exhibit 5.1   Case Problem–Computer Solution

FORMULATED LINEAR PROGRAM

Maximize P =

+ 300 X1   + 400 X2

Subject to:

C1:	+ 2 X1	+ 1 X2	<	120
C2:	+ 10 X1	+ 30 X2	<	900
C3:	+ 3 X1	+ 4 X2	<	360

SOLUTION TO LINEAR PROGRAM

Original Variable	Value
X1	54.00000
X2	12.00000

Objective Value: P = 21000.00000

Slack/Surplus Variable	Value
S1	0.00000
S2	0.00000
S3	150.00000

RIGHTHAND SIDE Sensitivity Anal.

CONSTR. No.	Type	Auxiliary Variable		Value of DUAL Variable	Lower Limit	Original Value	Upper Limit
1	<	S1	=	0.00	100.000	30.00	120.00	180.00
2	<	S2	=	0.00	10.000	600.00	900.00	2400.00
3	<	S3	=	150.00	0.000	210.00	360.00	None

OBJECTIVE COEFFICIENT Sensitivity

Main Variable	Optimal Value	DUAL Slack/Surplus	Lower Limit	Original Value	Upper Limit
X1	54.00	0.00	133.33	300.00	800.00
X2	12.00	0.00	150.00	400.00	900.00

measuring the effects on the objective function if additional resources were provided.

Linear programming is a deterministic modeling process. Note that in this case example, average values were used in formulating the constraint inequalities (i.e., average number of patient days per DRG, average number of nursing hours per DRG, and average number of diagnostic procedures per DRG). The limitation of using averages can be partly overcome by running the linear programming model multiple times using the limits of the range of the variables and the averages. The solutions at the limits of the variable ranges would represent worst-case and best-case conditions. Through this method, what-if analysis can be carried out for best-case, worst-case, and most-likely scenarios.

Sensitivity analysis can also help in evaluating the impact of using averages or estimates for parameters in the linear programming model without rerunning the computer software (Cook 1977, 187–95). Right-hand side ranging (see Exhibit 5.1) determines how much the right-hand side value of a particular constraint can be increased or decreased without changing the value of the dual variable or shadow price. Objective function coefficients (see Exhibit 5.1) determine the range over which the coefficients of each variable can vary without changing the values of these variables. For example, in the Northpark University Hospital and Medical Center case problem, the right-hand value of the inpatient days constraint can range from 30 to 180 days of available capacity without changing the dual variable value of $100. The coefficient for DRG-2 in the objective function (margin of profit for this DRG) can range from $150 to $900, and the optimal solution will still include 12 DRG-2 patients. Of course, the value of the objective function will change as the objective function coefficients change.

What-if analysis using multiple runs of the software with changed parameters can also be used to carry out sensitivity analysis.

There are limitations to the use of linear programming techniques. The following two conditions usually indicate that the model has been formulated incorrectly:

1. **No feasible solution.** It is possible to formulate a linear programming problem that has no feasible solution. This can occur when there are conflicting restrictions among the constraints.

2. **Unbounded solutions.** Unbounded solutions result from problem formulations in which the feasible region for solution extends infinitely in the direction of improvement of the objective function. There are no real-world problems in which the decision variables can assume infinite values.

Certain problems may contain multiple optimal solutions. More than one feasible solution will be obtained for linear programming problems in which the objective function is parallel to a constraint that includes an optimal extreme point. Consider for example:

$$\text{Minimize: } Z = 5X_1 + 4X_2$$
$$\text{Subject to: } \quad 10X_1 + 8X_2 \geq 30 \qquad \text{(A)}$$
$$2X_1 + X_2 \leq 6 \qquad \text{(B)}$$

In this problem, the objective function is parallel to constraint A, which is a lower boundary constraint in the solution space. Any point along line A represents an optimal solution to the problem (see Figure 5.3). Note that the *QuickQuant* software (see Exhibit 5.2) provides one optimal solution point, $X_1 = 3$ and $X_2 = 0$ and prints a message indicating that there are multiple optimal solutions.

Model Variations

Integer Programming

Linear programming models assume that the decision variables are continuous; that is, they can take on any fractional or decimal value. In real-world problems, this is often not the case. In the Northpark example, the decision variables are number of patients treated (for two DRGs). Obviously, it is not possible to treat a fraction of a patient. Cook states that linear programming may be used in such problems to provide approximate answers by rounding off the solution. However, doing so may result in a suboptimal or nonfeasible solution (Cook 1977, 126).

Integer programming solutions will eliminate this problem. Consider, for example, an alteration of the Northpark case problem (see next equation).

$$\text{Maximize: } NREV = 300D_1 + 400D_2$$
$$\text{Subject to:} \quad 2D_1 + D_2 \leq 120$$
$$12D_1 + 35D_2 \leq 900$$
$$3D_1 + 4D_2 \leq 360$$

Figure 5.3 Multiple Optimal Solutions

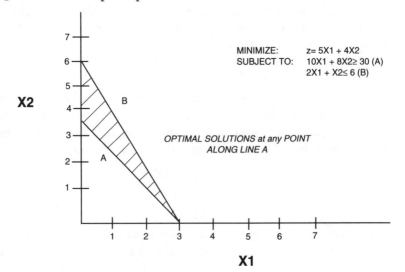

Exhibit 5.2 Multiple Optimal Solutions–Computer Output

```
                         FORMULATED LINEAR PROGRAM

Minimize C -

            + 5 X1            + 4 X2

Subject to:

  C1:      + 10 X1           + 8 X2                        >      30

  C2:      + 2 X1            + 1 X2                        <       6


                       SOLUTION TO LINEAR PROGRAM

                   Original
                   Variable        Value
                   -----------------------
                      X1           3.00000
                      X2           0.00000

                 Objective Value: C -    15.00000
             This problem has multiple optimal solutions.

                   Slack/Surplus
                     Variable        Value
                   -----------------------
                      S1           0.00000
                      S2           0.00000
```

Note that the coefficients of the second constraint (nursing hours) have been changed from 10 and 30 to 12 and 35, respectively.

The *QuickQuant* software has an integer programming solution capability that allows the problem to be formulated with one or more of the decision variables specified as integers.

Exhibit 5.3 shows the *QuickQuant* solution to this problem formulated first as an integer programming problem and second as a linear programming problem. Note that the linear programming solution overstates the value of the objective function by $51.72.

Mathematical Programming

As mentioned previously, linear programming is a special case of mathematical programming in which all elements of the model are linear. The solution of nonlinear mathematical programming models is much more complex and beyond the mathematical prerequisites for users of this book. Figure 5.4 depicts a simple, two-dimensional problem with a nonlinear solution space. Note that there are no longer points of

Exhibit 5.3 Solution to Integer Problem

FORMULATED INTEGER PROGRAM

Maximize P =

+ 300 X1   + 400 X2

Subject to:

C1:	+ 2 X1	+ 1 X2	<	120
C2:	+ 12 X1	+ 35 X2	<	900
C3:	+ 3 X1	+ 4 X2	<	360

DETAILED RECORD OF LINEAR PROGRAMS EVALUATED IN SOLVING INTEGER PROGRAM

Problem Number	Profit Upper Bound	Parent Problem	Branching Variable	Problem Status
1	19551.722			
2	19405.712	1	X1 (< 56)	
3	19500.000	1	X1 (> 57)	Integer

SOLUTION TO INTEGER PROGRAM

Original Variable	Value	Status
X1	57.00000	integer
X2	6.00000	integer

Objective Value: P = 19500.00000

FORMULATED LINEAR PROGRAM

Maximize P =

+ 300 X1   + 400 X2

Subject to:

C1:	+ 2 X1	+ 1 X2	<	120
C2:	+ 12 X1	+ 35 X2	<	900
C3:	+ 3 X1	+ 4 X2	<	360

SOLUTION TO LINEAR PROGRAM

Original Variable	Value
X1	56.89655
X2	6.20690

Objective Value: P = 19551.72270

Slack/Surplus Variable	Value
S1	0.00000
S2	0.00000
S3	164.48276

intersection where an optimal solution will be found. Readers interested in more information on mathematical programming models are referred to the "Additional Readings" at the end of this chapter for references to books that deal with this topic.

Staff Scheduling/Assignment Problems

Linear and integer programming can be used for certain types of staff scheduling models in health services organizations. Consider the following problem:

The director of Northpark University Hospital and Medical Center's walk-in primary care clinic is preparing a nurse staffing plan for the clinic. The clinic operates seven days per week from 7:30 a.m. to 4:00 p.m. According to the employee contract, registered nurses must work eight-hour shifts for five consecutive days, followed by two consecutive days off. A sampling study conducted by a management engineer provided the following data on staff requirements for each day of the week:

Monday	100 hours
Tuesday	110 hours
Wednesday	80 hours
Thursday	70 hours
Friday	60 hours
Saturday	30 hours
Sunday	20 hours

Figure 5.4 Mathematical Programming Problem with Nonlinear Solution Space

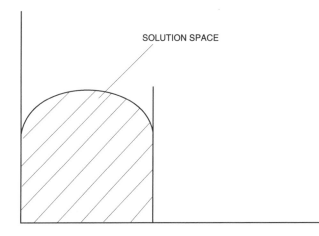

SOLUTION SPACE

The administrator wants to develop a staffing schedule that minimizes unused nursing staff hours. This problem can be solved by formulating a linear programming model as follows:

Minimize: Staff $= N_1 + N_2 + N_3 + N_4 + N_5 + N_6 + N_7$

Subject to:

$8N_1 + 0N_2 + 0N_3 + 8N_4 + 8N_5 + 8N_6 + 8N_7 \geq 100$	(Monday)
$8N_1 + 8N_2 + 0N_3 + 0N_4 + 8N_5 + 8N_6 + 8N_7 \geq 110$	(Tuesday)
$8N_1 + 8N_2 + 8N_3 + 0N_4 + 0N_5 + 8N_6 + 8N_7 \geq 80$	(Wednesday)
$8N_1 + 8N_2 + 8N_3 + 8N_4 + 0N_5 + 0N_6 + 8N_7 \geq 70$	(Thursday)
$8N_1 + 8N_2 + 8N_3 + 8N_4 + 8N_5 + 0N_6 + 0N_7 \geq 60$	(Friday)
$0N_1 + 8N_2 + 8N_3 + 8N_4 + 8N_5 + 8N_6 + 0N_7 \geq 30$	(Saturday)
$0N_1 + 0N_2 + 8N_3 + 8N_4 + 8N_5 + 8N_6 + 8N_7 \geq 20$	(Sunday)

where:

N_1 = number of nurses in the cohort working Monday–Friday

N_2 = number of nurses in the cohort working Tuesday–Saturday

and so forth.

Note that there is one constraint for each day of the week. Monday, for example, nurses could not be assigned from cohort N_2 (the group that works Tuesday to Saturday) or from cohort N_3 (the group that works Wednesday to Sunday). Consequently, values of zero are assigned as coefficients for these variables in the Monday constraint.

Note also that the coefficients and right-hand side values must use the same units of measurements, hours in this problem.

The solution to this problem (using integer programming) is shown in Exhibit 5.4. Ten nurses should be assigned to the Monday–Friday schedule and four nurses should be assigned to the Friday–Tuesday schedule to minimize nurse staffing requirements.

Certain types of scheduling and assignment problems can also be solved using the transportation/assignment model described in Chapter 6.

Computer Software

Linear programming software is readily available on the commercial software market. The software often will be part of a larger package of programs labeled "Operations Research," "Management Science," or "Decision Analysis."

Several spreadsheet programs have incorporated linear programming calculations as an option. Coefficients for the objective function and the constraint inequalities/equations are entered as columnar values

Exhibit 5.4 Example Problem—Integer Programming

```
                         FORMULATED INTEGER PROGRAM

Minimize C =

            + 1 X1          + 1 X2          + 1 X3          + 1 X4
            + 1 X5          + 1 X6          + 1 X7

Subject to:

  C1:       + 8 X1          + 0 X2          + 0 X3          + 8 X4
            + 8 X5          + 8 X6          + 8 X7                    >    100

  C2:       + 8 X1          + 8 X2          + 0 X3          + 0 X4
            + 8 X5          + 8 X6          + 8 X7                    >    110

  C3:       + 8 X1          + 8 X2          + 8 X3          + 0 X4
            + 0 X5          + 8 X6          + 8 X7                    >     80

  C4:       + 8 X1          + 8 X2          + 8 X3          + 8 X4
            + 0 X5          + 0 X6          + 8 X7                    >     70

  C5:       + 8 X1          + 8 X2          + 8 X3          + 8 X4
            + 8 X5          + 0 X6          + 0 X7                    >     60

  C6:       + 0 X1          + 8 X2          + 8 X3          + 8 X4
            + 8 X5          + 8 X6          + 0 X7                    >     30

  C7:       + 0 X1          + 0 X2          + 8 X3          + 8 X4
            + 8 X5          + 8 X6          + 8 X7                    >     20



                    BEST SOLUTION SO FAR (Not Confirmed as Optimal)

                    Original
                    Variable        Value           Status
                    ------------------------------------------
                       X1          10.00000         integer
                       X2           0.00000         integer
                       X3           0.00000         integer
                       X4           0.00000         integer
                       X5           4.00000         integer
                       X6           0.00000         integer
                       X7           0.00000         integer

                    Objective Value: C =      14.00000
```

in the spreadsheet, and the software will compute the solution values for the decision variables and the objective function. This type of software is particularly useful in what-if analysis, where changes in the coefficients and right-hand side values can be entered into the spreadsheet and the effects on the decision variables and objective functions are displayed. Exhibit 5.5 is a table of solutions for the Northpark University Hospital Medical Center case problem obtained by using the EXCEL spreadsheet (SOLVER) software package. The following scenarios are included:

1. The original problem formulation.
2. The margin for DRG-1 is reduced to $250 per patient because of higher costs.
3. The margin for DRG-2 is increased to $425 per patient because of improved efficiency.
4. Additional nursing service capacity (300 hours) is added through hiring.

Any number of combinations of changes in the coefficients and right-hand side values could be incorporated into this type of "what-if" analysis made easy through spreadsheet software.

There are many specialized software packages offered to health services organizations by commercial vendors. Some of these packages incorporate linear programming techniques. For example, Chapter 11 of the *Hospital Software Sourcebook* (McKenzie 1993) contains descriptions of 27 software packages in the category "food services and nutrition." Several of these packages provide computer-assisted menu planning based on linear programming, in which costs are minimized while nutritional requirements are met or exceeded. Chapter 11 of this book (McKenzie 1993) also describes nurse staffing software packages in which optimal staffing models (least cost) are developed given the constraints of personnel available for assignment.

Analysis, Interpretation, and Application of Results to Management Decisions

As a result of the linear programming analysis described above, the administrator of the surgical specialty division of Northpark University Hospital and Medical Center can now make a more informed decision about the planned marketing campaign. Using the original model formulation (see Exhibit 5.1), the optimum mix of the two high-volume procedures within service capacity available on the unit would be to add 54 patients for procedure DRG-1 and 12 patients for procedure DRG-2, a ratio of 4.5 to 1 in favor of DRG-1. Consequently, emphasis in the marketing campaign should be placed on efforts to attract additional DRG-1 patients.

Note that the model provides additional information to the administrator on the costs and constraints involved in providing these services. By using what-if analysis, as shown in Exhibit 5.5, the administrator can estimate the effects of changes in the way services are delivered. For example, if the margin for DRG-1 were to drop to

Exhibit 5.5   What-If Spreadsheet—Linear Programming

OBJECTIVE FUNCTION		CONSTRAINT #1			CONSTRAINT #2			CONSTRAINT #3			RESULTS		
											D1	D2	NREV
300	400	2	1	120	10	30	900	3	4	360	54	12	$21,000	(1)
250	400	2	1	120	10	30	900	3	4	360	54	12	$18,300	(2)
300	425	2	1	120	10	30	900	3	4	360	54	12	$21,300	(3)
300	400	2	1	120	10	30	1200	3	4	360	48	24	$24,000	(4)

NOTES: (1) Original formulation of case problem
(2) Margin for D1 drops to $250 per case
(3) Margin for D2 increases to $425 per case
(4) 300 hours of additional nursing capacity

$250 (because of increased costs, decreased efficiency, or a decrease in Medicare reimbursement), then net revenue would decline from $21,000 to $18,300 for these additional services. Similarly, if the margin for DRG-2 were to increase to $425 (because of improved efficiency or increase in Medicare reimbursement), then net revenue would increase by $300, to $21,300.

What-if analysis using the linear programming model also can be used to estimate the effects of adding additional service capacity. For example, in Exhibit 5.5, the addition of 300 hours of nursing service capacity would increase net revenue to $24,000.

Linear programming is an important tool for use in case-mix analysis and several other important resource allocation or scheduling problems in hospitals and health services organizations. Applications of the model to case-mix problems found in the literature are described in the mini-case reports that follow.

Case Studies from the Literature

Patient Mix Model (Brandeau and Hopkins 1984)

Stanford University Hospital (SUH) in Stanford, California, employed a linear programming model to determine how changes in the mix of patients by intensity level and payer class affect the hospital's finances and resource usage. This strategic planning model is used to answer a series of questions, such as:

1. How will net financial contribution and resource use change after a hospital modernization project?
2. How will hospital finances be affected by government legislation?
3. What is the marginal increase or decrease when a high-intensity patient is replaced with a low-intensity one?

The objective function for the model was the amount of net income needed to cover fixed expenses. Patients were divided into 14 groups representing different hospital services, payers, and service intensity level. The intensity level was determined by combining DRGs based on lengths of stay and average charges. Constraints were based on the amount of services available in each department and on the number of patients of each type (reflecting the hospital's commitment to serve a given population and patient demand).

The completed linear programming model yielded results for each of the 14 patient groups, illustrating the quantity of services patients consumed in certain departments according to days, hours, number of procedures, etc. For example, the average high-intensity Medicaid patient at SUH generates a loss in net income of $1,153. This same patient uses 12.58 routine bed days, 1.79 ICU/CCU days, 1.23 pediatric days, 1.12 anesthesiology procedures, 7.04 oxygen therapy hours, and so on. The linear programming model indicated that if there were more demand by OB/GYN and pediatric patients, it would be cost-effective for the hospital to admit them. Substituting a high-intensity medical-surgical patient for a low-intensity medical-surgical patient would increase net income by $2,900.

This patient mix model was used to answer many policy questions at SUH. The model explicitly links patient diagnosis with resource use and income.

Blood Allocation System (Sapountzis 1989)

The Regional Blood Transfusion Service (RBTS) of Glasgow and West of Scotland in Carluke, Great Britain, is a single monopoly blood-banking wholesaler. It is responsible for procuring, drawing, processing, storing, and distributing blood to the hospitals in its region. Under the auspices of Britain's National Health Service, each hospital must receive its blood from RBTS, who, in turn, allocates units to the hospitals according to the number of units requested. This RBTS center serves about 68 hospitals and annually collects about 150,000 units of blood.

The process of allocating units of blood from a regional transfusion center to the hospitals of its area must consider certain characteristics of the individual hospitals, such as the transfusion activity, demand, and the RBTS's policy concerning the distribution of units of blood, through a utility function.

Using a linear programming model, the optimal allocation of units of blood from an RBTS to the hospitals in its area was studied. Data collected contained information about each unit of blood, the blood type, the date of withdrawal, the hospital and the date it was sent, and finally, whether the unit had expired or not. Because the model considers the statistical distribution of expired units of blood, this method was found to improve the utility of expired units and to minimize the expected expiries of the units sent to hospitals.

As a result of this linear programming model, the RBTS can optimize the utilization of blood within its region and can allocate blood more efficiently to the hospitals that it serves, while taking into better account the expiration date of the units available. The author plans to expand the model to add additional factors including transportation time, costs, and distances.

Nurse Staffing Model (Leiken, Sexton, and Silkman 1986)

The Oxford Gerontology Center in upstate New York operates in two facilities, the Skilled Nursing Facility (SNF) and the Health Related Facility (HRF). Approximately 200–250 patients are divided equally between the facilities. The center provides 24-hour nursing and physician services; physical, occupational, and recreational therapies; and dietary, pharmaceutical, and social services.

The Center wanted to assess quality/cost trade-offs as they arise in nurse staffing and task assignment decisions commonly faced by nursing home administrators and industry regulators. The linear programming model employed by the Center included quality-related considerations such as restricting tasks to personnel at specified skill levels.

Each nurse at the Oxford Center was asked to identify his or her skill level (RN, LPN, aide), shift (day, evening, night), and facility (SNF, HRF). The 7 RNs, 23 LPNs, and 41 aides who participated in the study were then asked to identify those tasks that they felt they were capable of performing and to indicate the average amount of time required by them to execute each task on their shift in their facility. The sample contained 46 SNF patients (41 percent of the total) and 51 HRF patients (43 percent of the total).

The baseline, or minimum cost, solution assumed that personnel at every skill level are permitted to perform every task. The linear programming technique employed in this study determined the baseline cost for staffing both facilities for each shift to be $4,057/day. However, when six tasks were selected to be completed solely by RNs, the linear programming solution (as expected) called for more RNs under such a restriction. The total cost rose to $4,653/day (an increase of 14.7 percent) when this constraint was added. The administrator was then faced with a decision: either to impose the restrictions and accept the 14.7 percent increase in nursing wage costs, or not to impose the restrictions and keep nursing wage costs lower. At such a juncture, the medical experience and insight of management must come into play.

Additional Reports from the Literature

In addition to these case studies presented above, further research has been employed using linear programming techniques.

Sexton et al. (1989) studied a set of VA medical centers to evaluate their relative managerial efficiencies. Linear programming was used to identify resources underutilized and services that were inefficiently produced. The model showed that relative inefficiency existed in about one-third of the Veterans Affairs medical centers nationwide. Elimination of this inefficiency, without reducing the level of services provided, would save VA over $300 million annually on personnel, equipment, drugs, and supplies.

Lipscomb and Douglas (1986) used data from a national survey of dental practices in a linear programming model to determine whether cost efficiency in dental services production increases with practice size. They concluded that cost efficiency does increase with practice size, over the range from solo to four-dentist practices. The question of whether the apparent production efficiencies of a group practice are ultimately translated by the market into lower fees, shorter queues, or other nonprice benefits was left unresolved.

Lipscomb and Scheffler (1975) developed a linear programming model of dental care delivery used to examine the economic implications of introducing expanded-duty dental assistants (EDDAs) in three types of dental practices. The authors concluded that a dentist in solo practice can more than double net revenue by hiring an EDDA but will not increase productivity further by hiring additional EDDAs. Two- and three-dentist groups can also increase revenues by hiring EDDAs; however, beyond a certain point, an inverse relationship exists between the number of assistants hired and net revenue generated.

Barber, Branson, and Mahayni (1977) formulated a linear programming model to minimize the total travel time to hospitals for Rhode

Island residents. Optimal hospital locations with ideal bed distributions were derived from the model.

Greenwald, Woodward, and Berg (1979) studied the economic trade-offs among the various resources needed for appropriate care. Several strategies designed to achieve an optimal mix of investments in CT scanners and transportation resources in the South Chicago region were examined using linear programming. The linear programming model concluded that (1) the proper location of CT scanners is as important for cost containment as the optimal number, and (2) excess capacity in the utilization of a single resource—CT scanners—need not imply inefficiency in the overall delivery of the service. These findings help describe the importance of viewing health care as a package of interrelated services, both for providing access to appropriate care and for achieving cost containment.

Problems

5.1 The data in the tables below were obtained from the hospital's information system. They provide information about four of the hospital's DRGs.

Resource Requirements

	DRG-1	DRG-2	DRG-3	DRG-4
Hours of diagnostic services required	7	4	2	1
Inpatient days	5	2	1	0
Hours of nursing care	30	10	5	1
Pharmacy dollars	$800	$500	$150	$50

Resource Costs and Capacities

Resource	Cost	Maximum Available per Week
Diagnostic services	$100/hour	480 hours
Inpatient days	$500/day	170 days
Nursing care	$40/hour	1,000 hours
Pharmacy dollars		$50,000

DRG Margins

	Margin (Profit) per Patient	Minimum Number of Patients Who Must Be Treated per Week
DRG-1	$2,000	10
DRG-2	$1,000	15

DRG-3	$500	40
DRG-4	$300	160

Requirement: Answer the following questions.

a. What is the optimal number of patients the hospital should attempt to schedule weekly in each DRG category?

b. What would be the total operating margin generated if the hospital met this optimal weekly schedule?

c. How much additional operating margin would be provided by ten more hours per week of diagnostic services? Ten more inpatient days per week?

d. If the operating margin for DRG-4 could be increased to $500 through improved productivity, how would this affect the total weekly operating margin?

5.2 As director of Patient Services for Community Mental Health Center, you are planning casework assignments for the coming month. Your staff consists of three categories of professional personnel: visiting nurses, social workers, and psychologists. Data on availability and costs of your personnel are presented in the following table:

Personnel Category	Staff Hours Available Next Month	Average Hourly Cost
Visiting nurse	200	$35.00
Social worker	300	$28.00
Psychologist	100	$45.00

Your caseload may be handled in one of two ways—through home visitation or clinic appointments. The average home visitation case (including travel time) requires ten hours from a visiting nurse, 12 hours from a social worker, and five hours from a psychologist. The average clinic case requires five hours from a visiting nurse, 15 hours from a social worker, and four hours from a psychologist. A minimum of ten cases must be handled during the coming month.

Requirement: Find the following three solutions.

a. The least-cost solution

b. The solution that maximizes quantity of service rendered

c. The solution that maximizes allocation of resources (i.e., has the least number of unused staff hours)

Use integer programming in solving this problem.

5.3 An ambulatory care center has received funds to add 50,000 square feet to its present building. Management has decided to use the new space for relocation and expansion of the pharmacy, radiology department, and laboratory. It was decided that the laboratory should occupy no more than 50 percent of the new space. Also, the combined space allocated for radiology and the laboratory cannot exceed the space allocated to the pharmacy by more than 20,000 square feet. Each of the three departments must receive a minimum allocation of at least 10,000 square feet. The Center's management analyst provided the following net revenue figures for each of the three departments:

Pharmacy $12 per square foot
Radiology $20 per square foot
Laboratory $16 per square foot

Requirement: Determine how the space should be allocated to generate the maximum amount of net revenue.

References

Barber, B. K., M. H. Branson, and R. Mahayni. 1977. "Minimizing Travel Time to Hospital Beds in Rhode Island." Technical Report No. 10. National Technical Information Service. August.

Brandeau, M. L., and D. S. P. Hopkins. 1984. "A Patient Mix Model for Hospital Financial Planning." *Inquiry* 21 (Spring): 32–44.

Cook, T. M., and R. A. Russell. 1977. *Introduction to Management Science.* Englewood Cliffs, NJ: Prentice-Hall, Inc.

Greenwald, H. P., J. M. Woodward, and D. H. Berg. 1979. "Transportation or CT Scanners: A Theory and Method of Health Resources Allocation." *Health Services Research* 14 (Fall): 207–19.

Lapin, L. L. 1994. *QuickQuant Version 4.0.* Pleasanton, CA: Alamo Publishing Co.

Leiken, A., T. R. Sexton, and R. H. Silkman. 1986. "A Model to Assess the Quality-Cost Trade-off in Nursing Homes." *Health Services Research* 21 (2): 145–60.

Lipscomb, J., and C. W. Douglas. 1986. "Are Larger Dental Practices More Efficient? An Analysis of Dental Services Production." *Health Services Research* 21 (December): 635–61.

Lipscomb, J., and R. M. Scheffler. 1975. "Impact of Expanded-Duty Assistants on Cost and Productivity in Dental Care Delivery." *Health Services Research* 10 (Spring): 14–35.

McKenzie, J. R. (ed.). 1993. *Hospital Software Sourcebook.* Gaithersburg, MD: Aspen Publishers, Inc.

Sapountzis, C. 1989. "Allocating Blood to Hospitals." *Journal of the Operational Research Society* 40 (5): 443–9.

Sexton, T. R., A. M. Leiken, A. H. Nolan, S. Liss, A. Hogan, and R. H. Silkman. 1989. "Evaluating Managerial Efficiency of Veterans Administration Medical Centers Using Data Envelopment Analysis." *Medical Care* 27 (December): 1175–88.

Additional Readings

Anderson, D. R., D. J. Sweeney, and T. A. Williams. *An Introduction to Management Science: Quantitative Approaches to Decision Making.* St. Paul, MN: West, 1988.

Eppen, G. D., and F. J. Gould. *Introductory Management Science.* Englewood Cliffs, NJ: Prentice-Hall, 1987.

Hughes, W. L., and S. Y. Soliman. "Short-term Case Mix Management with Linear Programming." *Hospital & Health Services Administration* 30 (January–February 1985): 52–60.

Lee, S. M., L. J. Moore, and B. W. Taylor III. *Management Science.* Boston: Allyn and Bacon, 1990. Note particularly "Nonlinear Programming," 809–28.

Miller, L. *Operations Research and Systems Analysis at Rand 1968–1988.* Santa Monica, CA: Rand, 1989.

Phillips, D. T., A. Ravindran, and J. J. Solberg. *Operations Research: Principles and Practices.* New York: Wiley, 1987.

Rabinowitz, M., M. B. Dumas, and D. Valinsky. "A Two-Stage Optimization Model for In-Patient Transfers." *Operations Research* 24, 5 (1976): 871–83.

Render, B., and R. M. Stair Jr. *Quantitative Analysis for Management.* Boston: Allyn and Bacon, 1988.

Robbins, W. A., and N. Tuntiwongpiboon. "Linear Programming: A Useful Tool in Case-Mix Management." *Healthcare Financial Management* (June 1989): 114–16.

6

TRANSPORTATION AND ASSIGNMENT MODELS

ANY PROBLEMS in health services management involve matching units of demand to units of supply. A common example would be a staff assignment problem in which the skills of trained employees are matched to needed points of service within the organization in the most efficient manner. As a second example, a corporate system of hospitals and ambulatory care centers might have a contract for the provision of medical supplies and pharmaceuticals from a distributor with multiple warehouse locations. The corporation would be interested in the least-cost method of supplying units of the system.

Problems of this type can be solved employing the transportation and assignment modeling techniques described in this chapter. The transportation model is a special case of linear programming, but the model uses a simpler formulation and solution process. The term "transportation model" is used because early applications were made to problems in the manufacturing industry that involved shipment of materials between multiple warehouse sites and multiple plant sites while minimizing the cost of transportation.

Introduction of Case Problem

The director of Pharmacy Services for Tri-State Health Services Corporation is responsible for management oversight of a contract with a major supplier of intravenous fluids for the Corporation. There are four hospitals in the system supplied by the contract. The supplier has three warehouses in the region from which the IV fluids can be obtained. Transportation is by truck, and shipment costs are based upon the number of miles traveled for delivery.

The director is preparing an order to be placed with the supplier for next month's shipment of fluids to each hospital in the system. Requirements are as follows:

Hospital A	1,200 cases needed
Hospital B	1,500 cases needed
Hospital C	2,300 cases needed
Hospital D	2,400 cases needed

In placing the order, the director wants to include a shipment request that will minimize transportation costs for the system.

An Overview of the Transportation Model

Transportation models are formulated by constructing a two-dimensional matrix in which one dimension represents the sources of supply and the other dimension represents the points of demand. The available units of supply for each source are shown in the margins of the matrix on one dimension, and the needed units of demand are included in the margin on the other dimension. The units of cost for transportation between each supply point and each demand point are shown in the cells of the matrix.

Consider, for example, the following simple transportation cost matrix:

	Destination Points		Units
	D1	D2	Available
Sources of Supply S1	C1	C2	1,380
Sources of Supply S2	C3	C4	970
Units Needed	1,500	850	

Supply point S1 has 1,380 units available for shipment, and supply point S2 has 970 units available. Destination D1 requires 1,500 units, and destination D2 requires 850 units. Shipment costs per unit are shown in the cells of the matrix. For example, the cost to ship one unit from source S1 to destination D1 is C1.

Note that in this sample formulation, total demand and total supply are exactly equal, which will not often be the case. Unequal supply and demand conditions are discussed later in this chapter. Note also that in many transportation problems, costs are based upon a standard amount per unit of distance traveled in handling the shipment (e.g., cost per unit per mile). In such cases, distances between each point of supply and each point of demand are often used as surrogates for costs.

The solution to the transportation model will determine the number of units that should be shipped from each source to each destination to minimize shipping costs. The solution process involves establishing an initial solution matrix and then moving toward an optimum solution through a series of iterations. Each interim solution is tested until the solution matrix that meets the objective of minimal costs is obtained. Computer programs are available to carry out these repetitive computations that are cumbersome to do manually.

Model Formulation, Quantification, and Data Requirements

The director of Pharmacy Services for Tri-State Health Services can develop a least-cost shipment plan for the IV fluids' order by using the transportation model. Three sets of data are required to formulate the problem: demand requirements, supply available, and transportation cost for shipment.

Demand requirements for each hospital in the system for the coming month are known. As previously stated:

Hospital A	1,200 cases needed
Hospital B	1,500 cases needed
Hospital C	2,300 cases needed
Hospital D	2,400 cases needed

The director must determine the quantities available for shipment from each of the three warehouse locations operated by the supplier. These data, obtained by a phone call to the supplier's shipping manager, are as follows:

Warehouse #1	1,800 cases of IV fluids available to ship
Warehouse #2	2,400 cases of IV fluids available to ship
Warehouse #3	3,200 cases of IV fluids available to ship

The third data set required is the table of transportation costs between each supply point and each destination. The contract between Tri-State and the supplier calls for a standard shipment cost (by truck) of $0.02 per case of IV fluid for each mile traveled in making the delivery. The distances between each supply point and each destination are as follows:

Warehouse #1 to	Hospital A	60 miles
	Hospital B	50 miles

	Hospital C	110 miles
	Hospital D	40 miles
Warehouse #2 to	Hospital A	30 miles
	Hospital B	80 miles
	Hospital C	100 miles
	Hospital D	50 miles
Warehouse #3 to	Hospital A	50 miles
	Hospital B	70 miles
	Hospital C	140 miles
	Hospital D	90 miles

A management engineer working with the director of Pharmacy Services prepares the following transportation cost matrix for input into a standard transportation model computer software package.

| | Hospital | | | | Available |
	A	B	C	D	to Ship
Warehouse #1	1.20	1.00	2.20	0.80	1,800
Warehouse #2	0.60	1.60	2.00	1.00	2,400
Warehouse #3	1.00	1.40	2.80	1.80	3,200
Cases Needed	1,200	1,500	2,300	2,400	

Note that the shipment cost factors in the matrix were obtained by multiplying the miles between each supply point and each destination by the standard cost of $0.02 per case per mile. For example, to ship one case of IV fluid from Warehouse #1 to Hospital A, the cost would be 60 miles × $0.02 per mile = $1.20 per case shipped.

Solving the Case Problem

As stated above, transportation and assignment models are special cases of linear programming models that can be formulated and solved using techniques described in Chapter 5. However, as Cook (1977, 210) points out, transportation/assignment models have a special mathematical structure that can be solved by simplified computer procedures. The primary benefits of using these alternative solution techniques include (1) simplified problem formulation, and (2) faster computer processing with less memory required, allowing the program to handle larger problems.

Using *QuickQuant* software, the computer formulation and solution to the Tri-State Health Services pharmacy shipment problem are shown in Exhibit 6.1. Note that there are 12 possible shipment routes between the three warehouses and four hospitals. However, in the least-cost solution, only six of these routes will be used:

- 1,800 cases shipped from Warehouse #1 to Hospital D
- 2,300 cases shipped from Warehouse #2 to Hospital C
- 100 cases shipped from Warehouse #2 to Hospital D
- 1,200 cases shipped from Warehouse #3 to Hospital A
- 1,500 cases shipped from Warehouse #3 to Hospital B
- 500 cases shipped from Warehouse #3 to Hospital D

Total shipment costs for all deliveries would be $10,340.

This example problem was written with total demand and total supply equal to illustrate the most simple case for problem formulation and solution. In the real world, this is not a likely situation. In the section on model variations that follows, the equal supply-demand condition is removed and other model formulation conditions that are likely to be encountered in real-life applications are described.

Model Variations

Unequal Supply and Demand

For most operational problems, supply and demand for materials and/or services will not be equal. This condition is handled in the transporta-

Exhibit 6.1 Case Problem—Computer Solution

```
                     ORIGINAL PROBLEM DATA

=================================================================
  From   :                To Destination              :
  Source :      D1        D2        D3        D4       : Capacity
=================================================================
   S1    :     1.20      1.00      2.20      0.80      :   1800
   S2    :     0.60      1.60      2.00      1.00      :   2400
   S3    :     1.00      1.40      2.80      1.80      :   3200
=================================================================
 Demand  :     1200      1500      2300      2400      :   7400
=================================================================


                        OPTIMAL SOLUTION

=================================================================
  From   :                To Destination              :
  Source :      D1        D2        D3        D4       : Capacity
=================================================================
   S1    :     0.00      0.00      0.00   1800.00      :   1800
   S2    :     0.00      0.00   2300.00    100.00      :   2400
   S3    :  1200.00   1500.00      0.00    500.00      :   3200
=================================================================
 Demand  :     1200      1500      2300      2400      :   7400
=================================================================

              Minimum cost is C =   10340
```

tion model by establishing an extra row or column, generally referred to as a "dummy" row or column.

The solution process assigns all supply available with any surplus or shortfall assigned to the dummy row or column. A unit cost of 0 is assigned to all cells in the matrix in the dummy row or column.

Supply Exceeds Demand

Exhibit 6.2 is a reformulation of the Tri-State pharmacy shipment problem in which supply available from the three warehouses exceeds the amount required to be shipped by 600 cases of IV fluids—200 additional units at Warehouse #1 and 400 additional units at Warehouse #2. Note that the *QuickQuant* software automatically established a dummy column with zero unit costs, and the excess capacity is assigned to this column. In comparing the results to those of the original problem formulation, note that the shipment plan has changed and the total cost of shipment has been reduced from $10,340 to $9,860.

Demand Exceeds Supply

In Exhibit 6.3, the conditions are reversed. Demand at Hospital B is increased by 100 cases and demand at Hospital D is increased by 100 cases over the original problem formulation. Thus, the available supply is 200 cases short of the amount needed at the four hospitals in the

Exhibit 6.2 Supply Exceeds Demand

ORIGINAL PROBLEM DATA

From Source :	D1	D2	To Destination D3	D4	Dum*	:	Capacity
S1 :	1.20	1.00	2.20	0.80	0.00	:	2000
S2 :	0.60	1.60	2.00	1.00	0.00	:	2800
S3 :	1.00	1.40	2.80	1.80	0.00	:	3200
Demand :	1200	1500	2300	2400	600	:	8000

OPTIMAL SOLUTION

From Source :	D1	D2	To Destination D3	D4	Dum*	:	Capacity
S1 :	0.00	0.00	0.00	2000.00	0.00	:	2000
S2 :	100.00	0.00	2300.00	400.00	0.00	:	2800
S3 :	1100.00	1500.00	0.00	0.00	600.00	:	3200
Demand :	1200	1500	2300	2400	600	:	8000

Minimum cost is C = 9860

system. In this case, the computer software establishes a dummy row with zero costs. In the optimal solution, 200 cases of IV fluid are assigned from this dummy row to Hospital C, indicating that there would be a shortfall in the shipment to this facility. The director of Pharmacy Services would need to determine if this situation was acceptable or whether alternative ordering and shipping arrangements would need to be made.

Prohibited Routing

For some problems, certain combinations of shipment or assignment may not be permitted. In this situation, the prohibited route must be blocked in the initial problem formulation. This is accomplished by assigning a very large positive number as a cost factor if the objective is to minimize costs, or by assigning a very large negative number if the objective is to maximize profits or amount of service provided.

In the Tri-State case problem, assume that shipment from Warehouse #2 to Hospital C must be temporarily prohibited because of a dispute between shipping and receiving managers at the two facilities. Exhibit 6.4 shows this problem formulation with a very high cost factor ($5,000) inserted into the Row 2–Column 3 cell of the transportation

Exhibit 6.3 Demand Exceeds Supply

ORIGINAL PROBLEM DATA

From Source	D1	To Destination D2	D3	D4		Capacity
S1	1.20	1.00	2.20	0.80	:	1800
S2	0.60	1.60	2.00	1.00	:	2400
S3	1.00	1.40	2.80	1.80	:	3200
Dum*	0.00	0.00	0.00	0.00	:	200
Demand	1200	1600	2300	2500	:	7600

OPTIMAL SOLUTION

From Source	D1	To Destination D2	D3	D4		Capacity
S1	0.00	0.00	0.00	1800.00	:	1800
S2	0.00	0.00	2100.00	300.00	:	2400
S3	1200.00	1600.00	0.00	400.00	:	3200
Dum*	0.00	0.00	200.00	0.00	:	200
Demand	1200	1600	2300	2500	:	7600

Minimum cost is C = 10100

matrix. This changes the final routing in the optimal solution, and total shipping costs are increased from $10,340 to $11,060 under this scenario.

Alternative Optimum Solutions

There may be more than one optimum solution to the transportation problem, with the alternative solutions yielding the same results in the objective (e.g., lowest possible shipping costs). Note that there is a second optimal solution of the original case problem in this chapter, as follows:

- 1,800 cases shipped from Warehouse #1 to Hospital D
- 1,800 cases shipped from Warehouse #2 to Hospital C
- 600 cases shipped from Warehouse #2 to Hospital D
- 1,200 cases shipped from Warehouse #3 to Hospital A
- 1,500 cases shipped from Warehouse #3 to Hospital B
- 500 cases shipped from Warehouse #3 to Hospital C

Total shipping costs are still $10,340.

Assignment Problems

Certain management problems involve assigning employees to work-stations, one employee per station. Work assignments are to be made

Exhibit 6.4 Prohibited Routing

```
                         ORIGINAL PROBLEM DATA

============================================================================
 From   :                    To Destination                    :
 Source :       D1          D2          D3          D4          : Capacity
============================================================================
  S1    :      1.20        1.00        2.20        0.80         :   1800
  S2    :      0.60        1.60      5000.00       1.00         :   2400
  S3    :      1.00        1.40        2.80        1.80         :   3200
============================================================================
 Demand :      1200        1500        2300        2400         :   7400
============================================================================

                           OPTIMAL SOLUTION

============================================================================
 From   :                    To Destination                    :
 Source :       D1          D2          D3          D4          : Capacity
============================================================================
  S1    :      0.00        0.00       600.00     1200.00        :   1800
  S2    :   1200.00        0.00         0.00     1200.00        :   2400
  S3    :      0.00     1500.00      1700.00        0.00        :   3200
============================================================================
 Demand :      1200        1500        2300        2400         :   7400
============================================================================

                      Minimum cost is C =  11060
```

to minimize labor costs. The assignment model, which is a special case of the transportation model, can be used to solve these problems.

Consider the following example. A clinical laboratory has four different types of tests to be carried out using automated testing equipment. Four technicians are to be assigned to complete these tests. The salary rates for the technicians are as follows:

Technician A	$7.00 per hour
Technician B	$6.75 per hour
Technician C	$8.25 per hour
Technician D	$7.50 per hour

Because of different levels of training and experience, the technicians require different amounts of time to complete each test as follows:

	Test 1	Test 2	Test 3	Test 4
Technician A	30 minutes	75 minutes	15 minutes	45 minutes
Technician B	25 minutes	60 minutes	18 minutes	60 minutes
Technician C	18 minutes	90 minutes	12 minutes	45 minutes
Technician D	30 minutes	80 minutes	20 minutes	50 minutes

Your task is to assign the technicians to the automated equipment in the most cost-effective manner.

Assignment model software can be used to solve this problem. A matrix of costs must first be developed for input into the computer program. Note that this requires multiplying the time required for each technician to complete each test by that technician's salary rate. A word of caution: be sure to use the same units of measure. Since salaries are expressed in cost per hour and task completion times are expressed in minutes, conversion to a common unit is required. The resultant cost matrix is shown below:

	Test 1	Test 2	Test 3	Test 4
Technician A	$3.50	$ 8.75	$1.75	$5.25
Technician B	$2.81	$ 6.75	$2.03	$6.75
Technician C	$2.48	$12.38	$1.65	$6.19
Technician D	$3.75	$10.00	$2.50	$6.25

Exhibit 6.5 is the *QuickQuant* solution to this problem using the assignment model. The most efficient assignment matrix is:

Technician A assigned to Test 4
Technician B assigned to Test 2
Technician C assigned to Test 1
Technician D assigned to Test 3

Exhibit 6.5 Assignment Model

ORIGINAL PROBLEM DATA

Person :	T1	T2	Task T3	T4	:	Capacity
P1 :	3.50	8.75	1.75	5.25	:	1
P2 :	2.81	6.75	2.03	6.75	:	1
P3 :	2.48	12.38	1.65	6.19	:	1
P4 :	3.75	10.00	2.50	6.25	:	1
Demand :	1	1	1	1	:	4

OPTIMAL SOLUTION

Person :	T1	T2	Task T3	T4	:	Capacity
P1 :	0.00	0.00	Zero	1.00	:	1
P2 :	Zero	1.00	0.00	0.00	:	1
P3 :	1.00	0.00	Zero	0.00	:	1
P4 :	0.00	0.00	1.00	0.00	:	1
Demand :	1	1	1	1	:	4

Minimum cost is C = 16.98

Total cost for carrying out four tests is $16.98.

Note that transportation model software can also be used to solve this problem, with the condition that available supply and demand for each row and column have a value of one (i.e., one employee for each workstation).

Description of Available Computer Software

Transportation/Assignment model software is readily available on the commercial software market. As mentioned earlier, transportation and assignment problems are a special case of linear programming and can be solved using linear programming software.

As discussed in Chapter 5, commercial software packages may employ operations research components in their design. The *Hospital Software Sourcebook* (McKenzie 1993) provides descriptions of 49 software packages to support nursing administration. Several of these packages include nurse staffing components using assignment modeling techniques as described in this chapter.

Analysis, Interpretation, and Application of Results to Management Decisions

The transportation and assignment models described in this chapter provide tools for management to employ in controlling costs and optimizing the assignment of personnel within health services organizations.

In the Tri-State Health Services Corporation case problem, the director of Pharmacy Services now has information available from the transportation model to assist in the preparation of a shipment plan for IV fluids that will minimize shipping costs. In addition to using the model for operational planning, Tri-State corporate managers can employ this model for long-range analysis of alternative arrangements for ordering and shipping materials needed in the provision of health services. What-if analysis can be used to study alternative routing and transportation options in developing contracts with suppliers.

The assignment model provides another management tool designed to optimize the use of human resources in the provision of services. Staffing plans can be developed that will help reduce personnel costs and assist supervisors in using technical and professional staff in the most productive manner.

Case Studies from the Literature

Pharmaceutical Distribution (Harrison 1979)

The Cahill May Roberts Company (CMR), one of Ireland's largest wholesale distributors of pharmaceuticals, faced a difficult transportation problem. With five warehouses spread throughout the country, the firm had its head office and three warehouses in the Dublin area. The company supplied 400 customers in the Dublin area and over 800 customers in 300 outlying towns and villages. The customers, mainly retail druggists, were supplied by delivery vans, with a drop-off frequency varying from twice per day to once per week.

No coherent distribution plan for the whole company had been formulated. Customers often received their supplies from more than one warehouse. This illogical transportation system could not efficiently satisfy druggists' demands for products.

The implementation of a transportation planning model yielded the following results:

1. A 27 percent reduction in delivery and transportation cost

2. A $765,000 savings in overhead
3. A reduction of $125,000 in capital investments, with further savings anticipated
4. A 60 percent increase in customer service, leading to a sales increase of $2,457,000

CT Scanners (Greenwald, Woodward, and Berg 1979)

In these days of health care cost consciousness, the CT scanner has become a rallying point because of its high cost and rapid proliferation. Regulatory agencies are concentrating on restricting the deployment of new CT scanners. Several states have declared moratoriums for acquiring the devices. Certificates of need for their purchase are being granted with increasing reluctance.

The question of what constitutes a balance between high-technology medicine and support services is indeed a major issue in health policy. Thus, planners must make the decision of whether to allocate the region's resources to install more CT scanners or to promote easier transportation for persons requiring scans. The transportation model incorporating linear programming was used by health planners in the South Chicago region to evaluate this regional health planning problem. In this case, health planners were seeking to determine the mixture of investments in CT scanners and transportation services that would provide sufficient CT scanning for the local population at the lowest cost.

Problems

6.1 The ABC Hospital Supply Company packages and distributes sterile supplies from two plants' locations. Packaging costs are $5.25 per unit at Plant #1, and $5.27 per unit in Plant #2. ABC has a contract with Regional Health Systems Corporation that operates four hospitals. Listed below are the demand and supply requirements for the coming month along with the unit transportation costs for shipping from each plant location to each hospital.

Transportation Costs to Hospital

	A	B	C	D	Supply Available
From Plant #1	.09	.08	.06	.08	14,000 units
From Plant #2	.03	.10	.05	.07	12,000 units
Demand at Each Hospital	4,000	6,000	3,000	10,000	

Requirement: Develop a shipment plan that minimizes total costs for supplying the hospitals next month.

6.2 Five community health centers operated by the County Health Department send dialysis patients to three different dialysis treatment centers. The Health Department contracts with a van service to transport the patients from the community health centers to the treatment locations at a cost of $0.30 per mile per patient. Listed below are the number of patients requiring treatment, the treatment capacity of each dialysis center, and the distance in miles from each community health center to each dialysis treatment location.

Miles to Dialysis Center

	A	B	C	Patient Load
From Health Center #1	21	14	32	8
From Health Center #2	16	23	17	6
From Health Center #3	13	38	19	10
From Health Center #4	43	21	15	7
From Health Center #5	17	22	34	5
Treatment Capacity	6	20	10	

Requirement: Develop the least-cost transportation plan.

6.3 A multispecialty group practice has just added four new physicians to the practice. Each physician will be assigned to one of four medical staff committees. The physicians have been asked to rank their preferences for committee assignments. Their preferences are shown in the following table (1 = first choice; 2 = second choice, etc.).

Committees	A	B	C	D
MD 1	1	2	3	4
MD 2	1	3	2	4
MD 3	4	1	3	2
MD 4	4	2	1	3

Requirement: Assign the physicians to committees in a way that maximizes individual preferences.

6.4 Four community health centers in a regional system have decided to send all of their patients needing linear accelerator therapy to three locations in their region. They have contracted with an ambulance company that charges $1.00 per mile. Each location can handle only a certain number of outside patients per day. The following matrix shows the distances between the hospitals and the treatment locations.

Treatment Locations

	A	B	C	Patients
Health Center 1	17	31	41	5
Health Center 2	12	14	23	8
Health Center 3	46	32	13	7
Health Center 4	38	16	19	5
Places	8	12	5	25

Requirement: Find the optimal allocation of patients to locations of therapy.

6.5 Four physicians in the cardiology department of an academic medical center have agreed to spend one day a week staffing clinics in rural locations in the state served by the medical center. The table below shows the distance in miles between the homes of the physicians and the rural clinic locations.

Rural Clinics

	A	B	C	D
MD 1	16	46	15	33
MD 2	86	39	31	53
MD 3	21	22	41	62
MD 4	32	40	27	19

Requirement: Assign the physicians to the clinics to minimize driving distances for the physicians.

References

Cook, T. M., and R. A. Russell. 1977. *Introduction to Management Science*. Englewood Cliffs, NJ: Prentice-Hall, Inc.

Greenwald, H. P., J. M. Woodward, and D. H. Berg. 1979. "Transportation of CT Scanners: A Theory and Method of Health Resources Allocation." *Health Services Research* 14 (Fall): 207–19.

Harrison, H. 1979. "A Planning System for Facilities and Resources in Distribution Networks." *Interfaces* 9 (February): 6–22.

McKenzie, J. R. (ed.). 1993. *Hospital Software Sourcebook*. Gaithersburg, MD: Aspen Publishers, Inc.

Additional Readings

Ackoff, R. L., and M. W. Sasieni. *Fundamentals of Operations Research*. New York: John Wiley & Sons, 1968. Chapter 5: "Allocation Problems: The Assignment and Distribution of Resources."

Anderson, D. R., D. J. Sweeney, and T. W. Williams. *An Introduction to Management Science: Quantitative Approaches to Decision Making*. St. Paul, MN: West, 1988.

Cook, T. M., and R. A. Russell. *Introduction to Management Science*. Englewood Cliffs, NJ: Prentice-Hall, Inc., 1977. Chapter 7: "Transportation and Assignment Problems."

Eppen, G. D., and F. J. Gould. *Introductory Management Science*. Englewood Cliffs, NJ: Prentice-Hall, Inc., 1987.

Warner, D. M., D. C. Holloway, and K. L. Grazier. *Decision Making and Control for Health Administration: The Management of Quantitative Analysis*. 2nd Edition. Ann Arbor, MI: Health Administration Press, 1984. Chapter 3: "Simple Deterministic Analysis."

7

QUEUEING MODELS

W AITING IN line seems to be a necessary experience in modern society. Checking in at the airport, standing at the ticket counter in anticipation of a highly rated movie, checking out at the supermarket, or registering at a professional meeting are just a few of the many instances when long lines can pretty much be expected. Although these circumstances are often a source of frustration, most people accept the situation with reasonably good humor.

For consumers of medical services, however, the need to endure a long wait can potentially be more than a mere inconvenience. A delay of only a few minutes in the emergency room or the untimely completion of a laboratory procedure could be fatal. Even in more routine cases, the frustration of a long wait in the admitting department or a delay in response to a call for a nurse can affect recovery time by adding to the patient's agitation level.

Even when the patient's health is not threatened by excessive waiting, the reputation of the institution frequently is. Today's health care consumers tend to equate the quality of care they receive with the quality of service they experience. In today's competitive environment, the astute health care provider needs to be attentive to all details of the organization's operations, including the numerous areas in which waiting lines are present. Such areas are typically referred to as **queueing systems**. Queueing models provide health care administrators with a valuable analytical tool with which to evaluate these systems.

Introduction of Case Problem

In order to better understand the basic concepts of queues and queueing systems, consider a large fictitious preferred provider organization (PPO), Prime Health, operating in the Southwest. Like all PPOs, Prime Health realizes the importance of carefully managing the extent to which its primary care providers refer patients to specialists. Prime Health's contract with their primary care physicians therefore requires that before referring one of their patients to a specialist the primary care provider must obtain authorization for the referral from the PPO.

The primary care physician typically obtains the required authorization by having an office assistant telephone the PPO office, where a single authorization clerk is available to handle the request. If the authorization clerk is busy with another call, then the subsequent callers are placed on hold, and their calls are handled by the authorization clerk in the order in which they arrived. Because of the importance of receiving the required authorization, the office assistant never hangs up before talking with the authorization clerk. However, a survey conducted by the PPO among its provider network reveals that extreme dissatisfaction results if the wait exceeds five minutes.

Operation of such a system involves a number of costs:

1. The authorization clerk employed by the PPO earns a salary of $9.80 per hour including benefits.
2. The office assistant who places the telephone request for the authorization earns a salary of $8.35 per hour including benefits.
3. While the office assistant is on hold, he or she is unable to perform any additional productive functions for the office.
4. The cost associated with adding an additional telephone line to the PPO system is $50.00 per month, including prorated installation costs.

For such a system, a number of questions could be raised. The physician offices are quite interested in answering the following questions:

1. How often will the office assistant be placed on hold?
2. How long will the office assistant need to wait until the call is handled?
3. Will the office assistant ever receive a busy signal?

The PPO is also concerned with a number of issues. These might include

1. The amount of time that the authorization clerk sits idle;
2. The improvement in service that results from adding a second clerk;

3. The number of incoming lines needed to provide a particular level of service;
4. The fraction of incoming calls when the time on hold exceeds the maximum tolerable level of five minutes.

The ability to answer these and other questions depends on the assumptions that are made about the physical system under study. In some cases it is possible to obtain results analytically. These cases are described in this chapter. As the assumptions are loosened and more complex configurations are considered, it often becomes necessary to utilize simulation modeling in order to answer questions about the system. This approach will be covered in Chapter 11.

An Overview of the General Queueing System

The telephone system in the case problem is an example of a general queueing system. In such a general system, customers requiring some form of service emerge from the **calling population** and (assuming there is room and they do not feel the number of customers waiting is excessive) take their place in a waiting line or *queue*. They remain there until it is determined by some mechanism that it is their turn to obtain the required service from the **service mechanism.** (If the waiting time has become excessive, the customer might grow impatient and decide to leave without receiving the required service.) The service mechanism might consist of a single laboratory technician, several admitting clerks, a telephone operator, or several machines. The customer receives the required service from the service mechanism and then leaves the queueing system. This flow is depicted graphically in Figure 7.1.

Now in order to develop an appropriate queueing model, one must define clearly the three specific characteristics of the queueing system being analyzed. These characteristics comprise the process by which

1. customers are generated
2. customers form and wait in the queue
3. service is rendered

Each of these categories is now discussed.

Figure 7.1 The General Queueing System

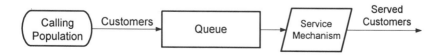

The Generation of Customers

Recall that customers arrive at the queueing system from the calling population. The **size** of this population will be either finite or infinite. An example of a finite calling population is the group of employees in a given company enrolled in a particular HMO plan. Although infinite calling populations rarely occur in fact, a calling population is often assumed to be infinite if the arrival pattern to the queueing system is unaffected by the customers already in the system. Patients arriving at a regional trauma center for service can typically be assumed to have come from an infinite calling population. An advantage of assuming the calling population to be of infinite size is the simpler mathematics that result.

Two other characteristics of the calling population are of interest. First is the notion of **homogeneity** of the population—that is, are the customers all coming to the facility for the same kind of service? The calling population associated with an emergency room is typically not a homogeneous population. Customers arrive with different levels of need, and frequently a triage nurse is employed to assess the specific needs of a newly arriving patient. Second is the question of whether the population can generate **batch arrivals**. Normally, an arrival is one individual, one customer. In some situations it is possible for two or more customers to arrive as a group. In the hospital, for example, people will frequently leave their office and travel to the cafeteria in a group. The simultaneous arrival of a group of customers is known as batched arrivals, and this situation must be modeled differently from one restricted to single arrivals.

In addition to characteristics of the calling population, the actual manner in which the customers emerge from the calling population must also be analyzed and modeled. In particular, the customers might emerge either **deterministically** or **stochastically**. If they emerge deterministically, then one must identify the deterministic pattern of arrival. If they emerge stochastically, then the random mechanism describing the arrival times must be identified. Again, arrivals to the emergency room would be an example of a stochastic arrival pattern. Deterministic arrivals are frequently associated with facilities where the arrivals are **scheduled**, although even in this case the actual arrival time could easily vary randomly about the scheduled time.

The Queueing of Customers

Upon entering the queueing system, a newly generated customer checks the status of the service mechanism. If the service mechanism is idle, then the newly arriving customer receives service immediately. Otherwise, it is necessary for this new customer to enter the queue. The capacity of the queue can be either finite or infinite. It is possible that a queue with a finite capacity could be fully occupied. In this case the newly generated customer is said to be **blocked** and cannot be admitted to the queueing system. An example would be a telephone system with only a finite number of hold positions. Once all hold positions are fully occupied, subsequent callers receive a busy signal, and are thus blocked from entering the system.

Even when space remains in the queue, a newly generated customer might decide that the line is too long and choose not to enter the queue. Such behavior is known as **balking**. Or a customer may grow tired of waiting in the queue and choose to leave before being served. This is known as **reneging**. In the telephone example, this would correspond to an office assistant who is on hold deciding to hang up before being connected to the PPO authorization clerk.

Finally, the rule by which customers in the queue are selected to be next for service is also of importance. One of the common rules is "first in, first out" (FIFO). Under this rule, customers are served according to the order of their arrival to the system. A second rule is "last in, first out" (LIFO). A common application occurs in computer systems, where instructions might be stacked in a queue and the last instruction entered is the first one to be processed. A third rule uses a priority system for determining which customer is served next. The triage function in an emergency room, in which the severity of patients is ascertained in order to determine the order in which they will be treated, is an example of the use of a **priority rule** for selecting the next customer in the queue to receive service.

Servicing the Customers

Several characteristics associated with the service mechanism play an important role in the process of modeling a queueing system. The first is the number of servers contained in the service mechanism. In the simplest case there will be a single server. More complicated systems will consist of service mechanisms with multiple servers, which may or may not be identical with regard to how they render service. These servers are sometimes referred to as **channels**.

A characteristic associated with the servers is the time required to render service to a single customer. This time can be either deterministic or stochastic. For the deterministic case, one must specify the constant value of service time. For the case of stochastic service times, one must determine the random mechanism that appropriately describes the service times.

Finally, there is a category of server characteristics that might be called **unusual server behavior**. One such behavior is the failure or breakdown of the server, a phenomenon most often associated with a piece of mechanical equipment. A second is a change in server rates, which can be a very subtle occurrence. Very often, the server's rate of meeting the customer's requirements is a function of the queue length. For example, the admitting clerk, seeing a long line waiting for her services, may try to increase her service rate. In some cases, servers get nervous when the waiting line gets longer and may actually slow down as a result. In any event, the model must account for this behavior if it is present in the system. A final behavior of servers that might need to be included in the model is the notion of **batch processing**. Just as a queueing system can have batch arrivals, it is also possible to have batch processing. This refers to a system in which more than one customer can receive service from one server at the same time. An example of batch processing would be a procedure by which a group of several patients receives instructions on how to fill out their registration forms, rather than having the clerk work with each patient individually.

Model Formulation, Quantification, and Data Requirements

It follows from the discussion of the general queueing system in the preceding section that a number of models could be formulated in order to analyze Prime Health's telephone system. The appropriate model depends upon the specific assumptions made about the system's characteristics. By making several simplifying assumptions about these characteristics, one can obtain the **basic single-server queueing model**. This model provides an excellent starting point for the analysis of Prime Health's telephone problem.

The set of assumptions about Prime Health's system that results in the basic model being appropriate can be summarized as follows:

1. The size of the physician network and their patient population gives rise to a potential pool of calls that is so large that it can be considered to be of **infinite size**.
2. The calls require the same kind of service so that the calling population can be considered **homogeneous**. Also, the calls arrive individually so there are **no batch arrivals**.
3. The arrival pattern of the incoming calls follows a **Poisson distribution**. (For a discussion of this distribution, see, for

Figure 7.2   The Basic Single-Server Queueing System

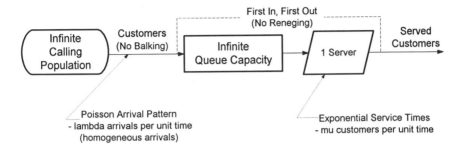

example, Berenson and Levine 1992, 245–48). In a given unit of time, the average number of arrivals is defined as lambda (λ).

4. There is an unlimited number of hold positions on the telephone so that the queue (and hence the system) can be considered to have **infinite capacity**.

5. Physician office assistants remain on the line until an authorization clerk answers (that is, there is **no balking** and **no reneging**).

6. Calls are answered in the order in which they arrive so that the service rule is "**first in, first out**" (FIFO).

7. There is a **single clerk** on duty to process the incoming calls.

8. The time required to service a call follows an **exponential probability distribution**. (For a discussion of the exponential distribution, see, for example, Keller, Warrack, and Bartel 1994, 203–6). Mu (μ) is defined as the average number of calls serviced per unit time.

9. There are **no unusual server behaviors**.

This model is presented graphically in Figure 7.2.

When these assumptions are made, the queueing system becomes a special case of the "birth-death process" (see, for example, Parzen 1962, 278–86), and a simple steady-state solution is easily obtained. The concept of **steady-state** means that the system has been operating long enough so that the fluctuations associated with startup of the system have disappeared. If the arrival rate is less than the service rate (that is, $\lambda < \mu$), then the following algebraic formulas can be obtained:

1. Probability of n customers in the system

$$P_n = \left(1 - \tfrac{\lambda}{\mu}\right)\left(\tfrac{\lambda}{\mu}\right)^n$$

2. Percent utilization

$$\rho = \left(\tfrac{\lambda}{\mu}\right)(100)$$

3. Average number of customers in the system

$$L = \frac{\lambda}{\mu - \lambda}$$

4. Average number of customers in the queue

$$L_q = \frac{\lambda^2}{\mu(\mu - \lambda)}$$

5. Expected time in the system

$$W = \frac{1}{\mu - \lambda}$$

6. Expected time in the queue (waiting time)

$$W_q = \frac{\lambda}{\mu(\mu - \lambda)}$$

7. Probability that the time in the queue, T, is greater than t

$$P[T > t] = \rho e^{-\mu(1-\rho)t}, \text{ where } \rho = \frac{\lambda}{\mu} \qquad \text{(E 7.1)}$$

(Note: If $\lambda \geq \mu$, the queue grows without bound, no steady state is reached, and the preceding formulas do *not* apply).

The application of these formulas to Prime Health's system requires the completion of two important steps. First, it must be verified that the pattern of arrivals follows a Poisson probability distribution, and the service process follows an exponential probability density function. Second, numerical values for the parameters associated with the formulas must be obtained.

Verification of the Poisson arrival pattern and exponential service process are essentially "goodness of fit" problems discussed in most statistics texts (see, for example, Berenson and Levine 1992, 470–73). The assumption will be made that the decision maker has appropriately determined that the patterns of arrivals and service are sufficiently well described by the Poisson and exponential distributions, respectively.

Two important parameters must be quantified—λ (the average arrival rate) and μ (the average service rate). Along with this quantification is the verification that arrival rate is less than service rate. Suppose that Prime Health has determined from a special study conducted during the past month that calls arrive at an average rate of 18 per hour. The same study reveals that the PPO operator requires an average of two minutes to process a given call. Thus, the average service rate is 30 per hour, which is indeed greater than the value of λ.

Prime Health will very quickly need some additional parameters as they look at the managerial implications of the system. In particular, they will need salary information for the PPO operator as well as the office staff people who place the calls for the physicians. They will also require data on equipment costs as they consider installing additional telephone lines or newer switching equipment. The financial data on salaries will be obtained from payroll records with the assistance of the accounting department. Vendors will be the likely source of data on equipment costs.

Solving the Case Problem

Although the basic single-server queueing model has sufficient algebraic simplicity to allow for hand solution, problem solvers typically employ one of the many software systems available for queueing analysis. *QuickQuant* can quickly solve for many of the quantities discussed above. The *QuickQuant* printout for the case problem is presented in Exhibit 7.1.

Note that the arrival and service rates have been entered into the *QuickQuant* program in units of callers per minute. This was done in order to obtain expected times in the system and queue that would also have units of minutes. A review of the printout and the extent to which it provides values for the system characteristics of interest is presented below.

1. Probability of *n* Customers in the System (P_n)

For the Prime Health system, being in the system means either talking to the PPO operator or being on hold. *QuickQuant* provides a table of exact and cumulative probabilities for each possible value of number of customers in the system.

One notes from the table that about 95 percent of the time there will be at most five persons in the system. This means, then, that the number of persons on hold will be four or less about 95 percent of the time. This has important managerial implications, as will be seen shortly.

2. The Percent Utilization (ρ)

Percent utilization is equal to 0.6, or 60 percent. Said another way, 40 percent of the time the system is empty and the server is idle. Again, the managerial implications of this fact will be important.

3. Average Number of Customers in the System (*L*)

The average is equal to 1.5 customers. This number indicates that if Prime Health's telephone system were monitored for a long period of

Exhibit 7.1 *QuickQuant* Solution to Case Problem

```
Parameter Values:
    Mean Customer Arrival Rate: lambda = .3
    Mean Customer Service Rate: mu = .5

Queuing Results:
    Mean Number of Customers in System: L = 1.5
    Mean Customer Time Spent in System: W = 5
    Mean Number of Customers Waiting
                   (Length of Line): Lq = .9000001
    Mean Customer Waiting Time: Wq = 3
    Server Utilization Factor: rho = .6
```

Number in System n	Probability Pn	Cumulative Probability
0	0.4000	0.4000
1	0.2400	0.6400
2	0.1440	0.7840
3	0.0864	0.8704
4	0.0518	0.9222
5	0.0311	0.9533
6	0.0187	0.9720
7	0.0112	0.9832
8	0.0067	0.9899
9	0.0040	0.9940
10	0.0024	0.9964
11	0.0015	0.9978
12	0.0009	0.9987
13	0.0005	0.9992
14	0.0003	0.9995
15	0.0002	0.9997
16	0.0001	0.9998
17	0.0001	0.9999

time, the weighted average of the number of callers talking with the authorization clerk or on hold would be 1.5, where the weight for a given value is the fraction of total observation time associated with that value.

4. Average Number of Customers in the Queue (L_q)

The average is equal to 0.9. This value indicates that in the long run the system operates in such a manner that there is the equivalent of slightly less than one person on hold. An alternative method for computing this value is given by

$$
\begin{bmatrix} \text{Average number} \\ \text{of customers in} \\ \text{the queue} \end{bmatrix} = \begin{bmatrix} \text{Average number} \\ \text{of customers in} \\ \text{the system} \end{bmatrix} - \begin{bmatrix} \text{Average number} \\ \text{of customers in} \\ \text{the server} \end{bmatrix}
$$

The number in the server is either 0 with probability 0.4 (recall that the system is empty 40 percent of the time) or 1 with probability 0.6 (1 − 0.4). Thus, the average number in the server is equal to (0)(0.4) + (1)(0.6) = 0.6. Then the average number of customers in the queue equals [1.5 − 0.6] = 0.9.

5. Expected Time in the System (*W*)

This value is given by five minutes and represents the average length of time that an office assistant must spend in order to obtain one referral authorization.

6. Expected Time in the Queue (Waiting Time, *W_q*)

The expected waiting time is given by three minutes. Each caller, then, will spend an average of three minutes on hold. Again, the consistency of this follows from the fact that expected time in the queue = (expected time in the system − expected service time). A service rate of 0.5 customers per minute equates to an average service time of two minutes per customer. Since the expected time in the system = five minutes, then expected time in the queue would be (5 − 2), or three minutes.

7. The Probability That the Time in the Queue, *T*, is Greater Than *t*

These probability values are not provided by *QuickQuant*. However, they can be easily computed by substituting the values of 0.3 and 0.5 for λ and μ, respectively, in Equation 7.1. The resulting equation is

$$P[T > t] = 0.6e^{-0.5(1-0.6)t} = 0.6e^{-0.2t}$$

where *t* is expressed in minutes (since λ and μ have been expressed in units of callers per minute). A spreadsheet can be used to evaluate this equation for selected values of *t*. The results are shown in Table 7.1.

The table reveals two interesting points. First of all, although the expected time in the queue is three minutes, nearly 33 percent of the time the office assistant will be tied up on hold for more than three minutes. In addition, recall the PPO survey that indicated that extreme dissatisfaction would result within its provider network if the time on hold exceeds five minutes. According to the table, this limit is exceeded more than 22 percent of the time. The PPO very likely will want to improve this performance.

Table 7.1 Probability That Time in Queue Is Greater than t for Selected Values of t (Basic Single-Server System)

t (minutes)	$P[T > t]$
0.0	0.600000
1.0	0.491238
2.0	0.402192
3.0	0.329287
4.0	0.269597
5.0	0.220728
6.0	0.180717
7.0	0.147958
8.0	0.121138
9.0	0.099179
10.0	0.081201

Model Variations

The preceding example illustrated the basic single-server queueing model. Several operational characteristics were computed by which management can evaluate its performance. In particular, it was found that more than 22 percent of the time that an office assistant calls for an authorization, the call will be placed on hold for longer than five minutes.

Prime Health, therefore, might want to explore ways to reduce waiting times and thus improve their telephone service. One obvious strategy would be to add a second authorization clerk to handle incoming calls. In addition, the basic model assumed an infinite queue capacity. This assumption is, of course, quite unrealistic. Telephone systems have only a finite number of hold positions. Therefore, the performance of the system with a finite queue capacity needs to be explored. This section will consider three variations of the case problem: the basic queueing system with multiple servers; the finite queue model with one server; and the finite queue model with more than one server.

The Basic Queueing System with Multiple Servers

Assume that the telephone system described in the case problem remains otherwise unchanged except for the addition of a second operator. The resulting system might be called a "basic multiple-server queueing system." The formulas presented for the single-server case problem example in the previous section no longer hold, and a new set of algebraic formulas must be derived for this system. These formulas are presented in Appendix 7.A.

While the algebraic complexity of this model would still permit hand solution, the availability of a software package is usually seen as a much more attractive approach. The *QuickQuant* system will therefore be used once again to obtain a solution. The printout of this solution is presented in Exhibit 7.2. Notice that the mean waiting time has dropped considerably, from three minutes with one clerk to approximately 0.2 minutes with two clerks.

As before, although *QuickQuant* provides much information of interest, it does not compute probabilities of time spent in the queue. For the present example this probability is of importance since callers are extremely dissatisfied when waiting time exceeds five minutes. For the single clerk system, waiting time exceeded five minutes more than 22 percent of the time. It is of interest to compute this probability with two clerks on duty.

From Appendix 7.A, observe that the probability of experiencing a waiting time, T, which is greater than t, is given by

Exhibit 7.2 *QuickQuant* Solution to Variation of Case Problem—Two Authorization Clerks

```
Parameter Values:
    Mean Customer Arrival Rate: lambda = .3
    Mean Customer Service Rate: mu = .5
    Number of Servers: S = 2

Queuing Results:
    Mean Number of Customers in System: L = .6593407
    Mean Customer Time Spent in System: W = 2.197802
    Mean Number of Customers Waiting
              (Length of Line): Lq = 5.934066E-02
    Mean Customer Waiting Time: Wq = .1978022
    Server Utilization Factor: rho = .3
```

Number in System n	Probability Pn	Cumulative Probability
0	0.5385	0.5385
1	0.3231	0.8615
2	0.0969	0.9585
3	0.0291	0.9875
4	0.0087	0.9963
5	0.0026	0.9989
6	0.0008	0.9997
7	0.0002	0.9999
8	0.0001	1.0000

$$P[T > t] = \frac{\left(\frac{\lambda}{\mu}\right)^S}{S!(1 - \rho)}P_0 e^{-\mu St(1-\rho)}$$

where $\rho = \frac{\lambda}{\mu S}$, $S =$ number of servers.

With $S = 2$ clerks, $\lambda = 0.3$ calls per minute, and $\mu = 0.5$ calls per minute, ρ will have a value of 0.3. The value of P_0 is found from the *QuickQuant* printout and is equal to the probability of 0 in the system, or 0.5385. (Alternatively, this value can be computed from the formula for P_0 given in Appendix 7.A. For greater accuracy the value obtained from the formula (0.538462), has been used in the following computations). The values of λ and μ have been expressed in units of calls per minute so that time can be expressed in units of minutes.

When these values are inserted into the above formula, one obtains

$$P[T > t] = 0.138462e^{-0.7t}$$

where t is expressed in minutes.

Any spreadsheet of choice provides a convenient software environment in which to evaluate this formula. The results of this analysis are presented in Table 7.2. The table indicates that fewer than 5 callers in 1,000 will wait longer than five minutes for an operator. In fact, an incoming caller will be immediately connected to an operator more than 86 percent of the time $(1 - P[T > 0])$. It would seem that the PPO can provide excellent service with two operators.

The Finite Queue Model

The analysis to this point has assumed that the telephone system has an infinite number of hold positions. In practice, of course, only a finite

Table 7.2 Probability That Time in Queue Is Greater than t for Selected Values of t (Basic Two-Server System)

t (minutes)	$P[T > t]$
0.0	0.138462
1.0	0.068758
2.0	0.034144
3.0	0.016956
4.0	0.008420
5.0	0.004181
6.0	0.002076
7.0	0.001031
8.0	0.000512
9.0	0.000254
10.0	0.000126

number of callers can be placed on hold. When all of the operators are busy and the capacity of the hold circuits has been reached, subsequent callers will receive a busy signal. A new model is needed to represent this situation.

When a queueing system has limited queue capacity, it is no longer necessary for the arrival rate (λ) to be less than the service rate (μ) in order to reach a steady-state solution. This follows from the fact that the system will have at most $N + S$ customers, where N = the queue capacity and S = the number of servers. Although formulas can be obtained for the system characteristics (see, for example, Hillier and Lieberman 1986, 551–54) the computations are sufficiently complex to merit use of a software package.

Consider first the case of a single authorization clerk. Assume that the telephone system has five hold positions, the arrival rate of incoming calls is 0.3 calls per minute, and the service rate is 0.5 calls per minute. The *QuickQuant* system produces the output shown in Exhibit 7.3.

Exhibit 7.3 *QuickQuant* Solution to Variation of Case Problem—Five Hold Positions, One Authorization Clerk

```
Parameter Values:
    Mean Customer Arrival Rate: lambda = .3
    Mean Customer Service Rate: mu = .5
    Number of Servers: S = 1
    Maximum Number of Customers in System: M = 6

Queuing Results:
    Mean Number of Customers in System: L = 1.298401
    Mean Customer Time Spent in System: W = 4.412728
    Mean Number of Customers Waiting
            (Length of Line): Lq = .7099212
    Mean Customer Waiting Time: Wq = 2.412728
    Traffic Intensity: rho = .6
```

Number in System n	Probability Pn	Cumulative Probability
0	0.4115	0.4115
1	0.2469	0.6584
2	0.1481	0.8066
3	0.0889	0.8955
4	0.0533	0.9488
5	0.0320	0.9808
6	0.0192	1.0000

With only one server and five hold positions there will be a maximum of six calls in the system. It follows, then, that the probability of n callers in the system will equal zero for values of n greater than 6.

Of particular interest is the value of $P(6)$, the probability of six persons in the system (in this case, five persons on hold). This corresponds to a full system. Subsequent callers to the system will not be admitted. Thus, $P(6) = 0.0192$ provides the probability that a caller will receive a busy signal.

Again, *QuickQuant* gives no information about waiting time probabilities. In fact, these probabilities are somewhat computationally complex and beyond the scope of this text. Thus, in evaluating the impact of a limited number of hold positions, the discussion will be limited to expected values. The expected time in the queue for this case is slightly longer than 2.4 minutes, compared with 3 minutes for the infinite queue case. But of course there is never a busy signal with an infinite queue, whereas with five hold positions a caller receives a busy signal nearly 2 percent of the time.

One can also evaluate a system with five hold positions and two authorization clerks. The *QuickQuant* output of the analysis is shown in Exhibit 7.4.

With the second clerk (and five hold positions), the probability of a busy signal is given by $P(7)$. This probability has dropped significantly from the single-clerk case, to a value of 0.0002. In addition, the expected time in the queue drops from slightly more than 2.4 minutes with one clerk, to just under 0.2 minutes with two clerks. Finally, it is interesting to note that with two clerks, the performance of the system with only five hold positions is not markedly different from the infinite queue case (compare Exhibits 7.2 and 7.4).

Description of Available Computer Software

The microcomputer-based operations research packages, *QuickQuant*, QSB+, STORM, and AB:QM, all contain modules for solving a variety of basic queueing models. While these modules differ slightly with regard to their output format and the specific models that are included, they all provide output describing average waiting times, average queue sizes, and utilization.

The formulas describing these basic models are readily available and relatively straightforward (see, for example, Hillier and Lieberman 1986). As a result, it is possible for the more mathematically inclined decision maker to utilize a spreadsheet or scientific programming language in order to obtain solutions to these queueing problems. Unlike

Exhibit 7.4 *QuickQuant* Solution to Variation of Case Problem—Five Hold Positions, Two Authorization Clerks

```
Parameter Values:
    Mean Customer Arrival Rate: lambda = .3
    Mean Customer Service Rate: mu = .5
    Number of Servers: S = 2
    Maximum Number of Customers in System: M = 7

Queuing Results:
    Mean Number of Customers in System: L = .6585564
    Mean Customer Time Spent in System: W = 2.195705
    Mean Number of Customers Waiting
            (Length of Line): Lq = 5.869769E-02
    Mean Customer Waiting Time: Wq = .1957051
    Traffic Intensity: rho = .3


        Number in                    Cumulative
        System n   Probability Pn    Probability
        ------------------------------------------
           0          0.5385          0.5385
           1          0.3231          0.8616
           2          0.0969          0.9586
           3          0.0291          0.9876
           4          0.0087          0.9964
           5          0.0026          0.9990
           6          0.0008          0.9998
           7          0.0002          1.0000
```

other operations research problem areas, basic queueing solutions can be obtained with minimal programming effort.

Analysis, Interpretation, and Application of Results to Management Decisions

The value of these queueing models is their ability to help managers resolve the conflict between their desire to provide high-quality service and their need to control costs. In the present example, the PPO certainly needs to be sensitive to the waiting time of callers, the frequency with which they get a busy signal, the utilization of the authorization clerks, and, of course, the overall cost of the entire system.

The PPO management can use the queueing models that have been discussed to assemble the data shown in Table 7.3. A maximum of three clerks has been considered because this configuration appears to provide the desired performance level. The questions to be resolved are how many clerks to employ (1, 2, or 3) and how many hold positions to install.

The first criterion might be to achieve a reasonable busy rate. Assume that a 2 percent busy rate is deemed the maximum acceptable. That is, on at least 98 percent of the calls, it is desired that the office assistants get connected directly with an authorization clerk or be put on hold. With one server, this would require five hold positions (or a total of six incoming lines). But the expected time on hold with such a system is slightly more than 2.4 minutes. This might be too long. In addition, a caller will be put on hold with probability .5693 (this is the sum of $P(1)$ through $P(5)$ in Exhibit 7.3). One server just does not seem to be appropriate.

Looking at two servers, the PPO management observes that two hold positions (or a total of four incoming lines) would be required,

Table 7.3 Summary of Operational Characteristics for Specific Combinations of Number of Clerks and Hold Positions

No. of Clerks	No. of Hold Positions	P(Busy)	Exp. Time in Queue (minutes)	Utilization Factor
1	0	0.375	0	0.375
1	1	0.184	0.75	0.490
1	2	0.099	1.35	0.540
1	3	0.056	1.81	0.566
1	4	0.033	2.16	0.580
1	5	0.019	2.41	0.588
1	6	0.011	2.60	0.593
1	7	0.007	2.73	0.596
1	8	0.004	2.82	0.598
1	9	0.002	2.88	0.599
1	infinite	0	3.00	0.600
2	0	0.1011	0	0.270
2	1	0.0294	0.101	0.291
2	2	0.0088	0.157	0.297
2	3	0.0026	0.182	0.299
2	4	0.0008	0.192	0.300
2	5	0.0002	0.196	0.300
2	6	0.0001	0.197	0.300
2	infinite	0	0.198	0.300
3	0	0.0198	0	0.196
3	1	0.0039	0.013	0.199
3	2	0.0008	0.018	0.200
3	3	0.0002	0.020	0.200
3	infinite	0	0.021	0.200

resulting in an expected waiting time of 0.157 minutes, which should provide a reasonably low probability of a wait longer than five minutes. A third hold position reduces the busy rate by about 70 percent, and at $50.00 per month might be a good investment. The probability of being put on hold is 0.1265 with two hold positions, and 0.1349 with three hold positions. (With an additional hold position, a caller gets a busy signal less frequently but gets put on hold more often.)

With three authorization clerks, a busy rate of less than 2 percent can be achieved with no hold positions (that is, three incoming lines). In this configuration there will, of course, be no time spent on hold.

At this point the PPO might look at the costs of the alternatives currently under consideration. The cost for a given configuration involves line cost, cost of providing service, and cost of waiting. Initially, the cost of waiting will be set equal to the office assistant's salary. Assuming a 40-hour week and an average of 4.333 weeks per month, then each month will contain 173.333 hours. The authorization clerk's salary, then, is $1,698.66 per month. Similarly, the office assistant's monthly salary is $1,447.33.

The monthly cost of waiting for a given alternative is found by multiplying the average number of customers in the system by the office assistant's monthly salary. And, the line cost is just the number of incoming lines multiplied by $50. The costs can be summarized as shown in Table 7.4. From an economic standpoint, a single clerk with five hold positions is to be preferred. But recall that the expected time on hold would be 2.41 minutes. The option of two clerks and two hold positions reduces this time to 0.157 minutes, for a net increase in cost of less than $700. The three-clerk option costs over $1,500 more and has a higher busy rate (however, with two clerks about 13.5 percent of the callers get put on hold). On balance, the "two clerks, two hold positions" configuration seems to be a reasonable choice.

Table 7.4 Monthly Cost Information for Three Alternative Configurations

Configuration	Monthly Cost of Lines	Monthly Cost of Clerks	Exp. No. in System	Monthly Cost of Waiting	Total Monthly Cost
1 Clerk, 5 hold positions	$300	$1,699	1.2984	$1,879	$3,878
2 Clerk, 2 hold positions	200	3,397	0.6414	928	4,525
3 Clerk, 0 hold positions	150	5,096	0.5881	851	6,097

Two final observations bear mention. First, it is not always clear which a caller prefers—a busy signal or being put on hold for extended periods of time (the soothing background of piped-in elevator music, notwithstanding). The PPO would probably want to investigate this. In particular, how long will a caller stay on hold before hanging up and trying the call later? Second, the apparently higher cost of multiple-server options results from the fact that waiting cost was set equal to the office assistant's salary. There probably needs to be a goodwill cost added in as well. As the cost of waiting is set to higher values, the reduction in waiting achieved by adding clerks will have increasing monetary value and the optimum configuration can change. (This is a subject of one of the problems at the end of the chapter.)

Managerial decisions about a system whose configuration is essentially that of a queueing system typically call for an appropriate blend of science and art. The manager's experience, judgment, and knowledge of the customers' particular "quirks" support the "art"; queueing theory, involving models such as those presented in this chapter, provides the "science" component. By skillfully drawing from both science and art, the health care manager can guide the organization in providing cost-effective, high quality of care and high quality of service.

Case Studies from the Literature

Quality Improvement (Dershin and Schaik 1993)

A midwest hospital was actively involved in an organizationwide quality improvement program for several years. As a result of a series of meetings with nursing and other hospital staff to identify processes within the hospital in need of improvement, the transportation service was identified as an area in need of attention. Patient transportation demands had increased, and there seemed to be no logic behind the staffing patterns, shift assignments, or equipment inventory.

The data gathered substantiated initial concerns; it was obvious that the system needed to be redesigned. This redesign involved three key elements: (1) improved communication and control, (2) a rational staffing model, and (3) data to monitor performance on a long-term basis. The goals were to reduce average transport time as well as the variability in this time, reduce operating costs, and increase customer satisfaction.

In order to obtain a rational staffing model, the hospital utilized queueing theory. Using this theory, it was possible to generate a graph of waiting time as a function of staffing level and average number of calls per hour (call loading). The results were surprising: the investigators saw that waiting time increased quite rapidly with call loading.

The system manager has now assumed a proactive approach to the problem. Data on demand for transporter services are now monitored. Using these data along with the queueing analysis results, the system manager can adjust shift assignments and further refine the transport process. Average transport time has been reduced, unnecessary transports have been eliminated, and staffing requirements have been reduced by almost two full-time employees.

Patient Waiting Time (Vemuri 1984)

The outpatient pharmacy at the Medical College of Virginia Hospital was interested in reducing the waiting time experienced by patients. To analyze the problem, they first gathered data on how the various personnel in the pharmacy spend their time in filling a prescription. These data could then be used to perform a queueing analysis and identify alternative solutions for improving the operation.

Because of the complexity of the system, it was felt that a queueing simulation study would be more appropriate than an analytical approach (the rationale for reverting to simulation is discussed in more detail in Chapter 11). Even when simulation is used, it is still necessary to identify the arrival mechanism as well as the service process. In this case, a Poisson model was chosen for the arrival mechanism, and an empirical distribution was used to model the service process.

The simulation model was used to evaluate a number of alternative configurations of the pharmacy—number of pharmacists, number of technicians, number of typists, etc. For each configuration, the model provides an estimate of average patient waiting time. After computing the cost for each configuration, the investigators can determine the configuration that provides a suitable waiting time at an acceptable level of cost.

Additional Reports from the Literature

Weiss and McClain (1987) used a queueing analytic approach to describe the process by which patients in acute care hospitals await placement into a nursing home. This waiting period is known as "administrative days" because the time spent in the acute care facility is for administrative rather than medical reasons. The situation was modeled using a state-dependent placement rate for patients who are backed up in the acute care facility. The model results were compared with empirical data obtained from seven hospitals in New York State.

Taira and Huang (1989) discuss the design and implementation of a clinical picture archiving and communications system (PACS) module within the radiology department of a 700-bed teaching hospital. The investigators viewed the system as a large queueing network that allows processes to operate concurrently in a coordinated and prioritized fashion. Preliminary evaluation shows that the system is accepted by radiologists and clinicians.

Rosenquist (1987) reports on a study in which the characteristics of examination time and interarrival time were determined for an emergency room radiology service. Two examples were analyzed that demonstrate the usefulness of queueing analysis in radiology. The first looks at the impact that a 5 percent annual increase in patients has on waiting time, while the second demonstrates the use of this technique for cost analysis. The author makes a strong case for the value of queueing analysis for department planning and management.

Problems

7.1 Patients arrive at your outpatient registration desk according to a Poisson distribution at an average rate of six per hour. The single registration clerk spends an average of five minutes with each patient (exponentially distributed). Arrivals are handled on a "first come, first served" basis.

Requirement: Answer the following questions.

a. What is the average number of patients waiting in line to be registered?

b. What is the expected total time required for a patient to complete the registration process (waiting and service time)?

c. What is the probability that there are more than two patients waiting in line to be registered?

7.2 A new "point of care" computer workstation has been installed in the ICU. Nurses arrive at this workstation (in a Poisson fashion) at an average rate of five per hour. Only one nurse can use the workstation at a time. The time required for a nurse to enter data into the workstation follows an exponential distribution with a mean of six minutes. For simplicity we feel that the basic queueing system model applies.

Requirement: Answer the following questions.

a. How many hours, on average, during a 24-hour period is the workstation idle?

b. What is the mean number of nurses waiting to use the workstation?

c. ICU nurses earn $20 per hour. What is the expected cost associated with the total time that a nurse spends waiting for access to the workstation and entering the data?

7.3 Refer to Problem 7.2. You are considering adding a second "point of care" workstation. To help in the decision you have obtained the *QuickQuant* output shown below.
Requirement: Determine

a. The probability that more than two nurses are waiting to use a workstation;

b. The most we would pay for the additional workstation. (Recall that ICU nurses earn $20 per hour.)

7.4 You are employed by a large multispecialty physician group to help them design their telephone system. Two operators are employed to handle incoming calls. The question is how many hold positions to have. Currently under consideration are five such hold positions. Calls come in at an average rate of 20 per hour and require an average of eight minutes for service.
Requirement: Use an appropriate computer package to answer the following.

QuickQuant Output for Problem 7.3

```
Parameter Values:
    Mean Customer Arrival Rate: lambda = 5
    Mean Customer Service Rate: mu = 10
    Number of Servers: S = 2

Queuing Results:
    Mean Number of Customers in System: L = .5333334
    Mean Customer Time Spent in System: W = .1066667
    Mean Number of Customers Waiting
            (Length of Line): Lq = 3.333334E-02
    Mean Customer Waiting Time: Wq = 6.666668E-03
    Server Utilization Factor: rho = .25


        Number in                    Cumulative
        System n    Probability Pn   Probability
        ------------------------------------------
           0           0.6000          0.6000
           1           0.3000          0.9000
           2           0.0750          0.9750
           3           0.0188          0.9938
           4           0.0047          0.9984
           5           0.0012          0.9996
           6           0.0003          0.9999
           7           0.0001          1.0000
```

a. What is the probability that a caller to the physician group will receive a busy signal?

b. What is the probability that no one is on hold?

c. What is the expected number of busy operators?

7.5 The physician group described in Problem 7.4 is considering adding an additional hold position.

Requirement: Answer the following.

a. With six hold positions, what is the probability that a caller will get through to an operator immediately without being placed on hold?

b. Your boss notes that with six hold positions a caller has a longer expected time in the queue than with five hold positions. Therefore, your boss argues, five hold positions are better than six hold positions. Do you agree? Explain.

7.6 Consider the case problem once again. Recall, in Table 7.4, that on the basis of cost, a system with one authorization clerk (and five hold positions) might be considered optimum (since it has the lowest cost of the three configurations considered). This resulted from the relatively low cost placed upon waiting time.

Requirement: Find the minimum hourly cost of waiting time for which a configuration with two clerks (and two hold positions) would have the lowest total monthly cost.

7.7 A large hospital operates a blood donation center five days a week. The donor arrival rate is eight per hour, and the time required to complete the donation is 45 minutes (including initial screening, donation time, and recovery). The donation center is staffed by phlebotomists who earn $10 per hour. The facility has sufficient work space to accommodate up to 12 phlebotomists. Assume that the goodwill cost of waiting is $7 per hour.

Requirement: Answer the following. What is the optimal number of phlebotomists that should be employed to minimize overall costs?

References

Berenson, M. L., and D. M. Levine. 1992. *Basic Business Statistics: Concepts and Applications*. 5th ed. Englewood Cliffs, NJ: Prentice-Hall, Inc.

Dershin, H., and M. S. Schaik. 1993. "Quality Improvement for a Hospital Patient Transportation System." *Hospital and Health Services Administration* 38 (1): 111–19.

Hillier, F. S., and G. J. Lieberman. 1986. *Introduction to Operations Research*. 4th Edition. Oakland, CA: Holden-Day, Inc.

Keller, G., B. Warrack, and H. Bartel. 1994. *Statistics for Management and Economics*. 3rd Edition. Belmont, CA: Duxbury Press.

Parzen, E. 1962. *Stochastic Processes.* San Francisco: Holden-Day, Inc.

Rosenquist, C. J. 1987. "Queueing Analysis: A Useful Planning and Management Technique for Radiology." *Journal of Medical Systems* 11 (6): 413–19.

Taira, R. K., and H. K. Huang. 1989. "A Picture Archiving and Communication System Module for Radiology." *Computer Methods and Programs in Biomedicine* 30 (2–3): 229–37.

Vemuri, S. 1984. "Simulated Analysis of Patient Waiting Time in an Outpatient Pharmacy." *American Journal of Hospital Pharmacy* 41 (6): 1127–30.

Weiss, E. N., and J. O. McClain. 1987. "Administrative Days in Acute Care Facilities: A Queueing-Analytic Approach." *Operations Research* 35 (1): 35–44.

Additional Readings

Baker, J. R., E. R. Clayton, and B. W. Taylor III. "A Non-Linear Multi-Criteria Programming Approach for Determining County Emergency Medical Service Ambulance Allocations." *Journal of the Operational Research Society* 40, no. 5 (1989): 423–32.

McQuarrie, D. G. "Hospitalization Utilization Levels. The Application of Queuing Theory to a Controversial Medical Economic Problem." *Minnesota Medicine* 66, no. 11 (1983): 679–86.

Moore, B. J. "Use of Queueing Theory for Problem Solution in Dallas, Tex., Bureau of Vital Statistics." *Public Health Reports* 92, no. 2 (1977): 171–75.

Naylor, C. D., C. M. Levinton, S. Wheeler, and L. Hunter. "Queueing for Coronary Surgery During Severe Supply-Demand Mismatch in a Canadian Referral Centre: A Case Study of Implicit Rationing." *Social Science and Medicine* 37, no. 1 (1993): 61–67.

Pratt, M. L., and A. J. Grindon. "Computer Simulation Analysis of Blood Donor Queueing Problems." *Transfusion* 22, no. 3 (1982): 234–37.

Scott, D. W., L. E. Factor, and G. A. Gorry. "Predicting the Response Time of an Urban Ambulance System." *Health Services Research* 13, no. 4 (1978): 404–17.

Appendix 7.A

Formulas for Basic Multiple-Server Queueing Systems

The derivation of key formulas for this queueing model begins with a formula for P_0, the probability of an empty system:

$$P_0 = \frac{1}{\frac{\left(\frac{\lambda}{\mu}\right)^S}{S!\left(1 - \frac{\lambda}{\mu S}\right)} + 1 + \frac{\left(\frac{\lambda}{\mu}\right)^1}{1!} + \frac{\left(\frac{\lambda}{\mu}\right)^2}{2!} + \cdots + \frac{\left(\frac{\lambda}{\mu}\right)^{S-1}}{(S-1)!}}$$

where S is the number of servers, and λ and μ are the arrival and service rates, respectively.

Once the value of P_0 has been obtained, other quantities of interest can also be computed. The computation of the probability of n persons in the system depends upon whether n is larger or smaller than s. In particular, one can obtain

$$P_n = P_0 \frac{\left(\frac{\lambda}{\mu}\right)^n}{n!}, \text{ if } n \le S$$

$$P_n = P_0 \frac{\left(\frac{\lambda}{\mu}\right)^n}{S! \, S^{n-S}}, \text{ if } n \ge S$$

Similarly, one can obtain a formula for the expected number in the queue as

$$L_q = P_0 \frac{\left(\frac{\lambda}{\mu}\right)^{S+1}}{S \cdot S! \left(1 - \frac{\lambda}{\mu S}\right)^2}$$

Then the expected time in the queue can be found from

$$W_q = \frac{1}{\lambda} L_q$$

The expected number in the system then follows as

$$L_S = L_q + \frac{\lambda}{\mu}$$

And the expected time in the system is

$$W_S = W_q + \frac{1}{\mu}$$

Finally, the probability that the time in the queue, T, is greater than t is given by

$$P[T > t] = \frac{\left(\frac{\lambda}{\mu}\right)^S}{S!(1 - \rho)} P_0 e^{-\mu S t (1 - \rho)}, \text{ where } \rho = \frac{\lambda}{\mu S}$$

Control

P ARTS I and II describe techniques for strategic planning and efficient allocation of resources. Once plans are set in place and resources are allocated, management must control the processes by which services are delivered. Part III presents three commonly used techniques for management control in health services organizations.

Chapter 8 describes techniques (PERT/CPM) for controlling the time and costs associated with completion of major projects in the organization. Applications include construction and remodeling of facilities as well as service development projects that require careful scheduling and monitoring of progress.

Continuous quality improvement is the watchword of most health care organizations competing in today's complex environment. To be effective, quality improvement programs require that quality be measured and monitored over time. Targets and benchmarks must be established, and organizational performance must be measured in reference to these standards. Statistical quality control (Chapter 9) provides a management tool for measuring quality on an ongoing basis. It can be applied both to clinical quality (e.g., infection rates, returns to surgery) as well as to service quality (e.g., waiting time, patient satisfaction).

Inventory control methods are described in Chapter 10. Inventory models assist management in planning and monitoring the cost-effective use of supplies and materials in the organization. The techniques can also be applied to control of the use of other institutional resources such as financial capital, clinical personnel, and support staff.

8

PROJECT CONTROL WITH PERT/CPM

H EALTH CARE executives are frequently responsible for managing a variety of projects, ranging in complexity from the implementation of a new outpatient program to the construction of a completely new inpatient building. Among the challenges that the executive faces are identifying the resources necessary to complete the project, properly sequencing these resources so they are maximally effective, and monitoring the progress of the project in order to ensure its completion in a timely manner. For small projects, it is often feasible for the executive to meet these challenges by drawing upon some combination of intuition, experience, qualitative observation of the project's progress, guesswork, and luck.

When the project is larger and more complex, however, the executive might profit from the application of a formal quantitative procedure for planning and controlling the project. Such a procedure is known as **PERT (Program Evaluation and Review Technique)** or **CPM (Critical Path Method)**. While not totally identical, these two quantitative techniques share many common attributes and provide the executive with a model to help in project planning and control.

Introduction of Case Problem

A significantly high number of measles cases has been reported during the last several weeks within the service area of Hamilton County Hospital. (This case is based upon Problem 3.9 in Warner, Holloway, and Grazier 1984, 87–88.) The director of the County Department of

Public Health has contacted the administrator of Hamilton County Hospital to enlist her assistance in implementing an immunization program in order to avert a serious measles epidemic. The public health director indicates that time is of the essence so it is important that the hospital administrator work quickly and efficiently to design, develop, and implement the program.

As the hospital administrator analyzes the problem, she realizes that several questions confront her:

1. What is the specific sequence of activities that must be accomplished?
2. How long will it take to complete the entire immunization effort?
3. Which activities represent the greatest bottlenecks to completing the project?
4. What is the likelihood that the project might require significantly longer than desired to be completed?
5. If the likely completion time is deemed to be excessive, are there ways that additional resources could be efficiently expended to shorten the project completion time?

An Overview of PERT/CPM

PERT and CPM represent two network-oriented approaches to planning, analyzing, and controlling a project. The two approaches, developed independently during the mid- to late 1950s, are quite similar, with the major distinction being how time and cost are incorporated into the model.

Both techniques begin with the identification of the steps of a project along with the sequencing relationship among these steps. A network diagram is then constructed and time estimates for each step, or activity, are obtained. Figure 8.1 provides an illustration of the general structure of this network diagram. In PERT three time estimates are assigned to each activity—an optimistic (minimum), most likely (modal), and pessimistic (maximum) value. The CPM approach uses only one time estimate.

The solution to the problem involves identifying that path (or paths) through the network requiring the largest total time to be completed relative to all other paths in the network. This path (or paths in the case of a tie), known as the **critical path**, determines the project completion time. In order to shorten this completion time, activities lying on the critical path(s) must be completed more quickly. Of course, as critical-path activity times are reduced, other paths may become critical and require the manager's attention. In a large project

Figure 8.1 General Structure of Network Diagram

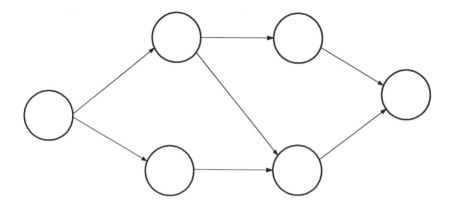

the problem of reducing the project's completion time may become quite complicated.

For PERT-oriented networks the three time estimates provide a basis for estimating a probability distribution for project completion time. In this way the analyst can obtain the probability that the project will be completed by a specified date. The single activity times used by the CPM method do not allow for such computations. Both techniques do, however, provide for project control. For each activity, the latest allowable start time necessary to keep the project on schedule can be computed. In this way, corrective action can hopefully be taken if project delays are detected.

Finally, under the CPM approach, the analyst can investigate strategies for completing the project in less than the normally required time. Shortening the completion time of an activity, known as "crashing," typically has a cost associated with it. It is possible to solve for the minimum-cost strategy for shortening a project's completion time (when feasible) to a desired value.

By way of a relatively simple example, consider a hospital that is beginning a new community outpatient clinic. Its first step would be to identify the components or tasks of the project as follows (a key word for each task is indicated in all capital letters):

1. Find and lease SPACE for the clinic.
2. HIRE a radiologist and laboratory director.
3. Purchase radiology and lab EQUIPMENT.
4. REMODEL the space.
5. INSTALL the equipment.

6. Hire NURSES and other personnel.
7. TRAIN personnel.
8. Design and implement PUBLICITY campaign.
9. FINAL preparation for opening.

Having identified these tasks, the hospital planners would then need to estimate activity completion times and costs. Using a CPM approach, they might obtain a normal and crashing time for each activity along with the cost associated with each of these times. In addition, they must establish a precedence relationship for each activity. This precedence relationship identifies the predecessor activities or tasks that must be completed before a new activity can begin. The results of their data gathering are summarized in Table 8.1.

Constructing the Network

The PERT/CPM network consists of arcs and nodes appropriately configured to represent the logical relationships among the activities making up the project. Two standard approaches can be taken in developing the network:

1. **Activity-on-Arc Approach**—Each arc represents an activity. The nodes correspond to events that mark the start or the completion of an activity.

2. **Activity-on-Node Representation**—Each node corresponds to an activity; arcs are used to connect two nodes where one node is an immediate predecessor activity of the second node.

While both approaches could be adopted, the activity-on-arc convention will be used in this text. Discussions of the activity-on-node

Table 8.1 Outpatient Clinic Task Data

Task Number	Task Description	Times (Weeks) Normal	Times (Weeks) Crashing	Predecessor Tasks	Costs Normal	Costs Crashing
1	SPACE	14	12	—	$ 5,000	$ 8,000
2	HIRE	13	12	—	10,000	12,000
3	EQUIPMENT	10	8	2	3,750	4,050
4	REMODEL	8	7	1,2	64,000	72,000
5	INSTALL	2	1	3,4	10,000	15,000
6	NURSES	5	3	—	3,500	4,400
7	TRAIN	4	3	6	10,000	12,000
8	PUBLICITY	11	8	—	25,000	26,200
9	FINAL	3	2	5,7,8	3,600	4,200

convention can be found in several management science texts (see, for example, Shogan 1988, 473–96; or Mathur and Solow 1994, Chapter 10). Thus, each node will correspond to either the beginning or end of a task.

The construction of the network for the outpatient clinic remodeling project begins by drawing a node, arbitrarily numbered 10, that marks the beginning of the project. The current discussion will adopt a "skip numbering" system for labeling the nodes. In this way if additional tasks are subsequently identified, they can be added to the network without having to entirely renumber the current nodes.

The analyst observes that four tasks—SPACE, HIRE, NURSES, and PUBLICITY—have no predecessor tasks. Therefore, these activities will flow directly out of the initial node (node 10) corresponding to the beginning of the project. Four arcs, then, are drawn out of this initial node, representing these four tasks. The network at this point appears as shown in Figure 8.2.

Now Task 3, "Purchase radiology and lab EQUIPMENT," has Task 2 as a predecessor activity. Therefore, this task is represented

Figure 8.2   Partial Network Diagram for Outpatient Clinic Project

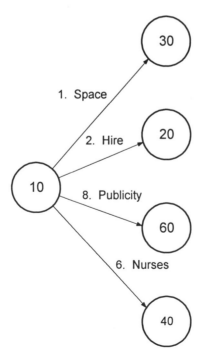

by the arc connecting nodes 20 and 50 (see Figure 8.3). But Task 4, "REMODEL the space," has Tasks 1 *and* 2 as predecessor activities. It would seem, then, that the arc representing this task needs to be drawn out of both nodes 20 *and* 30. This is not possible, however, and an alternative way of handling this situation is needed. The solution is to introduce a **dummy activity**, D1, which serves to link nodes 20 and 30 in order to maintain the desired logical flow (see Figure 8.3). This activity consumes no time and incurs no cost.

Drawing the rest of the network presents no unusual difficulty and proceeds quite smoothly. The final network is shown in Figure 8.4. Notice that each arc is labeled with the task name as well as the normal time required to complete the activity (in weeks). (The numbers adjacent to each node represent earliest expected completion time and latest allowable completion time for the events as described below).

Solving the Network

Once the network has been correctly drawn, the analyst can begin the solution phase. The goal here is to determine the completion time

Figure 8.3   Illustration of Use of Dummy Activity

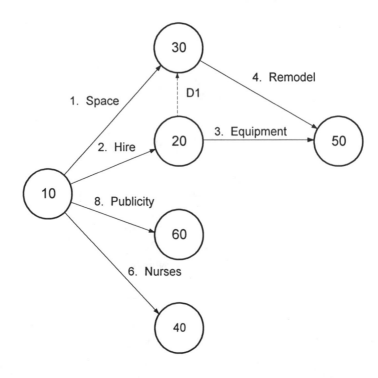

Figure 8.4 Outpatient Clinic—Complete PERT Network

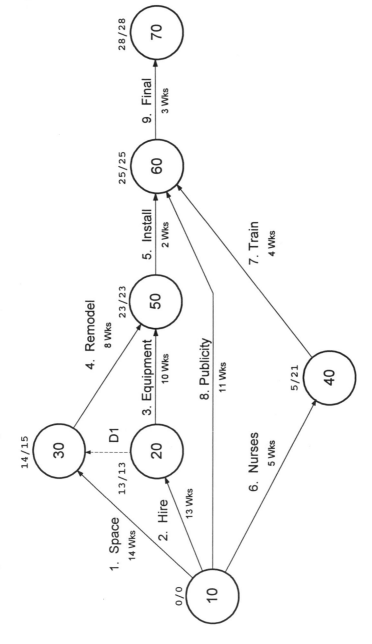

for the project and the path (or paths) through the network having the largest total completion time. This path (or paths in the case of a tie), the critical path, contains the activities that the analyst should concentrate upon in attempting to reduce the project completion time.

The analysis proceeds by computing two time values for each node (event)—T_E, (the earliest expected completion time for the event) and T_L, (the latest allowable completion time for the event). The value of T_E for the final event will provide the expected completion time for the project. These values are obtained by making two passes through the network—one moving forward through the network, and a second moving backward through the network.

The forward pass through the network yields values of T_E. The computation involves adding the times required to complete all activities leading up to a particular node. It is most easily accomplished iteratively, as shown in Figure 8.5. The value of T_E for Event 70 is equal to the value of T_E for Event 60, which is 25, plus the time for Activity 60–70, which is 3. Thus, T_E for Event 70 is 28.

The only complication occurs if two arcs enter an event node. In this case it appears to be possible to compute more than one value of T_E. A bit of reflection indicates that the definition of T_E—the earliest expected time that an event will occur—suggests that the largest of these possible T_E values should be assigned to the event. This follows from the realization that the event does not occur until all activities leading up to the event are completed.

By way of example, consider Figure 8.6. The value of T_E for Event 50 would seem to be computable as either 22 (T_E for Event 30, which is 14, plus the time for Activity 30–50, which is 8) or 23 (T_E for Event 20, which is 13, plus the time for Activity 20–50, which is 10). The larger of these two values, 23, would be assigned as the value of T_E for Event 50.

A backward pass through the network yields values of T_L for each event. The value of T_L for the final event of the network is set equal to the scheduled completion time for the project. If no such time has

Figure 8.5 Iterative Computation of T_E

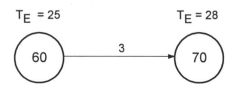

been specified, then this value of T_L is set equal to the value of T_E computed for the final event. The T_L values for the remaining events of the network are computed by an iterative process described below.

To illustrate, consider the portion of a network shown in Figure 8.7. The value of T_L for Event 40 is computed by subtracting 4 (the time to complete Activity 40–60) from the value of T_L for Event 60, which is 25. Thus, as shown in Figure 8.7, T_L for Event 40 is equal to 21.

The situation that creates a complication in this backward pass occurs when two or more activity arcs leave an event node. It would seem once again that more than one value of T_L could be computed. Since T_L is defined as the latest allowable time for the event in order to keep the project on schedule, it becomes clear that the appropriate value to assign for T_L is the smallest value.

As an example, consider Figure 8.8. The value of T_L would be found as the smaller of $(15 - 0 = 15)$, which corresponds to the top path, or $(23 - 10 = 13)$, which corresponds to the bottom path. Thus, T_L for Event 20 would equal 13.

Figure 8.6   Computation of T_E for Multiple Predecessor Events

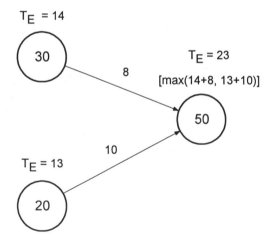

Figure 8.7   Iterative Computation of T_L

Figure 8.8 Computation of T_L for Multiple Successor Events

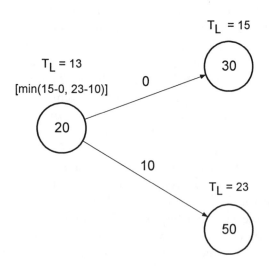

Finding the Critical Path

It is convenient to summarize the T_E and T_L values for each event of the project as shown in Table 8.2 (both T_E and T_L are expressed in weeks). The values of T_E and T_L are also included in Figure 8.4 adjacent to each node of the network. Table 8.2 also contains values of **slack** for each event. Slack is a quantity that indicates how much slippage could occur in the completion of an event without affecting the project's scheduled completion time. Mathematically, it is found by subtracting the earliest expected completion time from the latest allowable completion time. That is,

$$slack = T_L - T_E$$

Once the values of slack for each of the events in the project have been obtained, the critical path can be identified. The procedure is to first identify the smallest value of slack that has been computed. In the current example that value is 0. Next, a path is found from the beginning event to the final event that is made up of events all having this minimum slack value associated with them. If the work to this point has been performed correctly, such a path can always be found.

Referring to Table 8.2, it is in fact possible to identify a path through the network composed of events all of which have a slack of 0. Such a path consists of the events

10–20–50–60–70

Table 8.2 Outpatient Clinic Event Data

Event	T_E	T_l	Slack
10	0	0	0
20	13	13	0
30	14	15	1
40	5	21	16
50	23	23	0
60	25	25	0
70	28	28	0

In terms of the project tasks, this equates to

HIRE, EQUIPMENT, INSTALL, FINAL

This, then, is the critical path in the network. If this procedure leads to the identification of multiple paths, then the network has more than one critical path. The expected completion time for the project is found to equal 28 weeks, which is the T_E value for Event 70.

Shortening the Project Completion Time

If a completion time of 28 weeks is felt to be too high, the analyst would now begin to search for a strategy to reduce this completion time. In general, there will be a cost associated with doing this, and the goal would be to achieve a desired reduction at a minimum cost.

In the case of a small project, it might be feasible to identify this minimum cost strategy through trial and error. For example, if it were necessary to reduce the current project's completion time to 25 weeks, one would begin by examining the costs associated with shortening the completion times of the activities on the critical path. The cost for each activity is found from

$$\text{crash cost per week} = \frac{(\text{crashing cost} - \text{normal cost})}{(\text{crashing time} - \text{normal time})}$$

Then the crashing costs (per week) for the activities on the critical path—HIRE, EQUIPMENT, INSTALL, and FINAL—are $2,000, $150, $5,000, and $600, respectively (see Table 8.1). The lowest cost involves reducing EQUIPMENT by one week at a cost of $150.

Now the project requires 27 weeks and there are two critical paths—the original one, plus SPACE, REMODEL, INSTALL, and FINAL (10–30–50–60–70). By reducing the time for completing FINAL, both of these paths can be reduced at a cost of $600. At this point it turns out that there are three paths of interest:

- Path A: HIRE, EQUIPMENT, INSTALL, FINAL—26 weeks
- Path B: SPACE, REMODEL, INSTALL, FINAL—26 weeks
- Path C: HIRE, D1, REMODEL, INSTALL, FINAL—25 weeks

FINAL can be reduced no further. The relevant crash costs are as follows:

Activity	Crashing Cost per Week
HIRE	$2,000
EQUIPMENT	150
INSTALL	5,000
SPACE	1,500
REMODEL	8,000

The least expensive way to reduce Path A to 25 weeks is to crash EQUIPMENT by one week at a cost of $150. Finally, the optimum way to reduce Path B by one week is to crash SPACE by one week at a cost of $1,500. The project completion time has now been reduced to 25 weeks, at a cost equal to the sum of the crashing costs incurred at each stage of the process:

$$\$150 + 600 + 150 + 1,500 = \$2,400$$

For the present example, this cost represents a minimum. In general, this sequential trial-and-error approach to crashing a project to a desired completion time provides a feasible, but not necessarily lowest-cost, solution. The optimum crashing solution can always be found using an appropriate linear programming model (see, for example, Mathur and Solow 1994, Chapter 10).

Probability Analysis—The Role of PERT

Frequently the manager is interested in having a probability estimate associated with a particular scheduled completion date. The PERT approach to project control provides for such probability calculations by assigning three time estimates to each activity—an optimistic (t_o), most likely (t_m), and pessimistic (t_p) value. For the purposes of determining the critical path, these three values are averaged to obtain a single expected activity time (t_e). This average is computed from

$$t_e = \frac{t_o + 4t_m + t_p}{6} \qquad \text{(E 8.1)}$$

Once these values of t_e are obtained, they can be handled in the same way as the single time values in CPM.

The probability computations do make use of the three time estimates. The underlying theory is discussed in a number of texts (see, for example, Chapter 11 of Moder and Phillips 1970). For the current discussion it is sufficient to indicate that these three time values provide a measure of variability associated with activity time. This variability measure, in conjunction with the expected completion time, provides the basis for estimating probabilities.

To illustrate, consider a modification to the outpatient clinic remodeling problem involving several assumptions. First, assume that three time estimates for each activity are available. Second, assume that these estimates have the property that their average computed from Equation 8.1 is equal to the original single time estimate. Thus, a PERT analysis would yield identical results to those obtained thus far using a CPM orientation.

Assume further that the activities comprising the critical path have the following time estimates. (Recall that t_o, t_m, and t_p represent the optimistic, most likely, and pessimistic times, respectively. The value of t_e is the weighted average of these three time values, and variance will be discussed below. Note that the values of t_e equal the corresponding single time estimates in the CPM analysis.)

Task	t_0	t_m	t_p	t_e	Variance
HIRE	11	12.5	17	13	1
EQUIPMENT	8	10	12	10	.444
INSTALL	1	1.5	5	2	.444
FINAL	2	3	4	3	.111

The values of variance are computed from

$$\text{variance} = \frac{(t_p - t_o)^2}{36} \tag{E 8.2}$$

These values reflect the variability associated with each individual activity on the critical path. Assuming these activities are independent, the variability associated with completing the entire path, and hence the project, can be estimated as the sum of these individual variance values, or 2.

The expected time of completion for the project has already been found to equal 28 weeks. If the project completion time is assumed to have a normal distribution, then the probability that the project is completed in 25 weeks is equal to the area under a normal curve as shown in Figure 8.9. The shaded area can be found by referring to a cumulative normal distribution function table (see, for example, Moder and Phillips 1970, 315) using a z-value of −2.12 [which is (25 − 28) divided by the square root of 2]. The resulting probability is only 1.7 percent. Thus, if no measures are taken to crash the project, there is little chance that a deadline of 25 weeks would be met.

Model Formulation, Quantification, and Data Requirements

The case problem can now be continued. The Hamilton County Hospital administrator quickly realizes that a quantitative procedure like PERT/CPM would be very useful in helping her to successfully implement an immunization program within the tight time constraints imposed by the public health director. She therefore moves quickly to enlist her management engineer's assistance in developing an appropriate network model of the project.

A planning meeting is held, attended by the administrator, the management engineer, the public health director, and members of the hospital's infectious disease department. This group has sufficient expertise and experience to identify the tasks necessary to accomplish the desired level of immunization within the hospital's service area. Several meeting attendees have had experience with similar programs in other settings.

Figure 8.9 Probability of Completing Project in 25 Weeks

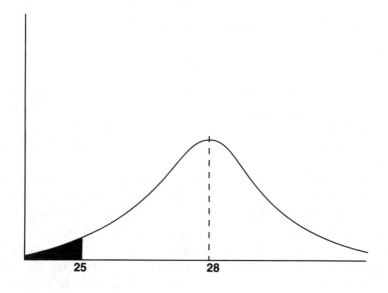

The meeting results in the identification of 19 specific tasks that must be completed:

1. Gather demographic data
2. Survey homes in the area
3. Estimate number of susceptible children
4. Review data that has been gathered
5. Select clinic sites
6. Schedule times at sites
7. Obtain vaccine and injection guns
8. Arrange for physicians and nurses
9. Arrange for hospital van and sound equipment
10. Obtain volunteers' assistance
11. Plan routes for hospital van
12. Develop educational material
13. Print educational material
14. Assemble educational material
15. Distribute educational material
16. Orient volunteers
17. Announce to households that clinic will open
18. Use sound equipment on hospital van to publicize clinic opening
19. Conduct the clinic

Having listed the required tasks, the group must now define their sequencing and obtain estimates of the time required to complete each one. This information will be obtained from a number of sources including past experience, input from staff members of the planning and marketing area, conversations with personnel at the County Department of Health, and some intelligent assumptions. Assume that the results of this data gathering effort yield the data listed in Table 8.3.

Having established the logical sequence of activities necessary to develop and implement the immunization program, the project team now proceeds to construct the network for the project. This process can be facilitated by using one of the several commercial graphics packages available for microcomputers (for example, *Flow Charting 4*, Patton and Patton 1994). The result is the PERT network shown in Figure 8.10. (Instead of being skip-numbered, the nodes have been labeled to coincide with the computer printout illustrated later in the chapter).

The construction of the network proceeds quite logically from the predecessor-tasks relationships listed in Table 8.3. The procedure is identical to that described in the previous section of the text. The

Table 8.3 Immunization Project Time Estimates and Sequencing

Task No.	Task Description	Optimistic Time (days)	Most Likely Time (days)	Pessimistic Time (days)	Predecessor Tasks
1	Gather data	0.5	1	1.5	—
2	Survey homes	4	6	14	—
3	Estimate number	3	4	11	1,2
4	Review data	1	2	3	3
5	Select sites	0.5	1	7.5	4
6	Schedule times	8	9	16	5
7	Obtain vaccine	2	3	4	6
8	Physicians and nurses	1	2	9	6
9	Arrange van	0.5	1	1.5	4
10	Get volunteers	1	3	5	6
11	Plan routes	2	4	6	4
12	Develop material	6	7	8	4
13	Print material	7	9	17	12
14	Assemble material	1	2	3	13
15	Distribute material	2	3	10	14
16	Orient volunteers	0.5	1	1.5	10
17	Announce opening	0.5	1	1.5	7,8
18	Publicize clinic	2	4	12	6,9,11
19	Conduct clinic	2	5	8	15,16,17,18

only complication that arises is the need to satisfy the predecessor relationship for Task 18. In order for Tasks 6 and 9 to both precede Task 18 while Tasks 7, 8, and 10 are preceded only by Task 6, the analyst must employ a dummy activity, D1, between nodes 06 and 08. Reference to Figure 8.10 illustrates the use of this dummy activity.

Solving the Case Problem

As a result of the planning meeting described above, the hospital administrator has essentially answered her first question regarding the specific sequence of activities that must be accomplished. These 19 activities have been tabulated (Table 8.3) and displayed graphically in the form of a network (Figure 8.10). The administrator can now proceed to answer her remaining questions by solving the network.

This case problem network can clearly be solved using the hand-calculation techniques described in the previous section of the text. From a practical standpoint, however, the process is greatly simplified by using appropriate computer software. In the *QuickQuant* PERT module, two input screens are used to enter the data from Table 8.3.

Figure 8.10 PERT Network for Immunization Project

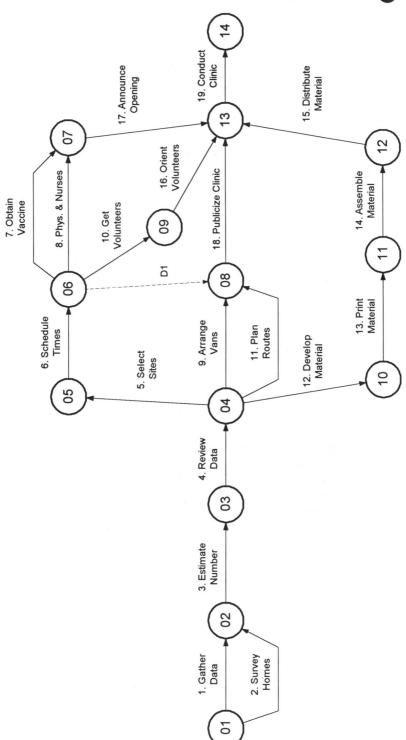

When the "Probabilistic Single Path Analysis" option within this module is chosen, several output screens (which can also be obtained in printed form) result. The hospital administrator can determine how long the entire immunization effort will take and which activities represent the greatest bottlenecks by referring to two of these output screens, displayed in Exhibits 8.1 and 8.2.

From Exhibit 8.1, it is clear that the immunization effort will require a total of 42 days. The critical path consists of the activity sequence 2–3–4–12–13–14–15–19. It is these activities that represent the greatest bottlenecks and that the project team needs to focus on first if they wish to shorten the completion time for the project. This report also provides six planning times that are useful for managerial control of the project. The value of "Exp. *t*" is the expected completion time for the activity. It is computed for each task using Equation 8.1. A discussion of these planning times appears in a later section of this chapter. Notice also that the dummy activity is included in the report.

The second report, Exhibit 8.2, presents information in terms of the events. The logical network connections are shown both in terms of other events as well as in terms of activities. In addition, three times are indicated for each event: "TE," "TL," and "Slack." Slack

Exhibit 8.1 *QuickQuant* Output Screen—PERT Activity Report

Activity			Events		Planning Times					
No	Code	Name	Beg.	End.	Exp. t	ES	LS	EF	LF	Slack
1	1	Gather Data	1	2	1.0	0.0	6.0	1.0	7.0	6.0
2	2	Survey Home	1	2	7.0	0.0	0.0	7.0	7.0	0.0
3	3	Estimate Nu	2	3	5.0	7.0	7.0	12.0	12.0	0.0
4	4	Review Data	3	4	2.0	12.0	12.0	14.0	14.0	0.0
5	5	Select Site	4	5	2.0	14.0	20.0	16.0	22.0	6.0
6	6	Schedule Ti	5	6	10.0	16.0	22.0	26.0	32.0	6.0
7	7	Obtain Vacc	6	7	3.0	26.0	33.0	29.0	36.0	7.0
8	8	Phys. & Nur	6	7	3.0	26.0	33.0	29.0	36.0	7.0
9	9	Arrange Van	4	8	1.0	14.0	31.0	15.0	32.0	17.0
10	10	Get Volunte	6	9	3.0	26.0	33.0	29.0	36.0	7.0
11	11	Plan Routes	4	8	4.0	14.0	28.0	18.0	32.0	14.0
12	12	Develop Mat	4	10	7.0	14.0	14.0	21.0	21.0	0.0
13	13	Print Mater	10	11	10.0	21.0	21.0	31.0	31.0	0.0
14	14	Assemble Ma	11	12	2.0	31.0	31.0	33.0	33.0	0.0
15	15	Distribute	12	13	4.0	33.0	33.0	37.0	37.0	0.0
16	16	Orient Vol.	9	13	1.0	29.0	36.0	30.0	37.0	7.0
17	17	Announce Op	7	13	1.0	29.0	36.0	30.0	37.0	7.0
18	18	Publicize C	8	13	5.0	26.0	32.0	31.0	37.0	6.0
19	19	Conduct Cli	13	14	5.0	37.0	37.0	42.0	42.0	0.0
20	D*1	Dummy--1	6	8	0.0	26.0	32.0	26.0	32.0	6.0

Expected Project Duration: 42

The following critical path(s) apply.

    2   3   4   12   13   14   15   19

Exhibit 8.2 *QuickQuant* Output Screen—PERT Event Milestone Report

	Event Connections		Times			Activity Connections	
Event	Predecessors	Successors	TE	TL	Slack	Ending	Starting
1	: none	: 2 2 -- :	0.0	0.0	0.0	: none	: 1 2
2	: 1 1 --	: 2 -- -- :	7.0	7.0	0.0	: 1 2	: 3 ----
3	: 2 -- --	: 3 -- -- :	12.0	12.0	0.0	: 3 ----	: 4 ----
4	: 3 -- --	: 4 4 4 :	14.0	14.0	0.0	: 4 ----	: 5 9
	:	: 4 -- -- :				:	: 11 12
5	: 4 -- --	: 5 -- -- :	16.0	22.0	6.0	: 5 ----	: 6 ----
6	: 5 -- --	: 6 6 6 :	26.0	32.0	6.0	: 6 ----	: 7 8
	:	: 6 -- -- :				:	: 10 D*1
7	: 6 6 --	: 7 -- -- :	29.0	36.0	7.0	: 7 8	: 17 ----
8	: 4 4 6	: 7 -- -- :	26.0	32.0	6.0	: 9 11	: 18 ----
	:	:				: D*1 ----	:
9	: 6 -- --	: 8 -- -- :	29.0	36.0	7.0	: 10 ----	: 16 ----
10	: 4 -- --	: 9 -- -- :	21.0	21.0	0.0	: 12 ----	: 13 ----
11	: 10 -- --	: 8 -- -- :	31.0	31.0	0.0	: 13 ----	: 14 ----
12	: 11 -- --	: 10 -- -- :	33.0	33.0	0.0	: 14 ----	: 15 ----
13	: 12 9 7	: 11 -- -- :	37.0	37.0	0.0	: 15 16	: 19 ----
	: 8 -- --	:				: 17 18	:
14	: 13 -- --	: none	: 42.0	42.0	0.0	: 19 ----	: none

Expected Project Duration: 42

is computed from $[TL - TE]$. These three time values also have managerial implications that are discussed later in this chapter.

In order to assess the likelihood that the project is completed within some specified time duration, the project team can consult the next portion of the computer output shown in Exhibit 8.3. This output presents representative fractile points associated with the project completion time. For example, if the desired completion time were 39.83 days, the probability of meeting this time would be 25 percent. For a project completion time not contained in Exhibit 8.3, the associated probability would be solved using a table of cumulative normal values, as described earlier in the chapter. Observe in Exhibit 8.3 that the mean and standard deviation of project duration are 42 and 3.23, respectively. Then a completion time of 40 days, for example, would have an associated Z-score of

$$Z = \frac{40 - 42}{3.23} = -0.619.$$

The cumulative probability of this Z-score is equal to approximately 26.8 percent, which is the approximate probability of meeting this completion time.

Finally, a graphical representation of the network is also provided by the *QuickQuant* program, as shown in Exhibit 8.4. The critical path (marked by double dashes) can be clearly seen in this figure as well as

Exhibit 8.3 *QuickQuant* Output Screen—Probability
Information

```
Critical Path:

  2     3     4    12    13    14    15    19

Mean Duration: 42          Standard Deviation: 3.23

              Fractile .01: 34.47
              Fractile .05: 36.7
              Fractile .10: 37.86
              Fractile .25: 39.83
              Fractile .50: 42.00
              Fractile .75: 44.17
              Fractile .90: 46.14
              Fractile .95: 47.3
              Fractile .99: 49.53
```

the values of "TE" and "TL" (explained later in this chapter) tabulated
in Exhibit 8.2.

Model Variation

The administrator has now answered four of her five questions. In
order to identify ways to efficiently shorten the project completion
time, she must now modify her model slightly. This model variation
calls for her to determine the costs for each activity, the shortest
possible completion time (crash time) for each activity, and the cost
of completing each activity in this shortened time period (crash cost).

To this end, assume that the administrator calls another meeting
of the project group and also includes a representative from the Accounting Department to assist in obtaining cost estimates. The group
collaborates to obtain the information displayed in Table 8.4. Appropriate software like the "Time-Cost Trade-off Analysis" option within
the PERT module of *QuickQuant* can now be used to examine the
cost of crashing the project to completion times less than 42 days. The
results of such an analysis are presented in Exhibit 8.5.

The *QuickQuant* program chooses activities sequentially to be completed within their crash time in decreasing order of their marginal
crash cost. For each resulting combination, the project time and project
cost are summarized. In addition, the activity (or activities) chosen to
be crashed at each stage are listed. If, for example, the project team

Exhibit 8.4 *QuickQuant* Output Screen—PERT Network

Heavy arrows give critical activities. TEs and TLs appear below events.

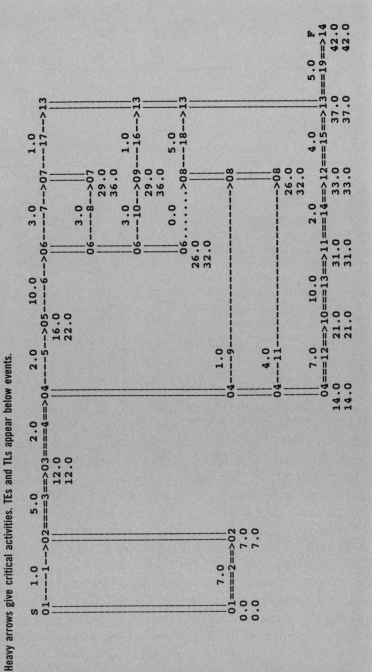

Table 8.4 Immunization Project Regular and Crash Planning Data

Task No.	Task Description	Expected or Regular Time (days)	Crash Time (days)	Regular Cost	Crash Cost
1	Gather data	1.00	1.00	$ 240.00	$ 240.00
2	Survey homes	7.00	5.00	1,400.00	2,200.00
3	Estimate number	5.00	4.00	840.00	1,008.00
4	Review data	2.00	1.00	480.00	720.00
5	Select sites	2.00	1.00	336.00	454.00
6	Schedule times	10.00	8.00	800.00	1,120.00
7	Obtain vaccine	3.00	2.00	288.00	432.00
8	Physicians and nurses	3.00	2.00	432.00	576.00
9	Arrange van	1.00	1.00	96.00	96.00
10	Get volunteers	3.00	2.00	432.00	576.00
11	Plan routes	4.00	2.00	672.00	1,008.00
12	Develop material	7.00	4.00	1,120.00	1,600.00
13	Print material	10.00	7.00	1,000.00	1,450.00
14	Assemble material	2.00	1.00	192.00	288.00
15	Distribute material	4.00	3.00	384.00	480.00
16	Orient volunteers	1.00	1.00	140.00	140.00
17	Announce opening	1.00	1.00	120.00	120.00
18	Publicize clinic	5.00	1.00	600.00	720.00
19	Conduct clinic	5.00	4.00	1,680.00	2,016.00

wanted to complete the project in 35 days, the total project cost would be $12,222. This figure is $970 more than the $11,252 cost associated with a completion time of 42 days. By referring to the "Last Activities Crashed" column in Exhibit 8.5 (and reading downward from Plan 1 through Plan 6), the team observes that a completion time of 35 days can be achieved by crashing Activities 14 and 15 each by 1 day, Activity 13 by 3 days, and Activities 12 and 3 each by 1 day. (See Table 8.4 for the descriptions of these activities.)

Exhibit 8.5 also reveals that the shortest possible completion time for the project is 29 days. Further reduction in the project completion time could only occur if the completion times for the individual activities were reexamined and even lower crash times were identified. In order to obtain the critical path(s) associated with a given crashing plan, one could perform a PERT analysis on the network using the crash times. In the general case, as crashing is introduced, the composition of the critical path(s) will change.

Exhibit 8.5 *QuickQuant* Output Screen—PERT Time-Cost Trade-off Analysis

Plan	Project Cost	Project Time	Time Savings	Last Activities Crashed	
1	11252.00	42.00	----	----	
2	11348.00	41.00	1.00	14	
3	11444.00	40.00	1.00	15	
4	11894.00	37.00	3.00	13	
5	12054.00	36.00	1.00	12	
6	12222.00	35.00	1.00	3	
7	12412.00	34.00	1.00	12	18
8	12652.00	33.00	1.00	4	
9	12930.00	32.00	1.00	5	12
10	13266.00	31.00	1.00	19	
11	14066.00	29.00	2.00	2	

Description of Available Computer Software

Solutions to PERT and CPM problems can be obtained with *QuickQuant*, QSB+, Storm, or AB:QM software. Of these four packages, only the *QuickQuant* system produces a graphical representation of the network and its associated critical path. The user essentially grows the tree on the screen in a sequential structured fashion. The three other packages require that the data be entered in a matrix or free form, and no graphical tree configuration is available.

Several more sophisticated (and more expensive) software products are available that fall into a category referred to as "project management" software. Noteworthy among these are three products—Computer Associates' CA-SuperProject 3.0c, Microsoft's Project 4.0, and Symantec's Time Line 6.0. A brief review of these products appeared in the August 1994 issue of *PC Computing*. A more comprehensive coverage of project management software appears in Badiru (1991).

Analysis, Interpretation, and Application of Results to Management Decisions

The hospital administrator has now resolved all five of her questions regarding the immunization project. She can proceed with the project with a relatively clear sense of direction regarding a number of issues: the sequence of tasks to be accomplished; the likely project completion time; probabilities associated with various completion times; the cost of completing the project; the activities that are likely to be bottlenecks;

and the most cost-efficient way to reduce the total project completion time. These issues are essentially planning issues.

PERT/CPM methods also offer valuable information for project control. For example, Exhibit 8.1 lists six key times for each activity: "Exp. t" is the expected completion time; "ES" and "EF" indicate the earliest times, respectively, that the activity can be expected to start and finish; "LS" and "LF" indicate the latest allowable times, respectively, that the activity can start and finish and still have the project remain on schedule; and "Slack" indicates the amount of slippage possible for the given activity. It can be computed from $[LS - ES]$ or $[LF - EF]$. As the project proceeds, the project manager can monitor activity start and completion times. If slippage is observed, it will be possible, one hopes, to take corrective action before the project is seriously delayed.

Similar management information is available in Exhibit 8.2, but from the perspective of the project events. Here "TE" and "TL" refer, respectively, to the earliest expected completion time for an event and the latest allowable completion time for the event in order for the project to remain on schedule. "Slack" is defined here as $[TL - TE]$ and once again is a measure of allowable slippage in the completion of the particular event.

Frequently the manager will run a new PERT analysis as the project progresses. This analysis will reflect actual completion times observed, new projected time estimates for uncompleted tasks, and in some cases new cost estimates. This type of analysis will provide information on how to complete the remaining portion of the project at the lowest cost and still meet the original completion date.

The use of a project management tool like PERT/CPM has provided Hamilton County Hospital with a framework in which to develop its measles immunization program. As a planning tool, these techniques provide an indication of how long the project will take and what resources need to be expended. As a control tool, the project manager can monitor the project's progress and take necessary steps to make modifications if delays appear likely. By using these methods, the hospital should be able to successfully complete its immunization efforts in a timely and economical fashion.

Case Studies from the Literature

Planning of Inservice Programs (D'Aquila 1993)

A nursing inservice department has responsibility for scheduling and planning inservice programs, seminars, and educational workshops. This planning process is always subject to delays, some of which could conceivably result in the need to cancel a program. However, such cancellations have repercussions, both on the inservice department and on those planning to attend.

The inservice department personnel soon recognized that a planning tool capable of anticipating possible delays and of providing for alternative strategies that would address these contingencies would be a very beneficial tool indeed. Although they are typically used in industrial settings, PERT and CPM were seen as potential planning tools to assist in this department's planning process for three main reasons: (1) scheduling workshops involves several distinct activities that are sequential and dependent upon one another for project completion; (2) there are also some definite independent activities; and (3) the PERT/CPM process would be a helpful framework in which to orient new nursing inservice instructors to the planning of their workshops.

The development of the PERT network involved first identifying 14 activities that comprised the workshop planning process. Once these activities were identified, three time estimates for each were obtained, and the dependence of each activity on other activities was also defined. A PERT network was then constructed and solved. Six activities comprised the critical path, whose completion time was found to be 6.2 weeks (with a standard deviation of 2.5 weeks).

The deadline that had been established for planning the workshop was ten weeks. The probability of meeting this deadline could then be computed, with the result equaling .937. The department thus realized that there was an excellent chance of completing the planning process before the ten-week deadline.

The department personnel also looked briefly at the question of crashing the planning activities in order to complete the process in less than ten weeks. Several difficulties became immediately obvious. First, costs were not recorded per project. Second, limited resources precluded crashing several of the activities. Finally, some of the activities simply could not physically be accomplished in less time. Therefore, no further effort was expended in trying to utilize crashing for this process.

The inservice department concluded that the use of PERT achieved better performance and successfully helped to avoid cancellation of programs. In addition, it was very useful in teaching a nurse the process of organizing a workshop.

Installation of Computer System (Fralic 1984)

When Braddock General Hospital decided to install a new hospital-wide patient information and communication system, the chief nursing officer (CNO) had to assume major responsibility for planning for the system for nursing and integrating the design into the hospital's overall plan. She immediately recognized that these responsibilities required a set of comprehensive and highly detailed activities. Much attention would have to be paid to estimates of time, cost, and function.

The CNO decided that the computer planning and installation represented a major undertaking that could not be worked into other routine nursing division activities. Rather, it required allocation of sufficient time and resources to be sure that the results would provide maximal benefit to the organization. She immediately recognized that a planning tool like PERT would offer a framework for completing the project.

A diagram of the project was constructed. While not a literal depiction of classical PERT, nevertheless the diagram represented a general and useful adaptation of PERT principles. Three key points were emphasized through the construction of this diagram: (1) a myriad of activities, all interdependent, are required to plan and install a computerized system; (2) planning needs to be deliberate and systematic if the installation is to serve the needs of the hospital, staff, and patients; and (3) a visual representation of the project, such as that offered by the PERT network, enables the nurse manager to professionally manage the project.

The network was solved and the critical path was identified. In summarizing the task of designing and implementing a computer system for the nursing division, the author concludes, "The task is always awesome. But, with proper planning, so are the results!"

Additional Reports from the Literature

Kost (1986) presents a case study in which CPM/PERT was used to plan and implement transcutaneous pCO_2 monitoring by a department of laboratory medicine. PERT techniques helped keep the project on track even though the initial estimate of the completion date was overly optimistic and the clinicians expressed intense demand to begin using the new monitoring technique. In addition to its value as a project management tool, PERT's use in this project helped to sharpen the participants' expertise in estimating and meeting deadlines.

An application of PERT to the analysis of problems in accounts receivable (A/R) has been reported by Wiles and Horwitz (1984). They indicate that isolated attempts to decrease the accounts receivable without analyzing the source or relationship of the problems may produce no results. However, the logic related to constructing a PERT network that describes the A/R process can help to identify ways to obtain a net decrease in the A/R payment cycle.

An adaptation of CPM to the delivery of patient care is described by Hofmann (1993). Although described as the critical path method, this application is representative of the nursing profession's use of this term, which is somewhat distinct from common usage in other fields. As Hofmann indicates, interdisciplinary teams work together to design a "critical path" or care plan that lays out the specific tasks to be followed on a day-to-day basis in caring for a patient in a particular diagnostic category.

As caregivers render care according to the care plan, they record variances, or differences between what is expected to occur and what actually happens, on the reverse side of the care plan form. No actual critical path is computed like that found in "traditional" PERT/CPM applications. Nevertheless, Hofmann reports that their pilot study of coronary artery bypass graft patients noted a lower rate of complications and a lower average length of stay. Additional paths will now be developed for other diagnostic categories.

Problems

8.1 The following process is planned for building a replacement outpatient clinic in a hospital:

Job	Completion Time (Weeks)	Predecessor Jobs
1. Obtain CON	20	None
2. Get cost estimates from contractor	4	1
3. Obtain necessary funding	16	2
4. Build the new clinic	32	3
5. Hire additional staff	16	3
6. Install equipment	6	4
7. Publicity	12	3
8. Train additional staff	4	5
9. Close old clinic	1	4,8

Requirement: Construct a PERT diagram for this project and compute the critical path, slack for each activity, earliest and latest start times, earliest and latest finish times.

8.2 The following process is followed in constructing a new ambulance entrance and waiting room for the emergency department of a community hospital:

Job	Completion Time (Weeks)	Predecessor Job
1. Pour foundation	5	None
2. Build walls	7	1
3. Build roof	5	2
4. Install the plumbing	3	2
5. Install wiring	4	2
6. Plaster walls	4	3,4,5
7. Paint walls	2	6
8. Install lighting fixtures	1	7

Requirement: Construct a PERT diagram for this project and compute the critical path, slack for each activity, earliest and latest start times, earliest and latest finish times.

8.3 The following process is planned for opening a new MRI unit for a hospital:

Job	Completion Time (Weeks)	Predecessor Job
1. Obtain CON	20	None
2. Relocate two x-ray machines	2	1
3. Remodel needed space	16	2
4. Hire MRI technician	12	1
5. Order MRI	20	1
6. Install MRI	5	1,2,3
7. Train existing personnel to use MRI	4	4
8. Schedule initial patients	1	6,7

Requirement: Construct a PERT diagram for this project and compute the critical path, slack for each activity, earliest and latest start times, earliest and latest finish times.

8.4 A project consists of a set of activities as described in the following table (all times are in weeks):

Activity	Optimistic Time	Most Likely Time	Pessimistic Time	Predecessor Activities
1	5	8	14	None
2	9	14	22	None
3	2	3	5	1
4	1	1	2	1
5	3	5	8	2

6	10	14	20	2
7	2	4	5	2
8	3	4	6	2
9	1	1	2	3
10	12	16	26	4,5
11	2	2	5	6
12	0	0	0	10
13	5	10	16	7
14	12	15	24	8
15	12	15	21	1
16	4	6	10	9
17	3	7	16	10
18	3	3	5	11,12
19	1	2	4	13
20	2	5	10	14
21	2	3	4	15,16,17

Requirements:

a. Construct the PERT diagram that models this network.

b. Determine the critical path and the expected completion time for the project.

c. A deadline for completing this project has been set at 50 weeks. Find the probability that this deadline will be met.

8.5 A project consists of seven activities with properties as shown in the following table (all times are in days):

Activity	Normal Time	Normal Cost	Crash Time	Crash Cost	Predecessor Activities
1	5	$ 80	4	$130	None
2	11	$ 75	8	$255	None
3	7	$165	6	$225	1
4	12	$ 48	10	$108	1
5	6	$314	4	$454	2,3
6	2	$100	1	$200	4,5
7	2	$100	1	$200	2,3

Requirements:

a. Construct the CPM network that models this project.

b. Determine the critical path, expected completion time, and total cost based upon normal times and costs.

c. Determine the optimum way to crash the project by two days, the corresponding critical path, and total cost when the project is crashed by two days.

References

Badiru, A. B. 1991. *Project Management Tools for Engineering and Management.* Norcross, GA: Institute of Industrial Engineers.

D'Aquila, N. W. 1993. "Facilitating Inservice Programs Through PERT/CPM." *Nursing Management* 24 (5): 92–96.

Fralic, M. F. 1984. "Using a PERT Planning Network to Manage a Nursing Service Computer System Installation." *Journal of Nursing Administration* 14 (12): 29–31.

Hofmann, P. A. 1993. "Critical Path Method: An Important Tool for Coordinating Clinical Care." *Joint Commission Journal on Quality Improvement* 19 (7): 235–46.

Kost, G. J. 1986. "Application of Program Evaluation and Review Technique (PERT) to Laboratory Research and Development Planning." *American Journal of Clinical Pathology* 86 (2): 186–92.

Mathur, K., and D. Solow. 1994. *Management Science: The Art of Decision Making.* Englewood Cliffs, NJ: Prentice-Hall.

Moder, J. J., and C. R. Phillips. 1970. *Project Management With CPM and PERT.* Second Edition. New York: Van Nostrand Reinhold Co.

Patton, K. A., and W. L. Patton Sr. 1994. *Flow Charting 4.* Morgan Hill, CA: Patton and Patton Software Corporation.

Shogan, A. W. 1988. *Management Science.* Englewood Cliffs, NJ: Prentice Hall.

Warner, D. M., D. C. Holloway, and K. L. Grazier. 1984. *Decision Making and Control for Health Administration: The Management of Quantitative Analysis.* Second Edition. Ann Arbor, MI: Health Administration Press.

Wiles, A., and R. M. Horwitz. 1984. "PERT Charts Pinpoint Problems in Accounts Receivable Management." *Healthcare Financial Management* 38 (9): 38–46.

Additional Readings

Johnson, K. C., and D. M. Priday. "The Single Most Important Event in a PERT Chart." *Radiology Management* 4, no. 4 (1982): 18–20.

Jones, R. H. "PERT/CPM Network Analysis: A Management Tool for Hospital Pharmacists Involved in Strategic Planning." *Hospital Pharmacy* 19, no. 2 (1984): 94–97.

Lovin, F. W. "Usage of PERT (Project Evaluation Review Technique) Networks in Medical Record Practice." *Journal of the American Medical Record Association* 59, no. 6 (1988): 48–51.

Valdiserri, R. O. "PERT: A Tool for Better Lab Planning." *Pathologist* 39, no. 7 (1985): 21–27.

Vanetzian, E. "Using PERT to Keep a Nursing Research Project Humming." *Nursing Research* 36, no. 6 (1987): 388–92.

Wesley, M. L., and A. Easterling. "Improving Clinical Care Through Project Management." *Nursing Administration Quarterly* 15, no. 4 (1991): 22–28.

Wilson, D. C. "Efficient OR Management ... The Program Evaluation and Review Techniques (PERT)." *Nursing Management* 15, no. 4 (1984): 42A, 42D–F, 42H.

9

STATISTICAL QUALITY CONTROL

OTAL QUALITY management (TQM) has become the watchword of health care organizations in all aspects of their operations. To compete effectively, providers of health services must simultaneously control costs and improve quality in response to the demands of purchasers of care, including business alliances, insurance companies, and managed care organizations. This delicate balancing act of cost and quality requires careful monitoring of key indicators of performance at both operational and strategic management levels.

Quality management efforts in health services organizations followed similar efforts in other segments of society. Business organizations who were losing their competitive edge, particularly in international markets, realized that they must be able to compete on the basis of both costs and the quality of products and services offered. A new philosophy of continuous quality improvement (CQI) emerged based on the works of industrial quality experts, including W. Edwards Deming, Joseph M. Juran, and Phillip B. Crosby (Rakich, Longest, and Darr 1992, 409).

The philosophy of TQM contains two guiding principles: all processes (clinical and administrative) can be improved, and the improvement must be continuous. The continuous improvement cycle includes the following steps:

- *Plan*: Measure current performance and determine areas for improvement.
- *Do*: Implement actions to improve the process.
- *Check*: Measure again to see if performance has actually improved.

- *Operationalize*: Put the new process into action and monitor performance continuously over time.

In its *Agenda for Change*, the Joint Commission on Accreditation of Healthcare Organizations (1993) states the need for both outcome and process quality. Key points of this agenda include

1. quality as a central, organizationwide priority
2. attention to customer needs
3. improvement of work processes through use of the system approach by cross-disciplinary teams
4. continuous measurement of performance
5. commitment to continuous improvement

TQM programs require effective monitoring and analysis of data, particularly measures of **customer satisfaction** (both clinical care and service quality) and **process performance** (clinical and administrative). TQM relies heavily on outcomes and inspection measures. These indicators allow management to perform time series comparisons and point the organization toward areas that need process analysis and improvement. Companies and organizations that have won the national Malcolm Baldrige Award for quality have developed sophisticated information systems and quantitative analysis of data to probe all areas of their operations—processes, products, and services.

Several analytic tools are available to health services managers for use in their TQM program, including flow process charts, fishbone diagrams to chart cause and effect, Pareto analysis to separate important events from more trivial ones, and scatter diagrams to explore possible relationships between variables. This chapter examines one of the most important and commonly used techniques, statistical quality control.

Statistical quality control analysis offers managers an organized process for monitoring variations in customer satisfaction and clinical and administrative performance. By monitoring small samples of key indicators taken at proper intervals, statistical analysis can be used to identify variations from expected standards and to detect the presence of assignable causes of these variations.

A variety of indicators can be monitored, including patient satisfaction, financial performance, system failures, and internal productivity.

This chapter describes statistical quality control in general terms and presents specific information on one commonly used tool, the quality control chart.

Introduction of Case Problem

ABC Regional Health Plan is an alliance of three hospitals, a large multispecialty medical group practice, and several related service units in long-term care and home health. Operating in an increasingly complex and competitive environment, the executive management team of ABC wants to systematically monitor key elements of the corporation's performance.

The chief information officer (CIO) of the corporation reports directly to the chief executive officer (CEO) and is responsible for information management, telecommunications, and management engineering within the health plan. The CIO has been charged with the development of an executive information system that will include statistical quality control charts to monitor the following indicators on a monthly basis:

1. Patient satisfaction as determined by regular surveys conducted in the clinical components of the health plan
2. Financial performance of more than 500 managed care contracts that the plan has in effect
3. Cash flow as measured by aged accounts receivable for revenue generated by units of the plan

An Overview of Statistical Quality Control

Quality control programs are designed to monitor the performance of organizational systems against predetermined standards. The framework for establishing such controls derives from general systems theory (Austin 1992, Chapter 2).

Organizational systems, administrative and clinical, consist of three essential components: one or more inputs, a conversion process, and one or more outputs. To introduce management control over the performance of systems, controlled feedback is used to adjust the future functioning of the system within predetermined standards.

Figure 9.1 is a diagram of an organizational system or process with controlled feedback provided by the following components:

1. A sensor element that collects data on system performance
2. A monitor that matches performance quantity and/or quality against standards
3. A control element that acts on data from the monitor to bring about necessary changes in system inputs and/or processes to bring the functioning of the system back within control limits

One commonly used technique for the monitoring process is statistical quality control. Acceptable performance standards must first be established. Actual performance is measured on a continuing basis and compared against the standard. Variations are examined to determine if they occurred by chance (random) or were the result of some other

Figure 9.1 Organizational System with Controlled Feedback

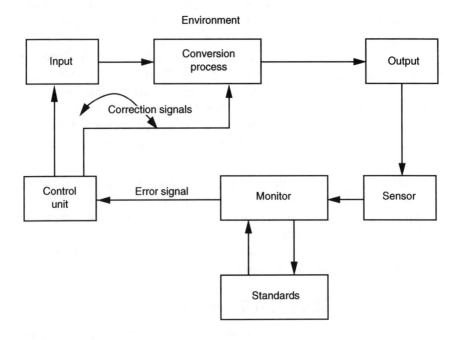

assignable cause (nonrandom) that can be corrected through management action.

Very few organizational processes will produce identical results every time. Random variation is inherent in these processes. For example, the rate of postsurgical wound infections can be expected to vary around some acceptable standard because of uncontrollable factors such as severity of illness or complications from other patient problems. However, when the infection rate exceeds an acceptable range of variation, then assignable causes are most likely to be present, and these need to be identified for corrective action.

Walter A. Shewhart, who worked as a statistician with the United States Department of Agriculture in the 1930s, is generally credited with the development of statistical quality control. Walter Shewhart observed that if an assignable cause entered a process, it would create a change, and that to spot this change a record of output quality would be required over time. He went on to consider that small samples taken at proper intervals would yield just the kind of information needed to detect the presence of an assignable cause of variation (Starr and Stein 1976, 161).

Statistical control charts are graphic tools for plotting performance data about established quality standards or past performance history with outliers falling outside an acceptable range of variation. Most control charts assume that the parent population of the variable being measured follows a normal probability distribution. (See Wonnacott and Wonnacott 1976, 91–99, for a discussion of normal probability distributions.) Computer programs for producing quality control charts that make this assumption should include a statistical test of the data for normality.

Figure 9.2 depicts a normal distribution of a set of values being monitored in a quality control process. The expected value is the mean of the distribution ($\bar{x}$). Variation is measured by the standard deviation from the mean (s). For a perfect normal distribution, 68 percent of the variation will occur within one standard deviation from the mean, 95 percent will occur within two standard deviations from the mean, and 99.8 percent will occur within three standard deviations from the mean.

Statistical control charts are developed by taking repeated samples of a variable to be monitored over time and plotting the distribution of the sample means in reference to the average of all observations. Data values are plotted in reference to a **center** and two limits, the **upper control limit (UCL)** and the **lower control limit (LCL)**. The center is the grand sample mean, which is the average of the individual sample means. It is common to set control limits that are two or

Figure 9.2 Standard Normal Distribution

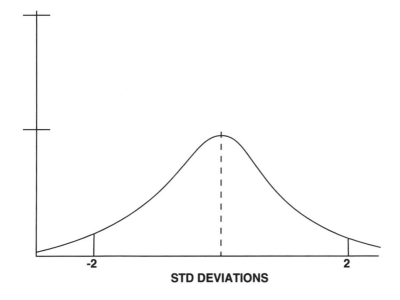

STD DEVIATIONS

three standard deviations from the grand sample mean. That is, the probability of a sample mean having a value more than two (or three) standard deviations higher or lower than the mean by random chance is less than 5 percent (or 1 percent) and there is likely to be an assignable cause for the deviation.

To illustrate the construction of a control chart, consider the following simple example. The city health department operates a drop-in, primary care clinic. The clinic manager has collected the following data on average waiting times for patients seeking service at the clinic. Waiting times for a sample of four patients per day have been collected for a five-day period.

WAITING TIMES (minutes)

Day	Pat. A	Pat. B	Pat. C	Pat. D	Mean	Range
1	25	18	23	24	22.50	7
2	32	30	26	22	27.50	10
3	14	21	20	25	20.00	11
4	20	26	16	19	20.25	10
5	18	23	25	20	21.50	7
				TOTAL	111.75	45

A statistical control chart is constructed that plots the values of the daily means for each day in the sample (see Figure 9.3). This is referred to as a mean or x-bar chart. The center line for the chart is computed as follows:

$$\overline{\overline{X}} = \sum \text{ of daily means/number of days}$$
$$\overline{\overline{X}} = 111.75/5 = 22.35$$

Upper and lower control limits are established at either two or three standard deviations from the center line to provide easy visual monitoring of points on the graph that are outside of these limits, or "out of control." That is, the probabilty of this occurring by random events is very low. The following formulas are used in constructing these control limits.

For three standard deviations:

$$UCL = \overline{\overline{X}} + 3\overline{R}/d2\sqrt{n}$$
$$LCL = \overline{\overline{X}} - 3\overline{R}/d2\sqrt{n}$$

For two standard deviations:

$$UCL = \overline{\overline{X}} + 2\overline{R}/d2\sqrt{n}$$
$$LCL = \overline{\overline{X}} - 2\overline{R}/d2\sqrt{n}$$

Figure 9.3 Statistical Control Chart (Mean)

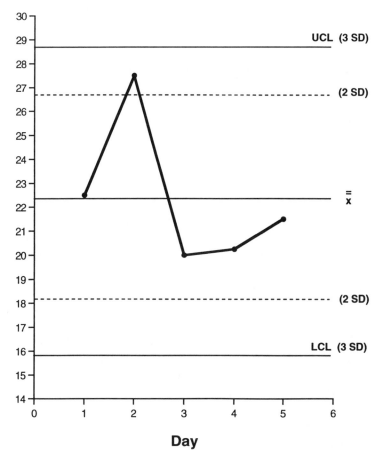

where

$\overline{R}\ =\ \sum$ of daily range value/number of days

$\overline{R}\ =\ 45/5 = 9$

$n\ =$ number of patients in daily sample $= 4$

$d2 =$ a constant value used in estimating the standard deviation $= 2.1$

(The $d2$ value is obtained from a table of industrial control chart factors—see Berenson and Levine 1992, Table E.13, 994).

Thus, at the three standard deviation level, the control limits are

$$UCL\ =\ 22.35 + 3(9)/2.1\sqrt{4} = 28.78$$
$$LCL\ =\ 22.35 - 3(9)/2.1\sqrt{4} = 15.92$$

And at the two standard deviation level, the control limits are

$$UCL = 22.35 + 2(9)/2.1\sqrt{4} = 26.64$$
$$LCL = 22.35 - 2(9)/2.1\sqrt{4} = 18.06$$

Note that in Figure 9.3, all five daily mean waiting times fall within the upper and lower control limits at the three standard deviation level. However, the mean waiting time for Day 2 is above the two standard deviation control line, with a probability of this occurring by chance of less that 5 percent.

Model Formulation, Quantification, and Data Requirements

Consider the following example. As a component of its Executive Information System, ABC Regional Health System managers have decided to monitor patient satisfaction in an ambulatory care center operated by the System. Each week five patients are selected at random and are asked to complete a patient satisfaction questionnaire before they leave the clinic. Responses are marked on a computer-scanned answer sheet. Respondents place a mark along a continuous line scale ranging from one to five, with one indicating lowest level of satisfaction and five indicating highest level of satisfaction. The computer scanner reads each recording of the continuous variable to the nearest 0.1 (for example, 3.5). A composite index is obtained by averaging the responses of each patient.

The Executive Information System includes a quarterly report showing responses to the patient satisfaction survey over a 13-week period. Results are presented in the form of a statistical quality control chart with initial computations made based on the actual history of patient satisfaction results. Listed here are the data entered into the system for the first 13-week period:

Week No.	Pat. 1	Pat. 2	Pat. 3	Pat. 4	Pat. 5
1	3.1	3.6	4.3	4.1	2.6
2	3.6	3.8	4.2	4.0	3.5
3	4.3	4.8	3.9	4.6	4.7
4	3.6	3.5	3.7	3.8	3.4
5	3.2	3.3	3.5	3.7	3.8
6	3.0	3.2	3.3	3.4	3.6
7	3.1	3.8	3.7	3.7	3.6
8	3.6	3.6	3.2	3.0	3.2
9	4.3	4.2	3.7	3.5	3.3

10	2.6	3.8	3.5	3.2	3.4
11	3.2	3.3	3.5	3.4	3.6
12	1.9	2.3	3.1	2.2	2.4
13	3.2	3.8	3.7	3.3	4.0

Solving the Case Problem

Exhibit 9.1 is a statistical control chart for the patient satisfaction data for this quarterly period using the *QuickQuant* software. The computer program uses three standard deviations from the mean in establishing the lower and upper control limits. *QuickQuant* employs a commonly used method for computing the upper and lower control limits. This method replaces reliance upon historical values with an estimate of the standard deviation computed according to well-established practices of industrial quality control. See Berenson and Levine (1992, 841–43) for a description of the formula and computations involved. The sample means for Weeks 1 through 13 are plotted graphically in reference to the overall average for the 13-week period. Note that in Week 3, the survey of five patients had an exceptionally high level of satisfaction (4.46), which exceeded the upper control limit. In Week 12, the satisfaction mean of 2.38 was below the lower control limit, indicating the need to investigate potential assignable causes for this low level of satisfaction.

As this monitoring process continues over time, a cumulative average of patient satisfaction can be used in constructing the control charts for subsequent quarters.

In addition to the mean (or x-bar) chart, the software can produce two control charts that monitor and control the level of variability in the process being monitored. These are the range (R chart), and the standard deviation (S chart). The standard deviation chart is preferable to the range chart because it is based on every measurement in the sample rather than just the two extreme values.

Exhibit 9.2 is the range chart and Exhibit 9.3 is the S chart for the example problem. Note that the greatest degree of variability is found in Week 1, where the range of the five patient satisfaction values was 1.7 and the standard deviation was 0.7.

The *QuickQuant* software also provides the capability to use a standard established by management as the reference point in constructing the control charts. Assume that management decides to establish a standard of at least 4.0 on the patient satisfaction index. Exhibit 9.4 is a control chart for the same 13-week period using this standard. Using this new standard, Weeks 6, 8, 10, and 12 have mean patient satisfaction values below the lower control limit. Note also that all mean values

Exhibit 9.1 Control Chart for Mean (3-Sigma Limits)

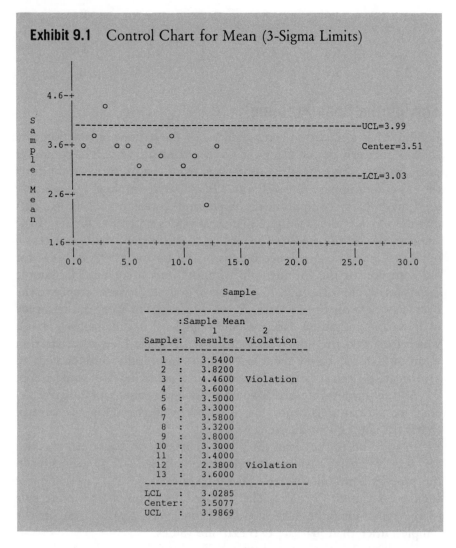

```
         |
         |
  4.6-+
         |      o
S        |
a        -----------------------------------------------UCL=3.99
m        |      o          o
p  3.6-+ o    o  o      o
l        |           o        o
e        |         o        o
         |                o
M        -----------------------------------------------LCL=3.03
e  2.6-+
a        |
n        |                o
         |
         |
   1.6-+----+----+----+----+----+----+----+----+----+----+
         |    |    |    |    |    |    |    |    |    |
       0.0  5.0  10.0  15.0  20.0  25.0  30.0
                       Sample
```

```
    -----------------------------------
                 :Sample Mean
                 :    1         2
    Sample: Results   Violation
    -----------------------------------
         1  :   3.5400
         2  :   3.8200
         3  :   4.4600    Violation
         4  :   3.6000
         5  :   3.5000
         6  :   3.3000
         7  :   3.5800
         8  :   3.3200
         9  :   3.8000
        10  :   3.3000
        11  :   3.4000
        12  :   2.3800    Violation
        13  :   3.6000
    -----------------------------------
    LCL    :   3.0285
    Center:   3.5077
    UCL    :   3.9869
```

except Week 3 are lower than the standard of 4.0. This would indicate to management that corrective action is required to meet the standard established.

Model Variations: The Attribute Chart

Attribute charts are used to examine products, services, or activities that either conform or do not conform to specifications. That is, the measurements take on "binary" values, conforming or nonconforming.

In constructing attribute charts, a series of samples of equal size are taken and the number of nonconforming events (or "defects") are

Exhibit 9.2   Control Chart for Range (3-Sigma Limits)

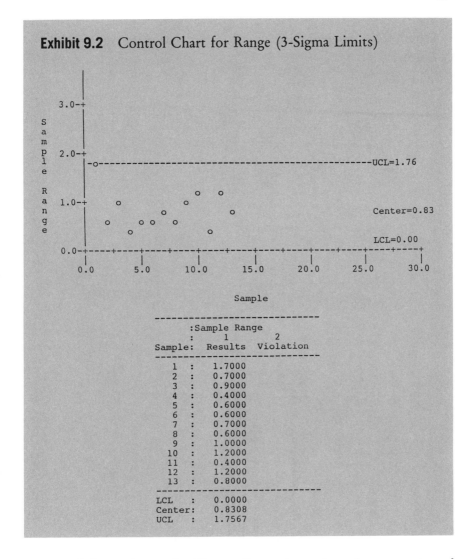

```
         |
 S  3.0-+
 a       |
 m       |
 p  2.0-+
 l     -o----------------------------------------------UCL=1.76
 e       |
 R       |
 a  1.0-+      o          o   o
 n       |            o                 o              Center=0.83
 g       |     o   o o   o
 e       |        o            o
         |                                             LCL=0.00
 0.0-+----+----+----+----+----+----+----+----+----+----+----+
         |    |    |    |    |    |    |    |    |    |    |
       0.0  5.0  10.0 15.0  20.0     25.0     30.0

                         Sample
```

```
               -----------------------------
                     :Sample Range
                     :    1        2
              Sample: Results  Violation
               -----------------------------
                 1  :  1.7000
                 2  :  0.7000
                 3  :  0.9000
                 4  :  0.4000
                 5  :  0.6000
                 6  :  0.6000
                 7  :  0.7000
                 8  :  0.6000
                 9  :  1.0000
                10  :  1.2000
                11  :  0.4000
                12  :  1.2000
                13  :  0.8000
               -----------------------------
              LCL    :  0.0000
              Center:  0.8308
              UCL    :  1.7567
```

measured for each sample. The attribute chart plots the *proportion* of nonconforming events in each sample against a center line and upper and lower control limits. This chart is often referred to as a "control chart for the proportion," or "*P*-chart." The center and control limits are computed as follows:

$$\text{Center} = \overline{P} = \text{the average proportion of defects}$$

$$LCL = \overline{P} - SL\sqrt{\overline{P}(1 - \overline{P})/n}$$

$$UCL = \overline{P} + SL\sqrt{\overline{P}(1 - \overline{P})/n}$$

Exhibit 9.3 Control Chart for Standard Deviation (3-Sigma Limits)

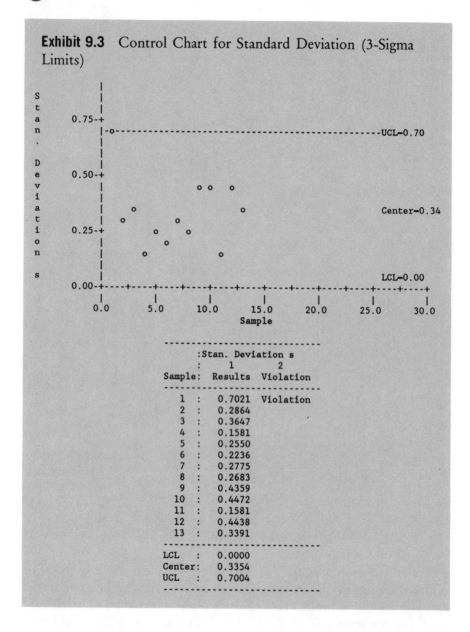

```
                      :Stan. Deviation s
                      :     1         2
              Sample: Results   Violation
              ------------------------------
                  1  :  0.7021   Violation
                  2  :  0.2864
                  3  :  0.3647
                  4  :  0.1581
                  5  :  0.2550
                  6  :  0.2236
                  7  :  0.2775
                  8  :  0.2683
                  9  :  0.4359
                 10  :  0.4472
                 11  :  0.1581
                 12  :  0.4438
                 13  :  0.3391
              ------------------------------
              LCL    :  0.0000
              Center :  0.3354
              UCL    :  0.7004
              ------------------------------
```

where

SL = standard deviation level (2 or 3)

n = size of each sample

Consider the following simple example:

Exhibit 9.4 Control Chart for Mean (3-Sigma Limits) Standard of 4.0

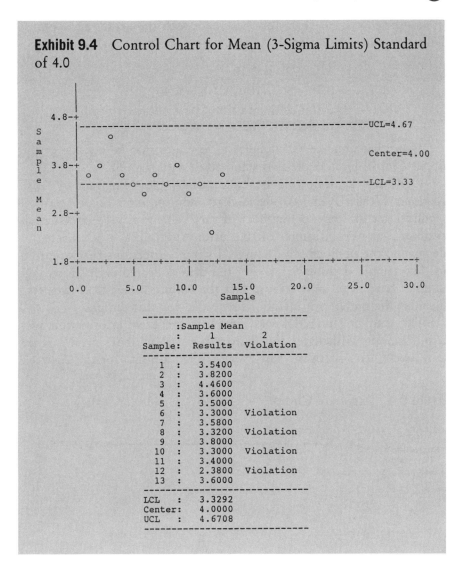

Sample	No. Examined	No. Nonconforming	Proportion
1	4	0	0
2	4	0	0
3	4	1	.25
4	4	0	0
5	4	1	.25
Totals	20	2	

Figure 9.4 is a *P*-chart for these data with the center and control limits computed as follows:

Center $= \overline{P} = 2/20 = 0.10$

$UCL = 0.10 + 2\sqrt{(.10)(.90)/4} = 0.40$

$LCL = 0$ (Since there cannot be a negative number of defects, this is set at zero.)

Note that none of the samples have values that lie outside of the upper control limit at the two standard deviation level.

Consider the following health care example. Managers of ABC Regional Health Plan have decided to monitor rates of postsurgical wound infections as a component of the Plan's executive information system. Each week, a sample of 100 current surgical cases is collected to determine the number of postsurgical wound infections that occurred in that sample. Exhibit 9.5 shows the data collected after 25 weekly samples have been drawn. Note that the column headed "N Defects" includes the number of infections recorded for that sample.

The data are entered weekly into the executive information system. Exhibit 9.5 includes the *P*-chart for this attribute produced by the *QuickQuant* software. The average infection rate for the 25-week

Figure 9.4 Attribute Chart

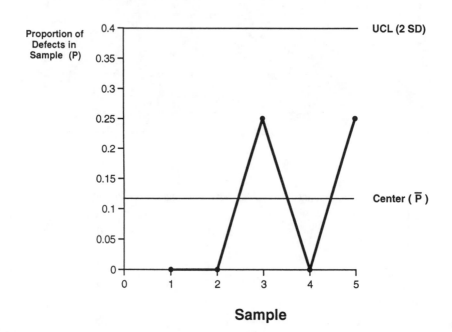

Sample

period was 1.76 percent. The chart shows rates below the average for most weeks, with no infections recorded for seven of the weeks. The highest rate was 7 percent in Week 2. Note a disturbing trend in Weeks 20 through 23, with the rate steadily increasing above the mean. However, corrective action may have been taken since the rate dropped to zero for Weeks 24 and 25.

These data can be monitored continuously over time, with the overall infection rate recomputed each time an additional weekly sample is added to the database. Targets can be set to seek continuous improvement in the infection rate as part of ABC's quality improvement program.

Description of Available Computer Software

Statistical quality control chart software is included in many operations research packages available on the commercial software market. In addition, statistical software packages such as SAS and SPSS include quality control chart components as well.

Executive information system (EIS) software is also available on the commercial market. The better EIS packages include good graphic output capabilities including presentation of time sequential information in control chart format.

Analysis, Interpretation, and Application of Results to Management Decisions

To compete in an era of market and managed competition, health services organizations must monitor carefully both their costs and the quality of their services. Statistical control charts provide an effective tool for monitoring these and other operational indicators on a continuous basis.

Control charts allow management to set standards of performance and view actual performance in relation to these standards through a user-friendly graphic presentation. When an indicator is out of control, a more detailed investigation to determine the assignable cause can be initiated. Corrective action can then be initiated through such actions as education or retraining of staff, reengineering of processes being used, implementation of better managerial control mechanisms, or some combination of these.

Garvin (1986) points out that maintaining a system within statistical control limits does not mean that the system is as good as it could be. Programs of improvement, including employee training and work

Exhibit 9.5   Control Chart for Proportion (3-Sigma Limits)

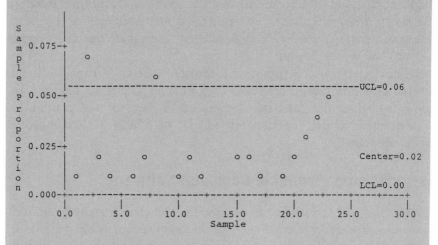

```
PROBLEM PARAMETERS

Number of Sample Sets = 25
Sample Sizes = 100

PROBLEM DATA
```

Sample:	:Observation : 1 N Defects		Sample:	:Sample Proportion : 1 Results	2 Violation
1 :	1.0000		1 :	0.0100	
2 :	7.0000		2 :	0.0700	Violation
3 :	2.0000		3 :	0.0200	
4 :	1.0000		4 :	0.0100	
5 :	0.0000		5 :	0.0000	
6 :	1.0000		6 :	0.0100	
7 :	2.0000		7 :	0.0200	
8 :	6.0000		8 :	0.0600	Violation
9 :	0.0000		9 :	0.0000	
10 :	1.0000		10 :	0.0100	
11 :	2.0000		11 :	0.0200	
12 :	1.0000		12 :	0.0100	
13 :	0.0000		13 :	0.0000	
14 :	0.0000		14 :	0.0000	
15 :	2.0000		15 :	0.0200	
16 :	2.0000		16 :	0.0200	
17 :	1.0000		17 :	0.0100	
18 :	0.0000		18 :	0.0000	
19 :	1.0000		19 :	0.0100	
20 :	2.0000		20 :	0.0200	
21 :	3.0000		21 :	0.0300	
22 :	4.0000		22 :	0.0400	
23 :	5.0000		23 :	0.0500	
24 :	0.0000		24 :	0.0000	
25 :	0.0000		25 :	0.0000	
Total :	44.0000		LCL :	0.0000	
Mean :	1.7600		Center:	0.0176	
S.Dev.:	1.9209		UCL :	0.0570	

redesign, when coupled with continuous monitoring and feedback (see Figure 9.1) enable the organization to seek quality improvements on a continuing basis.

The examples from the literature that follow describe how health care organizations are using this technology extensively in programs of continuous quality improvement.

Case Studies from the Literature

Infection Control (Classen et al. 1992)

Latter Day Saints (LDS) Hospital in Salt Lake City, Utah, performs more than 30,000 surgical procedures each year. A study was conducted to determine how the timing of antibiotic administration affects the risk of surgical wound infection rates.

The study utilized data from the HELP (Health Evaluation through Logical Processing) hospital information system. Patterns associated with the use of prophylactic antibiotics in surgical patients were tracked by recording all orders for antibiotic drugs, the time of drug administration, the duration of antibiotic usage, and the point of antibiotic discontinuance. The system records the exact time of antibiotic administration with respect to the time of initial surgical incision.

In this controlled study, 2,847 patients undergoing elective surgery were observed. The timing of antibiotic administration and the occurrence of surgical wound infections were examined. The administration of antibiotics up to 24 hours before the incision was defined as early administration; during the 2 hours before incision was defined as preoperative; during the 3 hours after incision was defined as "perioperative"; and more than 3 but less than 24 hours after the incision was defined as "postoperative."

Statistical monitoring and analysis were used to compare rates of wound infection according to the timing of antibiotic prophylaxis. For the study population, 44 surgical wound infections were detected (1.5 percent), broken down as follows:

Preoperative antibiotic administration	10 (0.6%)
Perioperative administration	4 (1.4%)
Postoperative administration	16 (3.3%)
Early administration	14 (3.8%)

Logistic regression analysis of the data supported the conclusion that antibiotic administration during the two-hour period before an operation was inversely associated with the occurrence of wound infections.

An estimated 27 wound infections could have been prevented at the time of this study had antibiotics been administered appropriately. Feedback was provided to LDS physicians, and practice patterns have been altered. Subsequently, 96 percent of all prophylactic antibiotics administered to surgical patients at LDS Hospital were given during the two hours before surgical incision. Statistical control charts can be used for continuous monitoring of infection rates.

Monitoring Employee Performance (Schnelle, Newman, and Fogarty 1990)

A statistical quality control system was used to manage nursing aide performance in nursing homes related to incontinence care. Eighty-seven subjects were recruited from four intermediate and skilled nursing bed facilities, ranging in size from 60 to 100 beds. All subjects in the study suffered severe incontinence. Data on patient incontinence frequencies were collected during a two-day assessment period that guaranteed that the patients' protective garments were changed on a one- or two-hour basis. Periodic monitoring and the use of statistical quality control charts permitted nurse managers to determine if the nursing aides were changing patients on either a one- or two-hour schedule, thus assisting in the assessment of the quality of care being rendered. The nurse manager was responsible for monitoring the sampling and for ensuring that the patients were being changed according to established standards.

Additional Reports from the Literature

Ciminera and Lease (1992) conducted a study to monitor reported medication errors at Montgomery Hospital in Norristown, Pennsylvania. As part of a continuous quality improvement program, control charts were used to analyze past and future occurrences of reported medication errors. Using control charts to monitor medication errors over time allowed Montgomery Hospital's pharmacy and therapeutics committee to identify problems, to manage intricate changes, and to quantify changes in incidences. The control chart was used as a tool to record progress toward goals (e.g., 15 percent reduction in missed doses) rather than a tool to maintain a steady state of control.

The Department of Radiology at Ochsner Clinic in New Orleans tested the effectiveness of continuous quality improvement techniques in radiology departments (Bluth, Havrilla, and Blakeman 1993). A project was initiated to improve the ability to interpret preoperative chest radiographs prior to surgery. All of the preoperative films were ordered by internists who determined, after seeing the patient, that the radiographic examination was warranted. An eight-member team was empowered to evaluate the existing process and make appropriate changes. Basic statistical analysis was employed using histograms, Pareto diagrams, and control charts. Data on the causes of delays in the process were also collected. Using data from the study, the process for obtaining and interpreting preoperative radiographs was modified. As a result, the percentage of chest radiographs interpreted before surgery improved from 83 percent to 98 percent. The average waiting period between patient check-in at the outpatient center and interpretation of the preoperative chest radiograph was reduced by 72 percent.

Summit Medical Center, a 223-bed hospital in Oakland, California, designed a six-step plan to improve quality in the central processing and distribution department (VanderVeen 1992). The project trained managers and staff to use Pareto charts, cause-and-effect diagrams, and statistical control charts in tracking quality control in the facility. The most important outcome was increased commitment to quality improvement by members of the department.

Problems

9.1 Develop a list of 25 indicators of quality for ABC Regional Health Plan to monitor through quality control charts as part of its Executive Information System.

9.2 Concerned with the frequency of recording omissions made by physicians on patients' medical records, the CIO at Mid-State Regional Medical Center has commissioned the administrative resident to study the problem. Bill Howell, the CIO, has given Susan Jones, the resident, the following information compiled by the Medical Records department in conjunction with the IS department. One hundred patient charts were selected at random each day for the 20 days of the study.

Day	No. Omissions	Day	No. Omissions
1	16	11	20
2	18	12	15
3	10	13	5
4	12	14	14
5	13	15	10
6	8	16	12
7	15	17	9
8	11	18	16

9	7	19	10
10	9	20	7

Requirement: Compute a *P*-chart and interpret the results.

9.3 The director of nursing at Logan Memorial Hospital complained of the repeated delays in receiving laboratory reports. The information systems manager decided to monitor the process over a 12-week period. Basic lab workups that can be generated and delivered back to the nursing stations within a two-hour period were considered viable for the study. Five tests were chosen at random from different units each week, and their return times (in minutes) were noted in the following composite index:

Week	Test 1	Test 2	Test 3	Test 4	Test 5
1	90	42	70	83	61
2	54	79	106	38	98
3	67	52	34	107	46
4	109	34	51	97	40
5	30	25	66	22	31
6	57	43	111	35	77
7	39	100	62	31	82
8	76	65	88	43	35
9	31	61	98	76	37
10	36	30	45	55	46
11	50	87	35	54	64
12	81	48	81	67	69

Requirement: Using *QuickQuant*, generate x-bar, range, and S-charts. Interpret the results and make suggestions on what management might do to correct any problems.

9.4 Hillsboro Women's Center is a 12-physician OB/GYN practice. The physicians are divided into three teams—the red team, the white team, and the green team. A patient selects one physician as her primary physician and, during her pregnancy, rotates among the four physicians on her doctor's team for prenatal care.

The clinic director suggested this team concept as a way to better ensure quality and timely care. Together with the medical staff, she is attempting to enact a "10-minute wait" rule; that is, no patient waits longer than 10 minutes after sign-in for an appointment with a doctor on her team. Accordingly, she is also implementing a study to evaluate the length of waiting time. Over a 15-week period, she takes a random sample of ten wait times per week.

Week	Obs 1	Obs 2	Obs 3	Obs 4	Obs 5	Obs 6	Obs 7	Obs 8	Obs 9	Obs 10
1	12	13	10	7	11	14	16	19.5	14	11
2	5	8	12	15.5	8	9	17	14.4	11	8
3	7.5	6.5	9	14	16	12.5	9	20	17	16
4	10	10.5	10.5	11	14	16	12	9.9	9.5	7.5
5	10	12	13.5	8	8.5	9	11	11.5	13	12
6	8	8.5	5	9	8	7.5	7.5	10	11	10
7	6	5	8	8.5	7	9	10	10.5	11	8.5
8	7	9	10	10	15	15	12	12	11.5	9
9	8	8	11	13	11.5	10	10	11	9.5	9
10	9	6	7.5	7	9	10	11	13.5	16	16.5
11	8.5	9	5	5.5	6	7.5	10	11	10	12
12	10	11	14	15	11	9.5	9.5	7.5	8	8
13	7.5	8	9	10	8.5	8.5	7	6	5	6
14	10	8.5	8.5	7	5	6	6.5	8	8.5	10
15	8	6	6	7.5	7	9	10	10	11	13.5

Requirement: Compute the appropriate statistical quality control charts. Discuss any problems discovered as well as how well the "10-minute wait" rule seems to be working.

9.5 Brookhaven Medical Center has just completed its first year of a total quality management program. The CEO is interested in knowing how many admissions became readmissions in the year immediately preceding the implementation of TQM (Year 1) and in the first year of TQM (Year 2).

	Month	# Readmissions/1,000 Admissions
Year 1	Jan	16
	Feb	18
	Mar	15
	Apr	11
	May	9
	Jun	8
	Jul	10
	Aug	9
	Sep	12
	Oct	8
	Nov	10
	Dec	11
Year 2	Jan	5
	Feb	6
	Mar	4

Apr	6
May	8
Jun	9
Jul	10
Aug	7
Sep	5
Oct	3
Nov	3
Dec	4

Requirement: Conduct the appropriate statistical quality control analysis for each year, make comparisons, and write a memo to the CEO with a description of the results.

References

Austin, C. J. 1992. *Information Systems for Health Services Administration*. 4th Edition. Ann Arbor, MI: AUPHA Press/Health Administration Press.

Berenson, M. L., and D. M. Levine. 1992. *Basic Business Statistics*. 5th Edition. Englewood Cliffs, NJ: Prentice-Hall.

Bluth, E. I., M. Havrilla, and C. Blakeman. 1993. "Quality Improvement Techniques: Value to Improve the Timeliness of Preoperative Chest Radiographic Reports." *American Journal of Roentgenology* 160 (5): 995–98.

Ciminera, J. L., and M. P. Lease. 1992. "Developing Control Charts to Review and Monitor Medication Errors." *Hospital Pharmacy* 27 (3): 192–97.

Classen, D. C., R. S. Evans, S. L. Pestonik, S. D. Horn, R. L. Menlove, and J. P. Burke. 1992. "The Timing of Prophylactic Administration of Antibiotics and the Risk of Surgical-Wound Infection." *The New England Journal of Medicine* 326 (30 January): 281–86.

Garvin, D. A. 1986. "A Note on Quality: The Views of Deming, Juran, and Crosby." *Harvard Business School Case No. 9-687-011*. Revised February 1990.

Joint Commission on Accreditation of Healthcare Organizations. 1993. *Implementing Quality Improvement: A Hospital Leader's Guide*. Oakbrook Terrace, IL: Joint Commission.

Rakich, J. S., B. B. Longest, and K. Darr. 1992. *Managing Health Services Organizations*. Baltimore, MD: Health Professions Press.

Schnelle, J. F., D. R. Newman, and T. Fogarty. 1990. "Statistical Quality Control in Nursing Homes: Assessment and Management of Chronic Urinary Incontinence." *Health Services Research* 25 (4): 627–37.

Starr, M. K., and I. Stein. 1976. *The Practice of Management Science*. Englewood Cliffs, NJ: Prentice-Hall, Inc.

VanderVeen, L. M. 1992. "Statistical Process Control: A Practical Application for Hospitals." *Journal for Healthcare Quality* 14 (2): 20–25, 28–29.

Wonnacott, T. H., and R. J. Wonnacott. 1977. *Introductory Statistics for Business and Economics*. 2nd Edition. Santa Barbara, CA: John Wiley and Sons.

Additional Readings

Andrews, S. L. "QA vs. QI: The Changing Role of Quality in Health Care." *Journal of Quality Assurance* (February 1991): 14–15, 38.

Berwick, D. M. "Sounding Board: Continuous Improvement as an Ideal in Healthcare." *New England Journal of Medicine* 1 (5 January 1989): 53–56.

Claus, L. M. "Total Quality Management: A Healthcare Application." *Total Quality Management* 2, no. 2 (1991): 131–48.

Donabedian, A. *Explorations in Quality Assessment and Monitoring. Vol. I: The Definition of Quality and Approaches to Its Assessment.* Ann Arbor, MI: Health Administration Press, 1980.

Green, D. K. "Quality Improvement Versus Quality Assurance." *Topics in Health Records Management* 11, no. 3 (1991): 58–70.

Iezzoni, L. I. "Monitoring Quality of Care: What Do We Need to Know." *Inquiry* 30 (Summer 1993): 112–14.

James, B. *Quality Management for Health Care Delivery.* Chicago: American Hospital Association, Health Research Education Trust, 1989.

Longo, D. R., and D. W. Avant. "Managing Quality." In *The AUPHA Manual of Health Services Management,* edited by R. J. Taylor and S. B. Taylor, Chapter 3. Gaithersburg, MD: Aspen Publishers, 1994.

Strasser, S., and R. M. Davis. *Measuring Patient Satisfaction for Improved Patient Services.* Ann Arbor, MI: Health Administration Press, 1991.

INVENTORY CONTROL

H EALTH CARE organizations use large quantities of supplies and materials in providing services to patients. Effective materials management is essential for both high-quality patient care and cost control. Major items of inventory include medical supplies, drugs and pharmaceuticals, emergency blood supplies, food, parts for equipment repair and maintenance, and office supplies.

Inventory management and control requires cost-effective procedures for ordering and stocking resources needed to meet the demand for services. Inventory models can assist the manager in establishing policies that balance the costs of procuring and storing materials with the need to have essential items available when needed.

Although the inventory model has been applied primarily to supplies and materials, it can also be used with other resources such as executive and technical talent or the cash needed to keep an organization liquid.

Introduction of Case Problem

The Springfield Ambulatory Care Center (SACC) is a rural health center affiliated with a comprehensive health plan and a provider network located 75 miles away in a major city. The Center provides primary health care and emergency services to residents of Springfield and refers patients requiring hospitalization or tertiary care to the urban facilities.

The business manager of SACC is contemplating the development of an inventory policy for the ordering and storage of a commonly used sterile supply pack for the Center. Since there are always competing demands for use of available cash, the manager wants to maintain an inventory level that will balance availability with lowest costs for ordering and storage of the item.

An Overview of Inventory Control: The Basic Economic Order Quantity Model

When the same supply item is stocked and used over time, the materials manager seeks to minimize the total costs for ordering and holding the item while insuring that there is always a sufficient supply on hand to meet demand from users of the item. Figure 10.1 is a graphic illustration of a simple order-inventory cycle. An initial order quantity (Q) is placed into inventory. The supply is continuously depleted over time until the reorder point is reached, and a new order is placed that will bring the supply back up to the initial order quantity (Q) when received. Note that the reorder point is determined by the lead time required to ensure that the stock is resupplied before the inventory on hand goes to zero. Many purchasing systems are designed so that an order is generated automatically when the inventory on hand reaches the reorder point.

With the advent of modern supply technology (on-line computer-ized ordering direct to the supplier; use of fax machines), the lead time for ordering materials from many vendors has been greatly reduced.

The demand pattern for drawing items from inventory in Figure 10.1 is uniform—that is, stock will be drawn from inventory at a continuous, uniform rate over time. In the real world, this assumption often is not valid. Demand may be completely random, or it may follow other patterns (see Figure 10.2 for examples). The lead time for reordering will be affected by the pattern of demand. The basic economic order quantity model discussed in this chapter and used in the case problem assumes a deterministic uniform pattern of demand. Probabilistic inventory models without these assumptions are described later in the section on "Model Variations."

To minimize costs, the order quantity must minimize the costs of ordering plus the costs of holding the material in inventory. The manager must determine the amount to order when the reorder point is reached.

Ordering costs include the costs of preparing the purchase order, sending it by mail or electronic medium to the vendor, maintaining records, and receiving and checking the material when it arrives.

Holding costs include the direct costs of storing and handling the material (space, forklift truck use and maintenance, warehouse

Figure 10.1 Order-Inventory Cycle

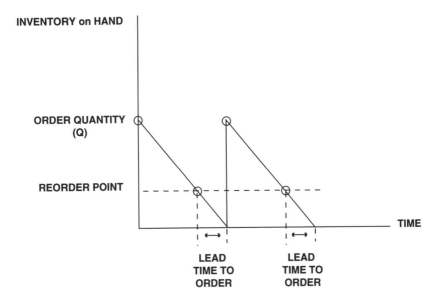

personnel, etc.); record-keeping and administrative costs; and the cost of invested capital. This latter cost is the opportunity cost associated with having cash tied up in inventory that might be used for short-term investment or other purposes in the organization.

Figure 10.3 is a graphic illustration of the basic economic order quantity (EOQ) model with uniform demand. Order quantity is plotted against costs for two functions. Note that holding costs of inventory start at zero and increase as the order quantity increases. Ordering costs decline as the order quantity increases since fewer orders would have to be placed. Total costs for the inventory system would equal holding costs plus ordering costs. Note that total costs are minimized at the point where holding costs and ordering costs intersect.

These functions are expressed in mathematical terms by the following formulas (Lapin 1994, 132):

total cost = annual ordering cost + annual holding cost
annual ordering cost = $(A/Q)K$

where

A = annual demand for item being ordered
K = cost each time an order is placed
Q = order quantity

Figure 10.2 Patterns of Demand for Inventory

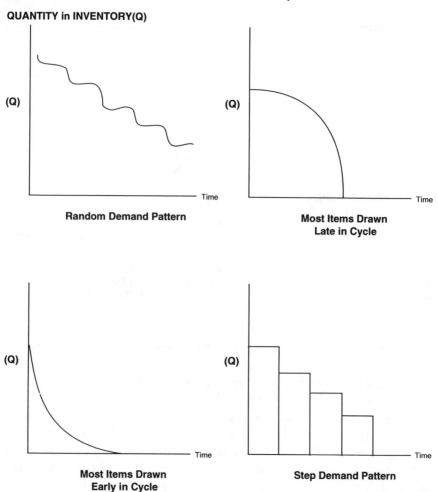

annual holding cost $= (Q/2)HC$

where

H = annual cost of holding one dollar in inventory (expressed as a percentage of the annual dollar value of inventory)
C = unit purchase cost of one item
Q = order quantity

The annual holding cost represents the cost of maintaining an inventory of supply items. The dollar value of the inventory on hand is

Figure 10.3 Economic Order Quantity (EOQ) Model

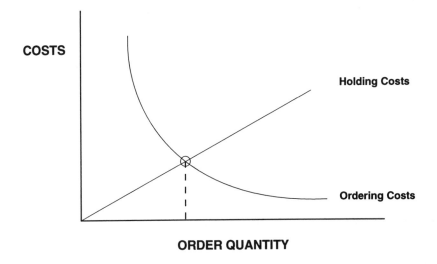

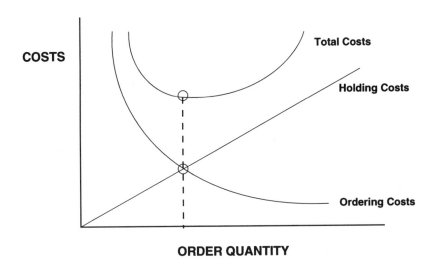

computed by multiplying the average inventory (Q/2) times the unit cost of purchasing one item (C). This average value of inventory is then multiplied by the annual cost of holding one dollar in inventory (H) to obtain a total annual holding cost.

The objective is to minimize total annual costs as follows:

$$TC = \frac{A}{Q}K + \frac{Q}{2}HC$$

Calculus is used to obtain the following formula for the economic order quantity:

$$Q = \sqrt{\frac{2AK}{HC}}$$

This value of Q provides the economic order quantity that minimizes the total annual costs of ordering and holding the item in inventory.

The reorder point is determined by analyzing historical information on lead time required from placement of an order to receipt of a shipment from the supplier. In the basic EOQ model, demand is uniform and the reorder point takes on a constant value (see Figure 10.1).

Model Formulation, Quantification, and Data Requirements

The business manager of Springfield Ambulatory Care Center, in consultation with a management engineer from the corporate office, obtains the following information to be used in an EOQ analysis:

1. A review of the past three years' usage of the sterile supply packs adjusted by projected growth in patient load yields an estimate of annual demand (A) of 6,000 sterile packs required per year.
2. The unit purchase cost (C) of the sterile packs is $20 per pack. There are no discounts available for ordering large quantities.
3. A cost study determines that the average cost of placing an order (K), including clerical time, computer costs, forms, and mailing, is $75 per order.
4. The average lead time for placing an order and receiving a shipment is one week.
5. The cost of holding items in inventory has two components:
   a. The direct holding cost includes storage, handling, record keeping, and administration. The cost study determines that this cost is $0.20 per sterile pack in inventory.
   b. The chief financial officer for the corporation provides information indicating that the cost of capital is 5 percent. This is the opportunity cost of holding one dollar of the value of items in inventory.

The EOQ model requires that holding cost (H) be expressed as the annual cost of holding one dollar value in inventory, computed as follows:

$$H = 0.05 + (\$0.20/\$20) = 0.05 + 0.01 = 0.06$$

Solving the Case Problem

These values can now be applied to the EOQ model as follows:

$$Q = \sqrt{\frac{2AK}{HC}}$$

$$Q = \sqrt{\frac{2 \times 6{,}000 \times 75}{0.06 \times 20}}$$

$$Q = 866 \text{ sterile packs per order}$$

These same results are obtained using the *QuickQuant* software package (see Exhibit 10.1). Note that the total annual cost of ordering plus the cost of holding sterile packs in inventory is \$1,039. Assuming even usage of the packs, a new order would need to be placed every 0.144 years, or approximately every 7.5 weeks.

One week is required for placing an order and receiving the shipment of sterile packs. The reorder point is computed as follows:

annual demand (A) = 6,000 packs
weekly demand   = $A/52$ = 6,000/52 = 115 packs

Stock should be reordered when Q approaches 115 units. Building in a safety factor for late shipment or sudden increase in demand, the reorder point might be set at $Q = 150$ units.

Note that this case problem presents the simple case of a deterministic demand model with no provisions for backordering an item that is out of stock. Backordering and probabilistic models with uncertainty about demand are discussed in the following section.

Exhibit 10.1 Inventory Analysis—Basic EOQ Problem (Deterministic)

```
Parameter Values:
    Fixed Cost per Order: k = 75
    Annual Number of Items Demanded: A = 6000
    Unit Cost of Procuring an Item: c = 20
    Annual Holding Cost per Dollar Value: h = .06

Optimal Values:
    Economic Order Quantity: Q = 866.0255
    Time Between Orders (year): T = .1443376 (7.5 weeks)
    Total Annual Relevant Cost: TC = 1039.23
```

Model Variations

Possibility of Shortages with Backordering Required

When supplier shortages are possible, a third item of cost must be added to the EOQ model. This is the annual cost of shortages. Therefore, total costs will be expressed as

$$TC = \text{annual ordering cost} + \text{annual holding cost}$$
$$+ \text{annual shortage cost}$$

To compute the annual shortage cost, a new variable (p) is added, which is the cost per year of being short one item of inventory. The revised model must now compute *two* order quantities:

Q = order quantity allowing for possibility of shortages

S = order level, the amount that will actually be shipped after backorder requirements have been determined

The relevant formulas for hand computation are as follows (Lapin 1994, 136–37):

$$TC = \left(\frac{A}{Q}\right)K + \frac{HCS^2}{2Q} + \frac{p(Q-S)^2}{2Q}$$

$$Q = \sqrt{\frac{2AK}{HC}}\sqrt{\frac{p+HC}{p}}$$

$$S = \sqrt{\frac{2AK}{HC}}\sqrt{\frac{p}{p+HC}}$$

As an example of this model, return to the case problem for this chapter with the added assumption that the supplier of sterile packs may occasionally experience shortages requiring backordering.

A study has determined that the daily cost of being short one item is $0.05. This cost is a combination of the cost of lost revenue if patient treatment is delayed and the cost of obtaining the sterile packs on an emergency basis if this should become necessary. Costs of this type generally must be estimated through previous experience and guesswork. Thus, the annual cost of being one item short is

$$p = 0.05 \times 365 \ \textit{days per year} = \$18.25 \ \textit{per item short}$$

This problem can be solved using *QuickQuant*; the results are shown in Exhibit 10.2. Note that the economic order quantity (Q) with backordering increases to 894 units. The order level (S) if a shortage

Inventory Control

occurs is 839 units. The number of units backordered would equal Q minus S, $894 - 839 = 55$ units.

Probabilistic Inventory Models

The basic EOQ model discussed previously in this chapter is deterministic. The model assumes that there is no uncertainty about demand requirements and makes the further assumption that demand continues uninterrupted over time. This section describes probabilistic inventory models without these assumptions.

Single-Period Model

This model can be used for problems in which demand occurs within a set period of time only. Unused items cannot be retained to meet future demand in another time period (Lapin 1994, 140–43). Examples include perishable food supplies, certain drugs, and blood plasma with expiration dates.

Consider the following example. A community hospital relies upon a regional blood bank in supplying blood units required in the emergency room and surgery department. The director of the laboratory for the hospital orders blood once per week to maintain a small inventory at the hospital. A cost study provides the following information:

Cost for each unit of blood ordered from blood bank $\ \ $ $ 45
Billing amount for each unit transfused $\ \ $ $ 80
Disposal cost for unused units of blood $\ \ $ $ 5
Emergency cost for obtaining backup unit when hospital
 supply is short $\ \ $ $100

Exhibit 10.2 Inventory Analysis—EOQ Model with Backordering (Deterministic)

```
Parameter Values:
    Fixed Cost per Order: k = 75
    Annual Number of Items Demanded: A = 6000
    Unit Cost of Procuring an Item: c = 20
    Annual Holding Cost per Dollar Value: h = .06
    Annual Cost of Being Short One Item: p = 18.25

Optimal Values:
    Economic Order Quantity: Q = 894.0443
    Economic Order Level: S = 838.8847
    Time Between Orders (year): T = .1490074
    Total Annual Relevant Cost: TC = 1006.662
```

A sampling study of past usage has determined that weekly demand is normally distributed with a mean of 250 units and a standard deviation of 35 units.

These data are entered into the *QuickQuant* software and the results are displayed in Exhibit 10.3. The optimal order quantity is 271 units per week, at a total cost of $13,391. The probability of a shortage occurring is .27.

Multiperiod Models

The multiperiod model is a hybrid combination of the basic EOQ model and the single-period probabilistic model. Demand continues from one inventory period to another (see Figure 10.1). However, uncertainty about demand can result in shortages or leftovers before a new shipment arrives. A new variable, **lead time demand**, is introduced. Lead time demand is expressed as a probability distribution measuring the uncertainty that demand will take place between the time an order is placed and the shipment arrives. Daily demand and lead time for an order to be filled may both be random. Thus, the demand during lead time is a random variable. In multiperiod models, the approach is to solve for optimum order quantity using average demand during the lead time for an order to be filled. The reorder point is chosen to obtain a desired safety level of stock on hand.

For an example of the multiperiod probabilistic model, consider the following modification to the initial case problem in this chapter.

The Springfield Ambulatory Care Center is developing an inventory policy for ordering and storage of sterile supply packs. However,

---

Exhibit 10.3 Single-Period Inventory Model

```
Parameter Values:
    Mean of Demand Distribution: mu = 250
    Stan. Deviation of Demand Distribution: sigma = 35
    Cost per Item Procured: c = 45
    Additional Cost for Each Leftover Item Held: hE = 5
    Penalty for Each Item Short: pS = 100
    Selling Price per Unit: pR = 80

Optimal Values:
    Optimal Order Quantity: Q = 271.35
    Expected Demand: mu = 250
    Total Expected Cost: TEC(Q) = 13391.7
    Expected Shortage: B(Q) = 5.8065
    Probability of Shortage: .2702703
```

in this example, demand is probabilistic, with lead time demand known to follow a normal distribution. The average lead time from placement of an order to receipt of a shipment of sterile packs is 5 days. Annual demand is 6,000 sterile packs. The Center is open 260 days per year; thus, daily demand for sterile packs averages 23. The average lead time demand for reordering is 23 units × 5 days = 115 units. A management engineer has analyzed sufficient data to determine that the standard deviation is 12.

Data are now entered into the *QuickQuant* software using the option called "Multiperiod EOQ Model (Backordering) with Normally Distributed Lead-Time Demand" (see Exhibit 10.4). Four of the input variables are the same as used in the basic deterministic EOQ model (see Exhibit 10.1):

Fixed cost per order	$75
Annual demand rate	6,000 units
Unit cost of procuring one pack	$20
Annual holding cost per dollar value	$0.06

Additional input values required by the computer software include the following:

Mean lead-time demand	115
Standard deviation of lead-time demand	12
Shortage cost per unit (the cost of obtaining one sterile pack from a local retail drug store)	$40

Exhibit 10.4 shows the results of the EOQ analysis for this problem. Optimal economic order quantity is 869 units, with optimal reordering to occur when the supply reaches 147 units. Total expected cost of ordering, holding, and shortages is $1,081. The probability of a shortage occurring is less than 1 percent.

EOQ Analysis with Quantity Discounts

Many suppliers will offer discounts to purchasers when certain quantities of items are ordered. In these situations, the economic order quantity must take into account the availability of these discounts in computing total costs (Shogun 1988, 649–52). Consider the following example.

The Fairfield Health System operates a durable medical equipment retail store as one unit of the system. The store is developing an order for wheelchairs from its supplier. The following parameters must be considered in deciding what quantity to order:

Exhibit 10.4 Multiperiod EOQ Model (Backordering)

```
Parameter Values:
    Mean Lead-Time Demand: mu = 115
    Std. Deviation for Lead-Time Demand: sigma = 12
    Fixed Cost per Order: k = 75
    Annual Demand Rate: A = 6000
    Unit Cost of Procuring an Item: c = 20
    Annual Holding Cost per Dollar Value: h = .06
    Shortage Cost per Unit: pS = 40

Optimal Values:
    Optimal Order Quantity: Q = 869
    Optimal Reorder Point: r = 147
    Total Expected Cost: TEC(r,Q) = 1081.511
    Expected Shortage: B(Q) = .014028
    Probability of Shortage: .004345
```

---

1. Annual demand for wheelchairs   1,500
2. Cost of placing an order $ 125
3. Unit cost per wheelchair $ 500
4. Holding cost per wheelchair per year (cost of physical inventory plus cost of capital tied up in inventory—computed at 20 percent of unit cost) $ 100
5. Shortage cost per unit per year (lost profit from failure to make a sale) $ 35
6. Lead time for placing an order (one month)   0.083 years

The supplier offers a quantity discount of 2 percent for orders of 250 to 999 units, and a discount of 5 percent for orders of 1,000 units or more.

The *QuickQuant* software does not include quantity discount computations. Therefore, the above problem was solved using QSB+ (Chang and Sullivan 1991) with the results shown in Exhibit 10.5. Note that the economic order quantity without discounts would be 61 units ordered. However, when quantity discounts are taken into consideration, the optimum order quantity becomes 250 wheelchairs, with a discount of 2 percent.

A Staffing Problem Example

As mentioned in an earlier section of this chapter, inventory models can be applied to problems involving other resources and are not limited to physical materials. Consider the following staffing problem.

Exhibit 10.5 Inventory Cost Analysis for Wheelchair

```
Input Data:
    Demand per year (D)                              =     1500
    Order or setup cost per order (Co)               =      125
    Holding cost per unit per year (Ch)              =       98
    Shortage cost per unit per year (Cs)             =       35
    Shortage cost per unit, independent of time (c) =       35
    Replenishment or production rate per year (P)    =        7
    Lead time for a new order in year (LT)           =     .083
    Unit cost (C)                                    =      490

Inventory Cost Analysis:
    Assigned order quantity          =       250
    Maximum inventory                =       250.000
    Maximum backorder                =         0.000
    Order interval                   =         0.167 year
    Reorder point                    =       124.500
         Ordering cost               =       750.000
         Holding cost                =     12250.000
         Shortage cost               =         0.000
    Subtotal of inventory cost per year =   13000.000
    Material cost per year           =    735000.000
    Total cost per year              =    748000.000

Without Discount:
    EOQ           =        61.237
    Total Cost    =    756123.750


Optimal Decision:
    Discount    =      2%
    Order       =     250
```

A large hospital must determine registered nurse staffing levels for the day shift of its operation. A study of the past six months of operation has determined that nurse staffing requirements per shift are normally distributed with a mean of 450 FTE nurses per shift and a standard deviation of 20. That is, 95 percent of the time, staffing requirements will vary between 410 and 490 nurses per shift.

The average salary including fringe benefits is $20 per hour, or $160 per shift for full-time nurses. However, when extra staffing is required, nurses must be paid overtime at a rate of $30 per hour, or $240 per shift.

This problem can be solved using the single-period probabilistic model described previously. The results using *QuickQuant* are shown in Exhibit 10.6. Note that the optimal staffing level would be 446, with an expected shortage of 10 nurses per shift. However, it would be more economic to cover shortages through overtime since there would be surplus staffing on days when fewer than 446 nurses were needed.

There are many other possible combinations of supply and demand conditions besides those described in these examples. Most inventory

Exhibit 10.6 Single-Period Inventory Model—Staffing Problem

```
Parameter Values:
    Mean of Demand Distribution: mu = 450
    Stan. Deviation of Demand Distribution: sigma = 20
    Cost per Item Procured: c = 160
    Additional Cost for Each Leftover Item Held: hE = 160
    Penalty for Each Item Short: pS = 240
    Selling Price per Unit: pR = 160

Optimal Values:
    Optimal Order Quantity: Q = 446.4
    Expected Demand: mu = 450
    Total Expected Cost: TEC(Q) = 76396.48
    Expected Shortage: B(Q) = 9.90802
    Probability of Shortage: .5714285
```

problems will involve multiple items of inventory rather than the single item problems described above. Demand may not always be normally distributed. These conditions must be included in the model construction and solved either through operations research software such as *QuickQuant* or through simulation techniques as described in Chapter 11.

Description of Available Computer Software

Most operations research software packages will include inventory modeling programs. In addition, a number of specialized materials management programs are available for use in the health services industry. *The Hospital Software Sourcebook* (McKenzie 1993) includes descriptions of 42 commercial software packages available in the area of materials management and inventory control.

Analysis, Interpretation, and Application of Results to Management Decisions

Information provided through inventory modeling enables materials managers to make most efficient use of resources by balancing the cost of ordering, holding items in inventory, and backordering when shortages occur.

In any business, inventories provide a continuing source of management problems. This is probably because of all the variables over which managers have control, stock levels are among the easiest to manipulate. Moreover, the capital investment in inventories is readily apparent, so that when working capital is in short supply, it is easy to achieve a reduction in the amount required by curtailing stocks. Unfortunately, such a policy is often a short-run optimization and may ultimately result in increased production or selling costs (Ackoff and Sasieni 1968, 178).

Modern systems of supply offered by many vendors on a "just in time" basis can help to reduce inventory requirements, provided good information on demand and usage is available. However, a 1994 *New York Times* article suggests that just-in-time inventory policies are losing favor in many companies (Norris 1994):

> The era of "just-in-time" inventories . . . may be coming to an end. That fad was based on the assumption that more could always be ordered, and quickly delivered, and that the price for such new inventory was likely to be no higher than the price of the old . . . . The trouble is that the mini-boom of last winter exposed the wishful nature of the theory. There have been shortages and rapid price hikes . . . . Suddenly, higher inventories seem to be prudent.

Case Studies from the Literature

Inventory Control at a Pharmaceutical Wholesaler (Sullivan and Schommer 1993)

A study was conducted to investigate the potential cost savings to a pharmaceutical wholesaler using the economic order quantity model. A regional pharmaceutical wholesaler that supplied pharmaceuticals and sundries to retail pharmacies in two states was selected for the study. Eleven brand-name, prescription-only products were randomly selected for the analysis.

Holding costs were determined by joint consensus of several of the company's executives and researchers based primarily on the cost of capital and interest rates. Since the company under analysis was small and had small purchasing and accounts payable departments, the ordering costs were lower. Annual demand was determined using the previous year's demand, while the purchase price of a product was the last price paid by the wholesaler. Order quantity was determined using the most recent order placed, concurring with the philosophy that the wholesaler usually orders approximately one month's worth of product when the reorder point is reached. Once these five parameters were determined, the EOQs for each product were determined.

The average yearly cost savings using EOQ was $31.92 per product. Because the wholesaler carried a stock of some 8,500 brand-name products, savings of $271,320 annually could be realized using the EOQ model. Undoubtedly, using EOQ can assist pharmaceutical wholesalers in minimizing holding and ordering costs, while improving efficiency in pharmaceutical distribution channels.

Inventory Control at a Nonprofit Community Hospital (VanDerLinde 1983)

An inventory control system that integrates the economic order quantity model was implemented at St. Luke's Memorial Hospital, a 146-bed nonprofit community hospital providing inpatient and outpatient services. Using a handheld computer that interfaces to the hospital's on-line perpetual inventory control database, a series of inventory management reports were developed for each drug line item in the hospital's pharmacy. These reports provide information on EOQ, EOQ proposed carrying cost, actual inventory carrying costs, safety stock, order point, and average inventory. From December 1980 to December 1981, the system facilitated a 46.5 percent reduction in standing inventory levels. The system demonstrated a greater return on inventory investment by substantial improvement in turnover and reduction of standing inventory levels and effectively reduced inventory operation costs.

Inventory Control at a Pediatric Teaching Hospital (Kwak, Durbin, and Stanley 1991)

The EOQ model was implemented at a 220+-bed pediatric teaching hospital in an effort to improve efficiency in inventory management. Specifically, the study was conducted to analyze and determine the optimal delivery of IV fluids based on data collected on the two highest usage items manufactured by Baxter Healthcare. The hospital belongs to a national buying group representing 23,947 hospital beds across the country. This large group has tremendous buying power and is in a situation to negotiate a very favorable contract with Baxter; thus, the costs incurred by placing an order are only the costs incurred within the hospital. Upon execution of the EOQ model, space and capital requirements can be reduced without compromising the quality of services rendered.

Inventory Control at an Acute Care Hospital (Ballentine, Ravin, and Gilbert 1976)

An inventory control study was conducted in the hospital pharmacy of St. Joseph Mercy Hospital in Ann Arbor, Michigan, a 558-bed acute care hospital. The 4,320-item inventory list was divided into A, B, and C groups according to the annual dollar value of the items. Two samples were selected for analysis, the first consisting of 10 percent of the total inventory, and the second consisting of 10 percent of Group A, the high-cost items. The EOQ for each was calculated to estimate the proposed annual inventory cost compared to the actual cost determined from past inventory records. In the first sample, there was a mean annual savings of $4.13 using the proposed annual cost. Most of the savings with the EOQ system were found to occur with the low dollar value, too frequently purchased items (B and C).

Problems

10.1 Macon's Pharmacy is located in an area with a number of retired people and has a large demand for durable medical equipment. The manager is currently developing an order for heavy-duty metal walkers from his supplier. He has compiled the following information from sales and inventory records:
Annual demand for walkers—200
Cost of placing an order—$90
Unit cost per walker—$125
Holding cost—8 percent of dollar value of inventory
   (Cost of capital 5 percent; Storage cost 3 percent)
Requirement: What quantity should he order? How frequently will orders need to be placed?

10.2 The pharmacy manager in Problem 10.1 is experiencing problems with backorders from the supplier of metal walkers. The annual cost of being short one walker is $15 profit lost on the inability to complete a sale. (Customers will use other pharmacies if the item is out of stock.)
Requirement: What quantity should be ordered under these conditions? What should be the reorder level?

10.3 Golden Home Health Care must determine home health aide (HHA) staffing levels for its daily operations (not including the 24-hour, 7-day-a-week on-call line). Analysis of last year's records show a staffing requirement with a mean of 15 HHAs and a standard deviation of 3. The average salary is $9 per hour, or $72 per shift. However, if overtime is required during an overworked week, home health aides are paid $16 per hour, or $128 per shift. Home health aide services are billed to patients at a rate of $18 per hour.
Requirement: Using EOQ, what is the optimal staffing level?

10.4 The manager of central supply for Johnstown Hospital is ready to place an order for prepackaged sterile supply cart packs for use on the surgical inpatient unit. Average daily demand for this item is 12, with a range of 9 to 15 per day. Each pack costs $80. The cost of placing an order through the hospital's purchasing department is $150. The average lead time from placement of an order to receipt of the material is 10 days, with a range of 8 to 12 days. Holding cost per dollar value of inventory is $0.08. Shortage cost per unit of inventory is $150 (the cost of obtaining packs on an emergency basis from another hospital or supplier).

Requirement: Compute the optimal order quantity and reorder point for this inventory item.

10.5 Metropolitan Health Care System contracts with a local college to conduct a training program for orderlies to be employed at hospitals in the System. The cost for each class offered is $15,000. The System has an annual demand for 200 new orderlies, with openings occurring uniformly over the year. All graduates of the training program who are waiting for an assignment are paid $1,000 per month.

Requirement: How many recruits should be trained in each class?

References

Ackoff, R. L., and M. W. Sasieni. 1968. *Fundamentals of Operations Research*. New York: John Wiley & Sons.

Ballentine, R., R. L. Ravin, and J. R. Gilbert. 1976. "ABC Inventory Analysis and Economic Order Quantity Concept in Hospital Pharmacy Purchasing." *American Journal of Hospital Pharmacy* 33 (6): 552–55.

Chang, Y., and R. S. Sullivan. 1991. *QSB+ Quantitative Systems for Business Plus*. Englewood Cliffs, NJ: Prentice-Hall Inc.

Kwak, N. K., E. Durbin, and D. Stanley. 1991. "An Inventory Model for Optimizing Purchasing of Intravenous Fluids for Hospitals: A Case Study." *Journal of Medical Systems* 15 (2): 171–81.

Lapin, L. L. 1994. *QuickQuant Decision Making Software*. Pleasonton, CA: Alamo Publishing Co.

McKenzie, J. R. (ed.). 1993. *Hospital Software Sourcebook*. Gaithersburg, MD: Aspen Publishers, Inc.

Norris, F. 1994. "Inventories Are Rising for the Right Reasons." *New York Times* (31 July).

Shogun, A. W. 1988. *Management Science*. Englewood Cliffs, NJ: Prentice-Hall.

Sullivan, D. L., and J. C. Schommer. 1993. "Improving Efficiencies in Pharmaceutical Distribution Channels Using the Economic Order Quantity Model." *Clinical Therapeutics* 15 (6): 1146–53.

VanDerLinde, L. P. 1983. "System to Maximize Inventory Performance in a Small Hospital." *American Journal of Hospital Pharmacy* 40 (1): 70–73.

Additional Readings

Abramowitz, P. W. "Controlling Financial Variables—Purchasing, Inventory Control, and Waste Reduction." *American Journal of Hospital Pharmacy* 41, 2 (1994): 309–17.

Haywood, B. G. "Understanding Economic Order Quantity." *Hospital Materiel Management Quarterly* 1, 4 (1980): 11–17.

"Inventory Management. Economic Order Quantity—Economic Order Period." *Radiologic Technology* 60, 1 (1988): 54–55.

Vincent, V., and M. Ranton. "Hospital Pharmacy Inventory Management: Economic Order Quanitity Model with Space Limitation." *Hospital Materiel Management Quarterly* 5, 3 (1984): 82–86.

Simulation: An Alternative Approach to Management Decisions

SIMULATION FOR FACILITY
AND PROGRAM PLANNING

by Tee H. Hiett

E ACH OF THE quantitative techniques presented in this textbook requires the collection, organization, and analysis of data
that are assigned to the input variables. These values are typically
considered to be deterministic single-valued numbers such as the fixed
cost, the variable cost, and the revenue in the break-even analysis of
Chapter 2. An input variable may also be assigned a parameter of a
probability distribution such as the mean of the distribution of the
time between arrivals and the mean of the distribution of the time
required for service in the queueing models of Chapter 7.

Each technique provides a process or a model for combining the
input variables. Some of these models are mathematical equations or
formulas such as those in the break-even analysis of Chapter 2 and
in the queueing models of Chapter 7. These models can easily be
adapted to computer spreadsheet programs, such as Excel. Other models, such as the decision analysis with decision trees in Chapter 4 and
the project control with PERT/CPM of Chapter 8, provide procedures for combining the inputs that make adaptation to spreadsheet
programs difficult. These more complex models have stimulated the
development of specialty computer programs such as the *QuickQuant*
program that accompanies this textbook. More refined (and costly)

specialty computer programs have been developed to accommodate the richness of very complex, realistic models.

Each model produces an output variable or variables providing information to the decision makers. These variables may be single-valued numbers such as the break-even point in the analysis in Chapter 2 and the economic reorder point of inventory control of Chapter 10. In some models, the analyst is interested in a range of possible values for the input variables, such as the four levels of demand with associated probabilities in the home health agency case of Chapter 3. These values may be entered in a table in a spreadsheet program, and when the program is executed, a value for the output variable is computed for each of the levels of the input. The latest versions of computer spreadsheets also provide the capability for solving a table of such values for the optimum, maximum, or minimum points. An example of this capability is the Solver program of the spreadsheet program Excel.

When an input variable is uncertain (i.e., dependent on chance or unpredictable factors), the analyst may want to use a probability distribution as the input variable instead of a deterministic single value. The fixed cost of the break-even analysis of Chapter 2 is an estimate of a cost to be incurred in the future. This estimated value can be considered to be the mean of a probability distribution, and an analyst may be interested in using all the other values over the range of that distribution instead of just a few values from the distribution. The four levels for the demand in the home health agency case of Chapter 3 could be fit to a probability distribution, and the entire range of those values with associated probabilities used in the model. One approach to introducing uncertainty with probability distributions is **Monte Carlo simulation.**

Conceptually, Monte Carlo simulation involves a series of iterations. At each iteration, a random value is taken from each input probability distribution or frequency distribution of observed data from a large sample. The random values are used to compute a value for the output distribution. The results of each iteration are retained, and at the end of the simulation, they are organized into relative frequency distributions. The number of computations and the amount of record keeping in simulation demand the use of a computer program. One program that provides this capability as an add-in for spreadsheet programs is @RISK (Morgan and Henrion 1990, 257).

A common use of Monte Carlo simulation is queueing models. For the formulas to apply in the case problem of Chapter 7, specific conditions had to be met. The distribution of the time between arrivals had to be exponentially distributed, and this distribution had to be consistent over the period simulated. The distribution of the time to provide services had to be exponentially distributed, and the same for all calls. The queue discipline had to be "first in, first out" (FIFO). Variations from these and other conditions would mean the derivation of different equations. In other than these simple cases, the development of analytical models such as the formulas used in Chapter 7 quickly becomes demanding. In complex processes involving several possible queues and different branches, such models may not even be obtainable. Simulation removes such constraints.

One of the first commercially available queueing simulation programs was IBM's General Purpose System Simulator (GPSS) in the early 1960s (Greenberg 1972, 7). Professional queueing model simulation programs, such as MedModel (Harrell et al. 1992, 21), are now available for microcomputers.

Increases in the power and availability of microcomputers, in the power and the ease-of-use of simulation programs, and in the interest in improving the delivery of health care services provide the potential for simulation to become a routine part of the quantitative techniques of managers in health care. In this chapter, the basic concepts of simulation are embedded in applications to models from other chapters in this book and one additional model. As meaningful simulation projects require the use of a computer and a specialty program, simulation concepts are also woven into the application of specialty programs. A major objective of this chapter is to prepare managers of health care services for the application of Monte Carlo simulation.

The Case Problems

Four cases are used to demonstrate the concepts of simulation. Spreadsheet models are developed using the break-even analysis model of Chapter 2 and the decision-analysis model of Chapter 3. Queueing model simulation is developed using the queueing model of Chapter 7 and a slightly more complex model of a medical clinic to demonstrate more features of queueing simulation.

The details of the first three cases and the applications of the results are presented in Chapters 2, 3, and 7. As each case is developed in this chapter, the details relevant to uncertainty and to simulation are reviewed. Where the applications of the results are significantly different from those in the original chapters, those differences are noted.

Computers are required for the creation and execution of the simplest simulation models. In this chapter, computer programs are used as the basis for defining the models and exploring the concepts of simulation. Some features of the programs are used to emphasize certain aspects of simulation. Other features are included to illustrate the ease of programming. No attempt is made to explore all the features of any of these programs. Additional information about the programs used in this chapter and about other computer programs relevant to simulation are included at the end of this chapter.

The simple spreadsheet models that clearly demonstrate many of the basic concepts of simulation are presented first. The queueing models that follow are built on the concepts of the spreadsheet models.

Spreadsheet Models

The case problems for break-even analysis and for decision analysis are examined using the program @RISK, an add-in program for the spreadsheet programs Excel and Lotus 1-2-3. In these cases, the basic steps for formulating the spreadsheet simulation models are the following:

1. Develop the model equations and enter them into a spreadsheet.
2. Identify input variables that are uncertain.
3. Assign a probability distribution to each uncertain input variable.
4. Run the model.

Break-Even Analysis

The spreadsheet model of the break-even analysis is presented in spreadsheet format in Exhibit 11.1. The input variables are the fixed cost for the project, the variable cost per enrollee per year, and the revenue per enrollee per year. The fixed cost and the variable cost are uncertain as they will be incurred in the future. The revenue per enrollee per year is certain because its value is set by the analyst.

One way to select a probability distribution for the input variable fixed cost is to estimate the maximum cost and the minimum cost—for example, $750,000 and $450,000. If these extreme values represent ±3 standard deviations about the mean, then 1 standard deviation would be $50,000. Assuming that the distribution is normally distributed about the mean, the probability distribution for the input variable is a normal distribution with a mean of $600,000 and a standard deviation of $50,000. As shown in Exhibit 11.1, the computer program @RISK provides the analyst with the opportunity to examine a graph of the probability distribution. The @RISK command "=RiskNormal(600000,50000)" is entered in Cell A7. The program will automatically identify Cell A7 as an input variable.

Exhibit 11.1 Inputs for Break-Even Analysis

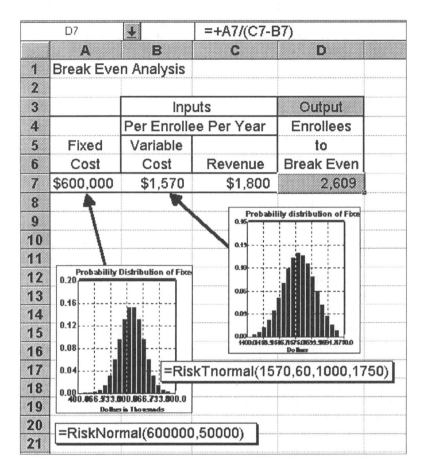

The probability distribution for the second input variable, variable cost per enrollee, can be determined in the same manner as the distribution for the fixed cost. This distribution is truncated at an upper limit of less than $1,800 to assure a positive value for profit, since a negative profit is meaningless. In this example, the upper truncation limit is set at $1,750. The lower truncation limit is $1,000, 9.5 standard deviations below the mean, effectively eliminating truncation at the lower end. A graph of this input distribution is shown in Exhibit 11.1. The @RISK command "=RiskTnormal(1570,60,1000,1750)" is entered in Cell B7 of the model.

Probability distributions for the input variables do not have to be normally distributed. @RISK provides 35 probability distributions, and

5 of these are truncated. During the formulation stage, any one of these distributions can be entered into the model and displayed in graphical form to assist the analyst in identifying an appropriate distribution.

The output variable is the number of enrollees to break even, shown by the formula in Cell D7 in Exhibit 11.1. The break-even point is determined by dividing the fixed cost by the profit per enrollee.

Solving the case problem   During simulation the computer completes a series of **iterations**, or repetitive steps. At each iteration, the computer selects a random value from the probability distribution for the fixed cost and a random value from the probability distribution for the variable cost. The computer then computes the break-even point as indicated in Cell D7 of Exhibit 11.1.

Computer simulation programs and spreadsheet programs have special subroutines for generating random numbers, usually on the interval 0–1. Simulation programs use these numbers for selecting values randomly from probability distributions. Some simulation programs have as many as 100 random number generators for producing up to 100 different series of random numbers.

Each random number generator uses a seed, or a beginning value, to initiate a series or sequence or **stream** of random numbers. For a given seed, a generator will produce the exact same stream of random numbers. Each different seed will produce a different stream of random numbers. Some computer programs, such as *QuickQuant*, provide an internal means for producing a different seed value each time the generator is started.

In @RISK, a value of zero in the "Random Number Generator Seed" in Exhibit 11.2 will generate a different stream of random numbers for each simulation. Each positive number will generate a unique stream of random numbers for a simulation, and will repeat that same stream for each simulation, if more than one simulation is run.

Simulations can be scheduled to terminate after a certain number of iterations or after certain conditions exist. Values entered into "# Iterations =" and "# Simulations =" shown in Exhibit 11.2 can be used to cause the process to terminate after these numbers of iterations and simulations. Simulations can also be canceled by the user anytime during the process.

After a certain number of iterations in a simulation, additional iterations do not significantly change the statistics of interest. Consider the following example with the break-even point project. Two variables are established, *MEANpre* and *MEANcur*. After every 50 iterations, the value in *MEANcur* is put into *MEANpre*, and the new mean of the

Exhibit 11.2 Settings for Break-Even Analysis Simulation

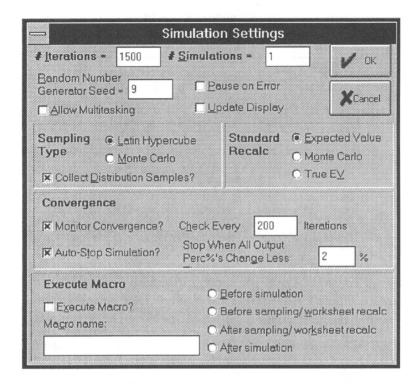

distribution of all break-even points is calculated and put into *MEAN-cur*. The percent change in the value of the mean from one iteration to the next can be calculated as ABS(*MEANcur* − *MEANpre*)/*MEANpre*) × 100. The percent change will become increasingly smaller as the number of iterations increases. The simulation process reaches a stable state, and the mean converges toward a narrow interval. An illustration of this convergence output variable break-even point for one simulation is shown in Figure 11.1.

In @RISK, convergence can be observed as the simulation progresses. By selecting the "Monitor Convergence" option and setting the number of iterations to be used for each check, the analyst can observe the convergence during the simulation. The percent change in contributions to the mean, the standard deviation, and the percentiles for each output distribution are computed at the specified number of iterations and are displayed on the screen.

Once a simulation has reached a stable state for each output variable, there is little reason to continue the process. The "Auto-Stop

Figure 11.1 Example of Percent Change in Mean

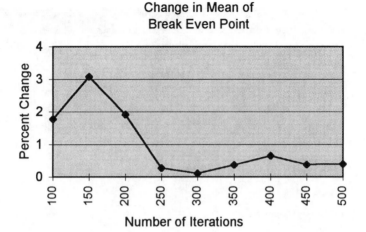

Change in Mean of
Break Even Point

Number of Iterations

Simulation" option of @RISK shown in Exhibit 11.2 can be used to terminate a simulation automatically as soon as the contribution to the output variables is less than the amount specified.

Model variations Simulation with spreadsheet add-in programs provides all the variations available in the original spreadsheet model. The very process of simulation provides a what-if analysis by identifying the range of values for the input variables. The input values can be varied by selecting different probability distributions with different parameters. For example, different parameters can cause the beta distribution to take on very different shapes and cover different ranges. With the graphics capability of microcomputers, such variations can be examined to aid in the search for the most realistic input distribution.

Simulation add-in programs also provide for additional what-if analysis. The "Simulation Settings" in Exhibit 11.2 can be used to set the number of iterations and the number of simulations. In the break-even analysis, the parameters for the probability distributions and the charge per enrollee are fixed throughout the single simulation. Values for the parameters of the input probabilities and for the charges can be entered into a table. The number of simulations is set equal to the number of records in the table. The number for each simulation is used to access the record number providing input values for that simulation.

Application of the results At the end of the simulation, the program organizes all the break-even points into a table and constructs a relative frequency distribution that can be interpreted as a probability distribution. Outputs of a simulation of the break-even analysis are presented in Exhibit 11.3. As shown in the frequency and the cumulative frequency distributions, the probability is high that the outcome will be much greater than 1,500 potential enrollees. This result is shown numerically in the small windows at the bottom of Exhibit 11.3. For the Target #1 Value of 1,500 enrollees, the program identifies the Target #1 Percent as 0.6189, less than 1 percent.

Also shown in Exhibit 11.3, for a Target #2 Percent of 50, the program identifies the Target #2 Value of 2,622 enrollees, slightly higher than the 2,609 enrollees calculated to break even at $1,800 per enrollee in Chapter 2. This statistic indicates that 50 percent of the time the number of enrollees required to break even will be greater than 2,622. As can be seen in the frequency distributions in Exhibit 11.3, the number of enrollees to break even can be as high as 5,000.

Decision Analysis

The steps for formulating the spreadsheet model for the decision analysis are the same as those for the break-even analysis model. There are, however, some distinctly different features in this model.

The original model for decision analysis is shown in spreadsheet format in Exhibit 11.4. All of the input costs in the model are deterministic, fixed-value variables. The only uncertain input value is the demand for PT services. To accommodate this uncertainty, four levels of demand with associated probabilities are included in the model, as shown in Exhibit 11.4.

Another approach to accommodating this uncertainty is to use the estimated levels of demand and associated probabilities in a computer program such as BestFit to fit the data to a probability distribution. As shown in Figure 11.2, a normal distribution with a mean of 112 and a standard deviation of 38 has been fitted to the input values.

As shown in Exhibit 11.5, the original model has been rearranged and the normal distribution used for demand. If there were compelling reasons for restricting the demand to the four values of the original model, those values could be used as input variables in the model. For the model in Exhibit 11.5, the demand is in the range of 14–242 visits and is normally distributed.

Solving the case problem The process for simulating this model is the same as that for simulating the break-even analysis model.

Model variations The variations available for this model are the same as those in the original model in Chapter 3 and in the simulation of the break-even model presented in the preceding section of this chapter.

Exhibit 11.3 Outputs for Break-Even Analysis

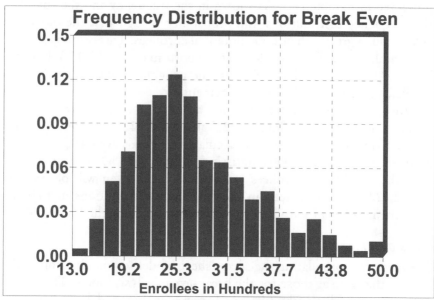

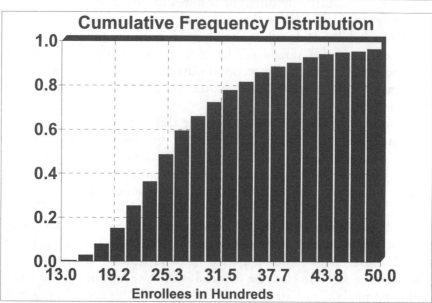

Name	/Break Even
Description	Output
Cell	D7
Target #1 (Value)=	1500
Target #1 (Perc%)=	.6189497%
Target #2 (Value)=	2622.265625
Target #2 (Perc%)=	50%

Exhibit 11.4   Original Model for Decision Analysis

| F13 | =+($E13*$E$12)+($D13*D12)+($C13*$C$12)+($B13*B12) | | | | | |

	A	B	C	D	E	F	G
1	**Decision Analysis**						
2							
3							
4	**Decision**		**Costs**				
5	**Alternative**	**Fixed**	**Variable**	**Revenue**			
6	Alt. A - Independent	$0	$60	$ 75			
7	Alt. B - Staff	($4,400)	$7	$ 75			
8	Alt. C - Services	($600)	$42	$ 75			
9							
10			**Inputs**			**Outputs**	
11	**Demand**	30	90	140	150	**Expected**	
12	**Probability**	0.1	0.4	0.2	0.3	**Profit**	
13	Alt. A - Independent	$450	$1,350	$2,100	$2,250	$ 1,680	
14	Alt. B - Staff	($2,360)	$1,720	$5,120	$5,800	$ 3,216	
15	Alt. C - Services	$390	$2,370	$4,020	$4,350	$ 3,096	

Figure 11.2 Normal Distribution Fitted to Input Data for Decision Analysis

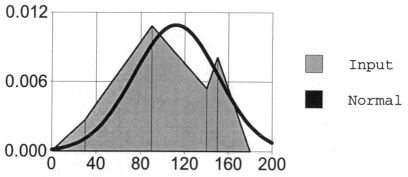

Comparison of Input Distribution and Normal(112,38)

Applications of the results The outputs shown in Exhibit 11.6 indicate that the means of Alternatives B and C are greater than the mean of Alternative A and that these two means are very similar. Thus information is similar to that produced by the solution in Chapter 3. The additional information of Exhibit 11.6 is that Alternative B has a greater risk than Alternative C. Alternative B has a wider range of outcomes with associated probabilities than does Alternative C.

Queueing Models

Analyzing queueing models with simulation is presented in three sections. The first section is devoted to simulating the PPO authorization model from Chapter 7 with *QuickQuant*, the computer program accompanying this textbook. The second section reviews steps for simulating the PPO authorization model with MedModel, one of the professional programs for simulating queueing models. The third section emphasizes more of the capabilities of queueing simulation by examining the steps involved in simulating a small clinic model with MedModel.

PPO Authorization Model with QuickQuant

The specific numerical data required to simulate the PPO authorization process with the *QuickQuant* program are the characteristics of the rate at which calls arrive for service and the characteristics of the time to process the calls. These data were collected by recording the date and

Exhibit 11.5 Inputs for Decision Analysis

E6	⬇		=+D6*C6	
A	**B**	**C**	**D**	**E**
1 Decision Analysis				
2				
3		Inputs		Outputs
4 Decision	Costs		Demand	Profit
5 Alternative	Fixed	Variable		
6 A - Independent	$0	$15	112	$1,680
7 B - Staff	($4,400)	$68		$3,216
8 C - Services	($600)	$33		$3,096

Independent / Demand - Normal(112,38)

the time each call arrived and the length of time required to process each call. In Chapter 7, emphasis was placed on the requirement that the arrival process follow a Poisson process. If an arrival rate is Poisson with a mean of λ, the distribution of the interarrival time (the time between arrivals) is exponential with a mean of $1/\lambda$. An arrival rate of

Exhibit 11.6 Outputs for Decision Analysis

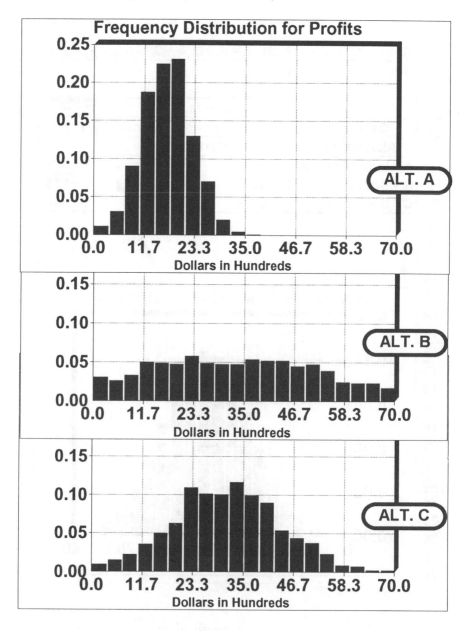

18 calls per hour translates into an arrival rate, λ, of 0.3 calls per minute. As shown in Figure 11.3, the program BestFit assigns the interarrival times to an exponential distribution having a mean of 3.3 minutes.

Figure 11.3 Input Data Fitted to Probability Distributions

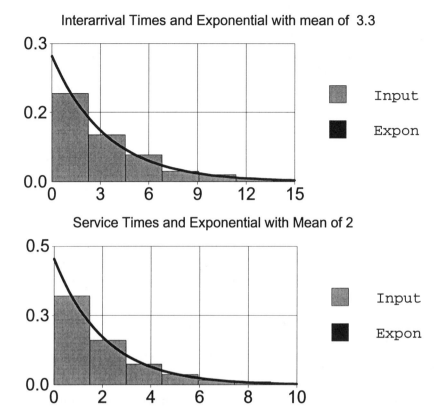

Interarrival Times and Exponential with mean of 3.3

Service Times and Exponential with Mean of 2

Also as shown in Figure 11.3, the service time, or time required to complete a call, is exponentially distributed with a mean of 2 minutes. This translates into a rate of 0.5 calls per minute.

In the case problem of Chapter 7, calls are taken from the queue on a "first in, first out" (FIFO) basis. In addition, physician office personnel do not "balk" nor "renege" but remain on the line (in the queue) until the receptionist at the PPO provides the necessary information. These conditions are standard in the *QuickQuant* program and cannot be modified.

Solving the case problem   Instructions for simulating queueing models with *QuickQuant* are given in the manual accompanying the program. A few points relevant to a discussion of simulation are included in this section.

The first option is the selection of the seed for the random number generator. Just as in the spreadsheet add-in simulation programs, a different seed for each session (or simulation) will cause the program to generate a different stream of random numbers for each session. Correspondingly, the same seed will generate the same stream of random numbers for each session.

After the "queueing" and the "enter new problem from the keyboard" options are selected, the user enters a name, including the path, for the problem. The user then identifies a single-server model by entering 1 as the number of servers and selects the probability distribution for the arrival time.

As shown in Exhibit 11.7, *QuickQuant* provides five options for probability distributions for queueing models. In this example, the user selects option 2, "Exponential Distribution," for the time between arrivals and enters the average number of calls per minute of 0.3. The exponential distribution is also selected for the service time, and the average number of calls per minute is 0.5.

After selecting the option to run the simulation, the user is asked for the number of simulation trials. This was the number of iterations in the @RISK program used to simulate the spreadsheet models. The range of iterations is 2–500.

Model variations   The variations available in the *QuickQuant* program are the number of servers, the arrival and service probability distributions, parameters of the distributions, the number of iterations per simulation, and the number of simulations.

Application of the results   The principal outputs of one simulation of 500 iterations with *QuickQuant* are presented in Exhibits 11.8 and 11.9. These outputs are basically the same as those produced by the analytical queueing models of Chapter 7 and provide the same managerial information.

Exhibit 11.7   *QuickQuant* Menu Of Probability Distributions

```
                 QuickQuant
       CHOICES FOR PROBABILITY DISTRIBUTION

    1. Supplied Table of Probabilities.

    2. Exponential Distribution.

    3. Normal Distribution.

    4. Uniform Distribution.

    5. Constant Value.

  X 6. Modified Beta Distribution (PERT).

  X 7. Triangular Distribution (PERT).
```

Exhibit 11.8   Outputs of One Simulation in *QuickQuant*

```
================== QuickQuant ==================
         Queuing Simulation Summary Results

PROBLEM: Single Server Queue


     Mean Number of Customers in System: L = 1.643867
     Mean Customer Time Spent in System: W = 5.654662
     Mean Number of Customers Waiting
                    (Length of Line): Lq = 1.027683
     Mean Customer Waiting Time: Wq = 3.535077
     Server Utilization Factor: rho = .6161844
```

A: Statistics

```
================== QuickQuant ==================
         Queuing Simulation Summary Results

PROBLEM: Single Server Queue


     Number of      Proportion of      Proportion of
     Customers      Time in System     Time Waiting
     ------------------------------------------------
         0             .3838              .5964
         1             .2126              .1518
         2             .1518              .0894
         3             .0894              .0674
         4             .0674              .0471
         5             .0471              .0126
         6             .0126              .0161
         7             .0161              .0119
         8             .0119              .0035
         9             .0035              .0020
                      (Continued)
```

B: Frequency Distributions

Comparing the statistics of Exhibit 11.8 with those produced by the analytical queueing model of Chapter 7 illustrates the need for repetitive simulations or for more iterations in a single simulation. The solutions of the analytical equations of Chapter 7 produce the values for steady-state operation of the model. These values are independent of the initial startup conditions of the model. Simulation provides approximations of those values.

The steady-state value for the mean number of calls in the single-server system is 1.5, as computed in Chapter 7 and shown in Exhibit 7.1. Normally, the true steady-state conditions of a process are not known, and simulations are used to estimate them. One estimate of the number of calls in the system after 500 iterations is 1.64, as shown in Exhibit 11.8. Additional simulations will produce other values near 1.5, the known steady-state value.

Exhibit 11.9 Additional Outputs of One Simulation in *QuickQuant*

Distribution of Waiting Time

```
=============== QuickQuant ===============
    Waiting Time Histogram for Simulation Results

PROBLEM: Single Server Queue

                                          *=16  n=500

4
*                         Fractile  .01:  0.000000
*                                   .05:  0.000000
*                                   .10:  0.000000
*                                   .25:  0.000000
*                                   .50:  1.64888
*                                   .75:  5.436783
* 1                                 .90:  9.791787
*2498731 61111                      .95: 13.26872
6*411 875989824153336   111324 11 1  211
                                    .99: 20.30753
*******
+-----+-----+-----+-----+-----+-----+-----+
0     5    10    15    20    25

            Nearest Waiting Time

                          Minimum:  0.000000
                          Maximum: 22.93726
                             Mean:  3.535077
                           S.Dev.:  4.638757
```

Log of Iterations

```
                              QuickQuant
                        Log of Queuing Simulation
```

PROBLEM: Single Server Queue

Customer	Time Between Arrivals	Cumulative Time at Arrival	Cumulative Time when Service Begins	Identity of Server	Service Time	Waiting Time
1	8.74	8.74	8.74	1	0.29	0.00
2	0.82	9.55	9.55	1	2.19	0.00
3	5.50	15.05	15.05	1	0.53	0.00
4	2.08	17.13	17.13	1	0.14	0.00
5	8.54	25.67	25.67	1	2.21	0.00
6	2.76	28.43	28.43	1	0.71	0.00
7	1.65	30.07	30.07	1	1.50	0.00
8	9.84	39.92	39.92	1	12.20	0.00
9	2.22	42.14	52.12	1	1.09	9.98
10	2.21	44.35	53.21	1	1.39	8.86

(Continued)

The values produced by additional simulations can be used to estimate an interval containing the steady-state value with a specific confidence. Replicating the single-server queueing simulation 10 times each with 150 iterations produced values for the average number in the queue of 1.5, 1.14, 1.25, 1.35, 1.43, 1.19, 0.83, 1.27, 1.87, and 2.28. The mean of these numbers is 1.41, and the sample variance is 0.16. The $t_{9,0.95}$ value is 1.83. The 90 percent confidence interval is then

$$1.416 \pm \left(1.83\sqrt{(0.16/10)}\right)$$

or 1.17–1.64. In this example, the average number of calls in the queue for the steady-state condition is known to be 1.5, which is in the computed interval. It is worth emphasizing that in the usual case, the value of the steady-state condition would not be known.

The distribution of waiting time in Exhibit 11.9 contains some of the information generated in Table 7.1. The .90 fractile indicates that 90 percent of the waiting was less than 9.79 minutes, or that 10 percent of the waiting was greater than 9.79 minutes.

As shown in Exhibit 11.9, *QuickQuant* also provides the output of each entity process in the simulation. These data can be saved into a raw data file for additional analyses with a spreadsheet program or with any standard statistical program such as SPSS.

PPO Authorization Model with MedModel

The more detailed and more realistic the queueing model, the greater the requirements for data collection and analysis. In contrast to the simple PPO authorization model, the magnitude of a project such as a diagnostic clinic or an emergency department demands a systematic approach. One such approach is implicit in the following steps:

1. Develop flowcharts and flow diagrams.
2. Collect and analyze sample data:
   a. Time of each arrival
   b. Relevant characteristics of each arrival
   c. Time to provide service to each arrival at each service area
3. Formulate the model.

These steps will be reviewed and applied to the PPO telephone authorization case. Then the steps will be applied to a medical clinic.

The development of the queueing model begins with the information required to construct relatively simple charts. Actually, the charts themselves are models of the process. The advantages of using charts in simulation are the same as their use in other projects to improve quality. First, the models provide a guide to the collection and organization of data. Second, they provide a clear visual representation of the process, reducing ambiguity. When the managers, workers, and analysts engaged in the analysis of the process examine the charts and diagrams, they will see the same steps.

Process charts and diagrams have been used by industrial engineers in health care as one means of improving work methods. Bennett, one of the early industrial engineers applying these techniques in health care in the early 1960s, wrote a classic "how to" book using these charting techniques to improve methods in hospitals (Bennett 1974, 7–33). In 1966, Smalley and Freeman devoted a chapter of their seminal work on hospital industrial engineering to using such charts to improve work methods (Smalley and Freeman 1966, 181–98). The use of these charts in health care increased as the number of industrial engineers (or management engineers) in hospitals increased during the decades of the 1960s and the 1970s. During the 1980s, the number of industrial engineers employed in health care peaked and began to decrease.

The adoption of continuous quality improvement (CQI) or total quality management (TQI) by health care managers in the late 1980s brought a resurgence of interest in process charts and in process diagrams. (It is interesting to note that in TQM and CQI the focus is on improving quality, whereas the industrial engineers focused on improving *work*.) Gaucher and Coffey, in their book on TQM in health care, devote a chapter to methods for improving quality, which included process charts and diagrams (Gaucher and Coffey 1993, 369–78). Berwick et al. include several examples of quality improvement studies, each of which includes process charts (Berwick, Godfrey, and Roessner 1990, 221–76).

Typically, the construction of a process chart model begins with the analyst following the flow through the process and identifying the significant steps. Each step is classified as start, action, delay, or decision and represented by a symbol, as shown in Figure 11.4. A symbol is drawn for each process step, and arrows connecting the symbols represent the direction of the flow from one step to the next. Sufficient information to identify a step is written inside the symbol.

For a simulation model, additional data are required about each step in the process. To generate arrivals for the simulation, analysts must have information about the distribution of the time between the arrivals to the process. This information is gathered by collecting the times of consecutive arrivals and computing the time between arrivals, usually in minutes. These data are converted into relative frequency distributions.

Figure 11.4 Process Chart Symbols

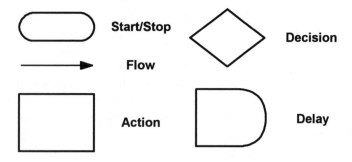

If entities in the process have characteristics that influence the sequence of the process steps or the time to provide the services at any step, these characteristics are usually recorded at the time of arrival. For patients, such characteristics might include age, sex, and condition or illness.

Because the frequency of arrivals to the process might be related to time of day, day of week, or season of the year, the date is usually recorded when the time of arrival is recorded.

To model the time each entity requires for service at each action step, analysts must have the distribution of the length of time to provide services at each action step. If the distribution of the length of time to provide services is a function of a characteristic of the entity (such as age, sex, etc.), that characteristic is recorded along with the time to provide the service.

To have the simulation model assign resources, such as doctors and nurses, at each action step, the analysts must know how the resources are used at each step. Typically, information about who is providing the services is recorded along with the time to provide the service.

To model entity flow through a queue, analysts must have information about how entities are processed in that queue. Entities may move through the queue on a "first in, first out" (FIFO) basis or a "last in, first out" (LIFO) basis. Entities may have characteristics that give them a priority position in a queue. Entities may also have a characteristic, such as a life-threatening condition, that causes them to circumvent a queue.

Normally, data about the length of time entities spend in queues are not required for the development in the simulation model. However, such operating statistics as the average number in the queue, the average length of time in the queue, the maximum number in the queue, and the distribution of the length of the queue are useful in validating a simulation model. The simulation model should produce operating statistics similar to those produced in actual operations.

Model formulation   Two process charts for the PPO telephone authorization case are presented in Figure 11.5. The first model is adequate for the single-server model. The second model is more appropriate if the project is to be expanded to include a second receptionist. In the latter case, a procedure would be required for routing calls to equalize the workload.

In this project the entities moving through the area are the telephone calls. A diagram illustrating the flow of this process is shown in Figure 11.6. The queue is depicted as a bank of lights along a wall, with an illuminated light representing a call waiting. The calls move from the queue to the receptionist and leave when the call is terminated. This diagram adds little to an understanding of this simple

Figure 11.5   Process Charts—Telephone Authorization Model

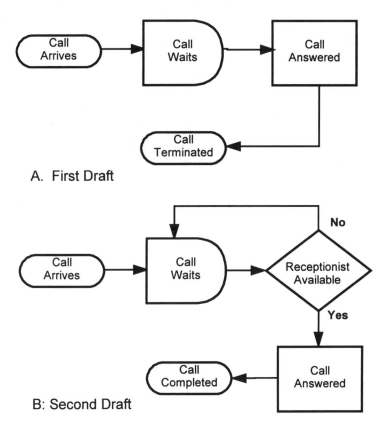

A. First Draft

B: Second Draft

process, but it is an essential element in modeling with programs such as MedModel.

The simulation model is formulated in MedModel with the options of the "Build" menu shown in Exhibit 11.10. The build options used in the PPO authorization process are the following:

Build Options	Activity	Source of Information
Background Graphics	Prepare Layout	Process Diagram
Locations	Identify Locations	Process Diagram
Path Networks	Identify Flow	Process Diagram
Processing	Describe Process	Process Chart
Arrivals	Schedule Calls	Historical Data

As indicated in Exhibit 11.10, the "Background graphics" option is used to enter the layout of the area. A layout can be drawn with the drawing capabilities of MedModel or can be scanned into a file from an engineering or architectural drawing and imported into the simulation program. A layout can also be constructed with another graphics program and imported into MedModel. In this example, the layout, consisting of a telephone receptionist sitting at a computer, is drawn in Microsoft's PowerPoint program and imported into MedModel. The graphics capability of MedModel was used to add the title for the model and for the names of the variables used in the model and displayed on the layout.

The "Locations" and the "Path Networks" options are used to model the flow diagram of Exhibit 11.10. The locations are identified by clicking the mouse button at the appropriate locations on the layout

Figure 11.6 Process Diagram—Telephone Authorization Model

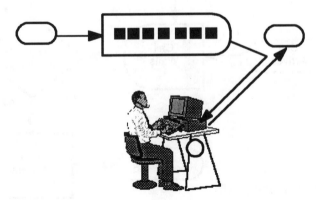

Exhibit 11.10 Incorporating Layout and Process Diagram into the Simulation Model

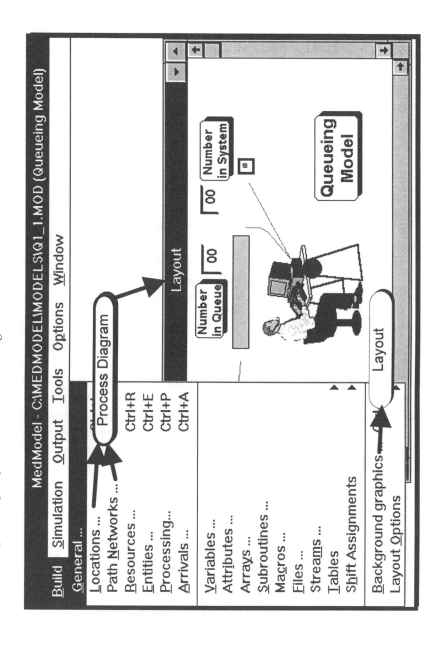

and typing a unique name for each location. In this example, the four locations are **entrance, queue, receptionist,** and **departure**.

The lines on the flow diagram are called "paths" in this simulation program, and they are created by clicking the mouse on the beginning point and then the ending point of each path. In this example, the three paths are between the entrance and the queue, between the queue and the receptionist, and between the receptionist and departure.

As illustrated in the upper segment of Exhibit 11.11, the "Processing" option of the "Build" menu is used to specify the steps of the "Process Chart." The "Operation" segment of the "Process" window shows the two operations for a call at the receptionist location. First, the operation "DEC (Queue—counter)" causes a variable named Queue—counter to be decremented. The operation "E(2,5)" obtains a random number using the random number generator 5 and uses that number to select randomly a number for an exponential distribution with a mean of 2. The resultant value is the number of minutes required to process the call.

As shown in the lower segment of Exhibit 11.11, the "Arrivals" option is used to establish the frequency and number of calls. The location for the call to enter the system is selected by clicking on the "Location" bar and selecting the name of the location from the list of established locations. The column for "First Time" is the number of minutes between starting and the arrival of the first call, in this example, 0 minutes. Thereafter, each arrival caused the next arrival to be scheduled until 100 calls have been processed. The value in the "Frequency" column determines the time between arrivals. The value can be typed directly or can be selected by clicking the mouse button through a number of windows and entering the parameter or parameters for the selected distribution. As shown in the lower segment of Exhibit 11.11, MedModel provides 100 random number generators (streams).

Solving the case problem As shown in Exhibit 11.12, simulation is started by selecting the "Run" option of the "Simulation" menu. As the simulation progresses, the icon for a call moves along the path of the layout. If the receptionist is busy, the icon will remain in the area identified as the queue until the receptionist is available. The icons move from the queue to the receptionist, are delayed for the time required to complete the call, and then move to the departure location.

As with the simulation programs @RISK and *QuickQuant*, MedModel provides the opportunity to run a simulation for a specific number of calls. A simulation can be canceled at any time during the process.

Exhibit 11.11 Incorporating the Process Chart and Arrival Data into the Simulation Model

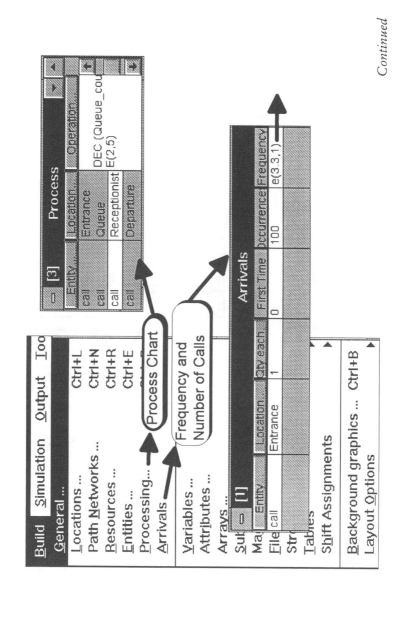

Continued

Exhibit 11.11 Continued

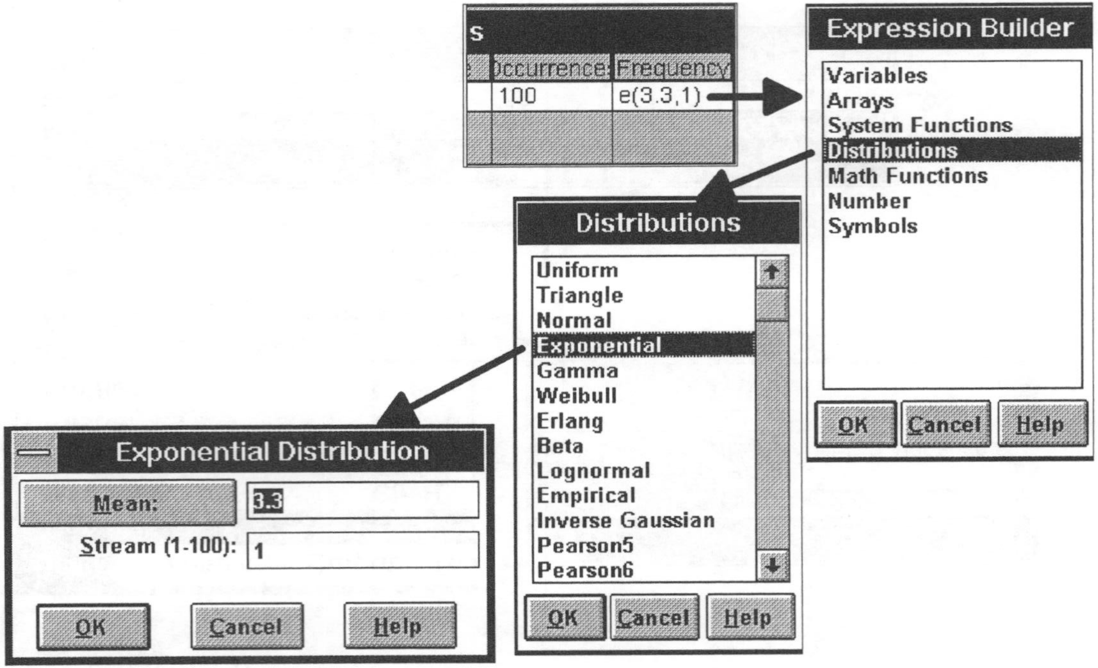

Exhibit 11.12 Simulation Menu and Replication Options

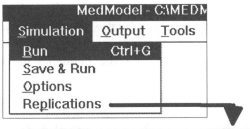

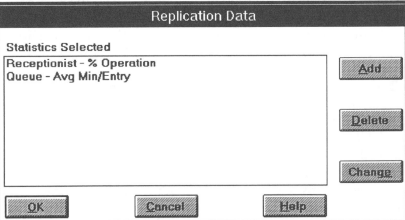

The "Replications" option of the "Simulation" menu of Exhibit 11.12 can be used to capture statistics for each simulation. One statistic of interest in simulating this process with *QuickQuant*, the average number of calls in the queue during each simulation, is included in the MedModel simulation.

Model variations   The simulation model described reflects the basic process of the queueing model of Chapter 7 and of the simulation model in *QuickQuant* in the previous section. Professional queueing simulation programs provide the capability to produce realistic models. In this simple model, only a few variations seem reasonable without more information. Examples of variations that might be introduced to make this model more realistic include the following:

- Have the receptionist work eight-hour days.
- Add a second receptionist either full-time or part-time.
- Have the receptionist take time for lunch and for breaks during the day.

If there is no interest in the utilization of each receptionist and both receptionists work for the entire period simulated, adding a second receptionist full-time can be accomplished by incrementing the capacity of the location Receptionist. Simulating the model with this capacity will produce estimates of the values produced with the equations of Chapter 7, similar to the results of simulating the queueing model with *QuickQuant*.

A second receptionist to assist the first can be added by creating a second location, Receptionist2, and changing the path as illustrated in Exhibit 11.13. Logic for the routing from the Queue is to either Receptionist or Receptionist2, depending which has the longest unoccupied time. If the two receptionists are on duty for the entire simulation, this process change will produce results similar to those of increasing the capacity of location Receptionist.

The two receptionists can be scheduled for different times during the hours of 8 to 5. As shown in the shift editor in Exhibit 11.14, the primary receptionist works from 8 to 12 with a 30-minute break. After a 1-hour lunch hour, the receptionist works from 1 to 5 with a second 30-minute break. The part-time receptionist works from 10 to 3:30 with two 30-minute breaks.

Further analysis of the data could indicate additional characteristics of the system that should be included in the model for additional realism. If supported by the data, the following variations could be introduced into the model:

- Have the arrival rates of calls differ by time of day.
- Have the arrival rates of calls differ by day of week.
- Have the telephone system and the computer subject to random breakdowns.

Application of the results   Professional queueing simulation programs routinely produce a large number of operating statistics. In addition, these programs provide for the collection of almost any statistic of interest to the analyst. Examples of some standard outputs of MedModel are provided in Exhibits 11.15, 11.16, and 11.17.

The basic report shown in Exhibit 11.15 is the result of the last of 20 simulations of 200 calls each, which simulated 10 hours and 33.01 minutes. The basic report includes statistics about the four locations of the model. In the telephone authorization model, the location named Queue has the capacity for 20 telephone calls. During this simulation, the average time a call was in the queue was 3.16 minutes, and the maximum number of calls waiting in the queue was 7.

The content history of the queue during one simulation of 200 calls is shown in Exhibit 11.16. The queue was empty (0 content) approxi-

Exhibit 11.13 Two Receptionists in Telephone Authorization Model

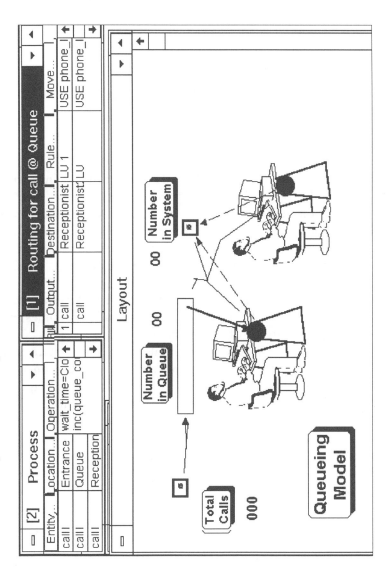

Exhibit 11.14   Work Schedules for Telephone Authorization Model

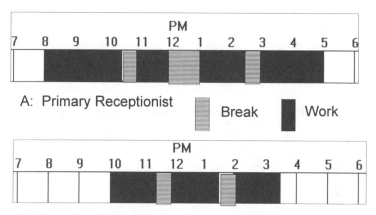

A: Primary Receptionist   ▦ Break   ■ Work

B: Part-time Receptionist

mately 60 percent of the time. About 12 percent of the time, the queue had only 1 call; about 10 percent of the time, the queue had 2 calls.

Information about the average number of minutes in the queue during 20 replications of a simulation is presented in Exhibit 11.17. The values are presented in three segments. The statistics for the average of the 20 replications show that the mean of the daily means was 3.28987. The 90 percent confidence interval about the mean is 2.79065–3.7891. The values for the means of the replications in rank order are shown in the lower segment of the figure. This wide range of values indicates the need for replications of the simulation.

Normally, when a process is simulated, a steady-state value for a statistic such as the average number of calls in the queue is not known. In this example, the steady-state value of the average number of calls in the queue was developed with the equations in Chapter 7 and was known to be 3. The average for one simulation was 1.83495. If the analyst had not continued with additional simulations, the results would have been very misleading. The same can be said for the value of the other extreme, 7.3517. If the analyst had terminated the process with that single simulation, the results would have been misleading. The overall results of the simulation indicate that a best estimate for the average time in the queue is 3.29 minutes, and 90 percent of the time, the true value is included in the interval 2.79–3.79.

Clinic Model with MedModel

This hypothetical model represents a clinic located in a hospital and staffed with one nurse and one doctor. Patients for the clinic come

Exhibit 11.15 Basic Simulation Report

```
Replication     :   20 of 20
Warmup Time     :    0 Hours    0.00 Minutes
Simulation Time:    10 Hours   33.01 Minutes
```

SINGLE CAPACITY LOCATIONS

Name	Scheduled Hours	Total Entries	Final contents	Avg Minutes Per Entry	Std Dev	Avg Opn Minutes Per Entry	% Operation
Entrance	10	200	0	0.00	0.00	0.00	0.00
Receptionist	10	200	0	2.10	2.17	2.10	66.42
Departure	10	200	0	0.00	0.00	0.00	0.00

MULTICAPACITY LOCATIONS

Name	Scheduled Hours	Capacity	Total Entries	Avg Minutes Per Entry	Avg Contents	Std Dev	Max Contents
Queue	10	20	200	3.16	1.00	1.64	7

Exhibit 11.16   Distribution of Queue Levels

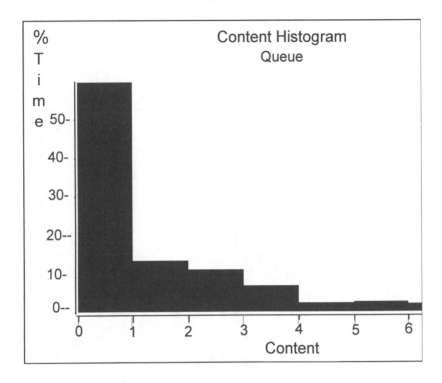

from different units within the hospital and from physicians in a professional office building owned by the health system. Patients are received at the clinic between the hours of 8:00 a.m. to 2:00 p.m. so the clinic can close by 4:30 p.m. without incurring overtime. Doctors referring patients are complaining about not being able to send patients after 2:00 p.m. The doctor at the clinic is complaining about the workload and about working overtime. He wants a second doctor employed at the clinic at least from the hours of noon until 4:00 p.m. He also wants patients to be accepted up until 3:00 p.m. With the second doctor to relieve him, he can take a full lunch hour and return to work until 5:00 p.m. The hospital administrator has just returned from a national meeting where she attended a presentation on queueing model simulation. She has asked the hospital management engineering staff to investigate the proposed process changes using simulation.

Model formulation   The process for formulating this model is the same as that for formulating the telephone authorization model. The value of process charts and process diagrams can be seen by examining the

Exhibit 11.17 Results of 20 Replications of 200 Iterations Each

```
MULTIPLE REPLICATION SUMMARY

Statistics for:
                         Reps     Mean      Median    Std Dev   Std Err
                         ----     ----      ------    -------   -------
Queue - Avg Min/Entry     20    3.28987    3.03105   1.29128   0.288738

Confidence Intervals for:  90%               95%                 99%
                         -----             -----               -----
Queue - Avg Min/Entry  2.79065 - 3.7891  2.68564 - 3.89411  2.46432 - 4.11

Data for:
                       Sorted Data
                       -----------
Queue - Avg Min/Entry
                       1.83495  1.96565  2.12035  2.31725  2.3393   2
                       2.4494   2.615    2.67875  2.90465  3.15745  3
                       3.43075  3.8058   3.81465  3.85825  4.03725  4.
                       4.7489   7.3517
```

process chart depicting the steps in the process in Figure 11.7. The steps in this chart are keyed by numbers to the locations in the process diagram in Figure 11.8. The diagrams of the flow of the doctor and of the nurse have been drawn to scale on transparencies so they can be placed on the layout with the patient flow as desired.

After collecting data about the process, the analyst collects data about the time to provide service to the patient at each step. The nurse registers the patient at Step 3 and prepares the patient for the doctor in Step 5. A normal distribution with a mean of 8 minutes and a standard deviation of 1 minute fits the data from the registration step. The time to prepare the patient for the examination is normally distributed, with a mean of 5 minutes and a standard deviation of 1 minute.

The doctor examines the patient in Step 7 and reviews the results with the patient in his office in Step 8. In examining the data, the analyst finds there are two different groups of patients in regard to the time required for the examination. Patients under 65 years of age require less time than patients 65 and older. The exponential distribution with a mean of 18 minutes and a standard deviation of 3 minutes fits the time to examine geriatric patients. The normal distribution with a mean of 13 minutes and a standard deviation of 3 minutes fits the time to examine other patients. The time to review the results with a patient from either group is normally distributed with a mean of 18 minutes and a standard deviation of 5 minutes. Data are collected about

Figure 11.7   Process Chart: Clinic Model

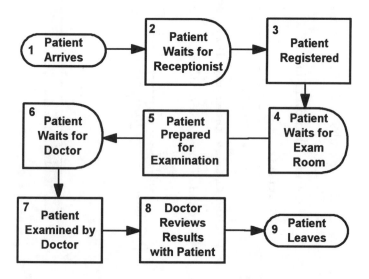

Figure 11.8 Process Diagram: Clinic Model

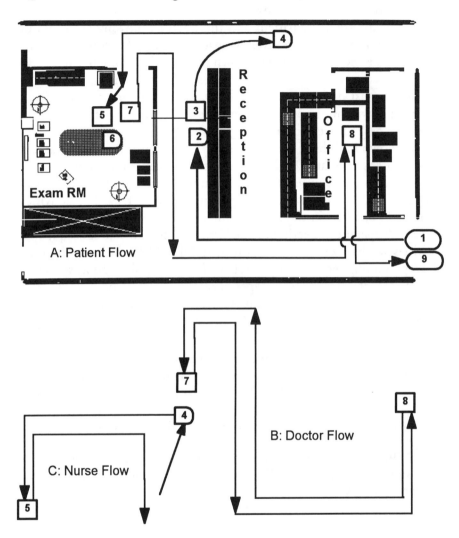

patient arrival times and are converted to minutes between arrivals. The exponential distribution with a mean of 35 minutes between arrivals fits the sample data.

Additional data collected at the time of arrival include the age of the patient. Those under 65 years of age are classified as Type 2 patients and those 65 and over are classified as Type 1 patients. Analysis of these data indicate that 60 percent of the patients are Type 1, and the remaining 40 percent are Type 2. No apparent pattern of arrival by type was discernible.

The layout and the flow of the process diagram in Figure 11.8 are entered into the model as shown in Exhibit 11.18. In this model, only two paths are used, the patient and the doctor following segments of the same path, and the nurse following a separate path. Icons representing the nurse and the doctor are shown in Exhibit 11.18. Icons have also been selected to represent the patient standing (walking and waiting at the receptionist desk), sitting (in the waiting room and in the office), and lying down (on the examination table). The standing icon will move along the paths indicated on the layout as the simulation progresses.

As shown in Exhibit 11.19, the model requires only seven locations because Steps 5, 6, and 7 take place in the examination room.

The steps of the process chart are entered through the "Processing" option of the "Build" menu as shown in Exhibit 11.19. The activities of Steps 5, 6, and 7 in the Exam_rm (examination room) are entered into the "Operation" section of the "Process" menu. The six sequential activities in the Exam_rm, shown in Exhibit 11.19, indicate the type of programming required in professional queueing simulation software. The statements can either be typed directly or can be built with statement builders, a feature that reduces typing and typing errors.

- "GRAPHIC 3." The icon is changed to a patient lying down on the examining table.
- "n(5,1,3)." The nurse prepares the patient. The time required is normally distributed with a mean of 5 and standard deviation of 1. Random number stream 3 is used to generate the time for this step.
- "free nurse." The nurse is released to return to the registration desk.
- "TYPE=type_distribution(4)." A type category of 1 or 2 is assigned to the patient. Random number stream 4 is used to generate this value.
- "GET DOCTOR." The patient waits for the doctor.
- "if TYPE=2 then N(13,3,2) else N(18,3,2)." If the patient is Type 2, the time for the examination is randomly selected from a normal distribution with a mean of 13 and a standard deviation of 3, using the random number stream 2. If the patient is Type 1, the time for the examination is randomly selected from a normal distribution with a mean of 18 and a standard deviation of 3, using the random number stream 2.

It is assumed the type of patient is distributed randomly throughout arrivals. As shown in Exhibit 11.20, a discrete probability table is entered in the model to assign patient type randomly in the Exam_rm activities. This assignment could have been made when the patient first arrived.

Exhibit 11.18 Incorporating Layout and Process Diagram into the Clinic Simulation Model

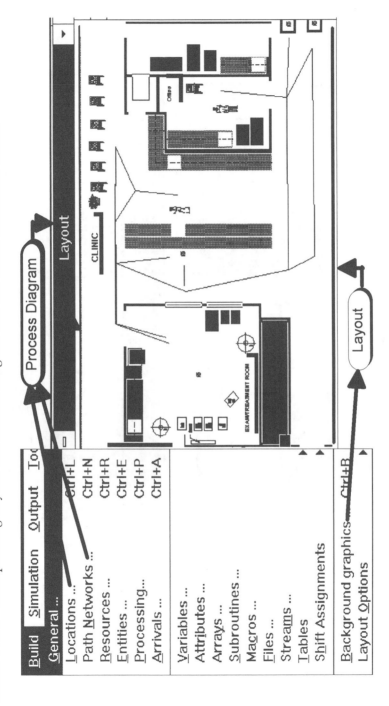

Exhibit 11.19 Identifying Clinic Locations and Incorporating Process Chart Steps into the Clinic Simulation Model

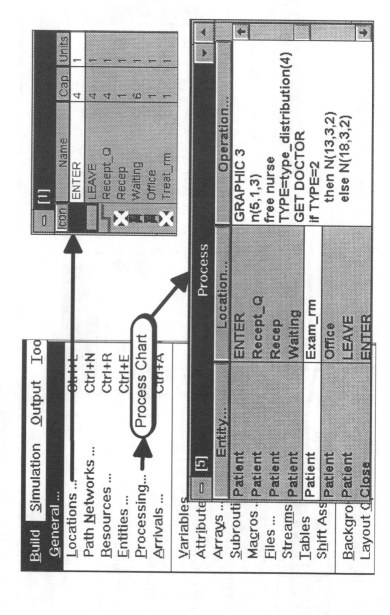

Exhibit 11.20 Identifying Distribution for Type of Patient

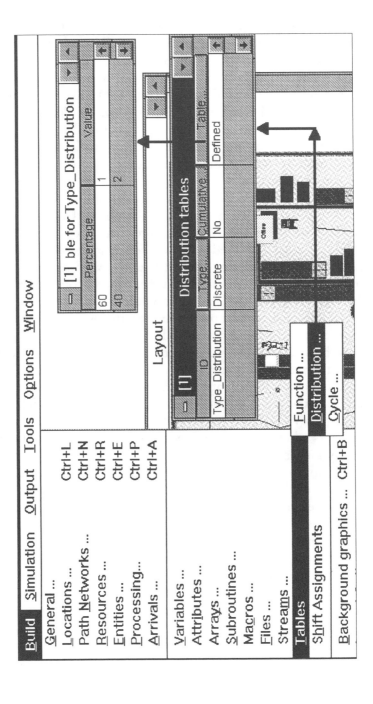

In this model, different random number streams have been selected for different activities. In Exhibit 11.19, random number stream 3 is used for nursing activities, stream 2 is used for doctor activities, and stream 4 is used for assigning patient type. Random number stream 1 is dedicated to patient arrival times.

The clinic receives patients between the hours of 8:00 a.m. and 2:00 p.m. The nurse in the clinic works from 8:00 a.m.–4:30 p.m., or later if required. She takes breaks as time is available during the day and has 30 minutes for lunch at noon. The doctor also works from 8:00 a.m.–4:30 p.m., or as required to examine all patients. He takes a 15-minute break in the morning and in the afternoon and has 30 minutes for lunch at 12:30 p.m.

Although professional queueing simulation programs simplify the task of creating models as shown in Exhibits 11.19 and 11.20, it is incumbent on the analyst to make sure that, at each step, the model reflects the actual or desired activities. For example, in this clinic model, the doctor and nurse stay each day until every patient admitted is examined. This policy creates overtime, which is one of the problems to be examined. The model should reflect this policy.

In MedModel, when a patient arrives, the program first determines if another arrival should be scheduled, then executes any logic associated with the arrival. An iteration of a simulation can be programmed to stop after running for a specific number of hours or after processing a specific number of patients. Neither of these methods for ending the day reflect the policy being simulated in the clinic model. The clinic has the policy that patients are not admitted after 2:00 p.m. and that all patients admitted are examined. The number of patients processed each day ranges between 3 and 17.

One approach to modeling this policy is to schedule 20 patients, more than could possibly be needed in one day. The logic in Exhibit 11.21 will examine the scheduled time of arrival of the next two patients. If the second patient would arrive after 2:00 p.m. (360 minutes after opening), the time between arrivals for that patient and all remaining patients to arrive is set to 0 by setting the variables named "next" and "following" to 0. After the next patient is admitted, the variable "Quantity" is set equal to 0, which means that no more patients will be admitted. Through this logic, the program removes all the patients not already admitted without advancing the clock. The program then continues until all the patients in the clinic are examined.

The variables "next" and "following" used in the logic of the arrivals are created with the initial values as shown in Exhibit 11.21. Also in Exhibit 11.21, the values "E(35,1)" mean a number randomly selected

Exhibit 11.21 Programming Arrivals in the Clinic Model

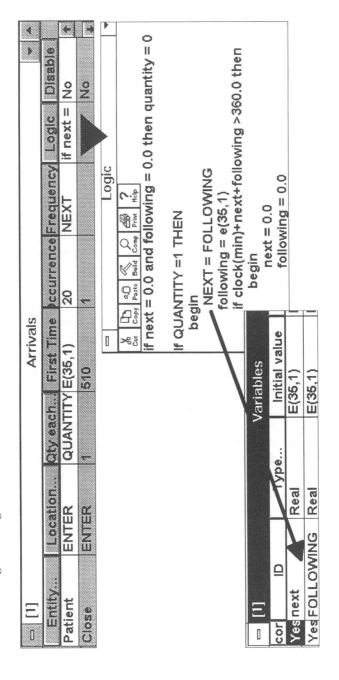

from an exponential distribution with a mean of 35 minutes, using random number stream 1.

Solving the case problem   One of the major differences between this model and that of the telephone authorization model is the information conveyed by animation. Animation brings a dynamic and dramatic quality to the analysis. During simulation, icons representing patients arrive at the entrance and move along the paths to the next activity. The nurse and the doctor also move along paths to their next activity. The number of figures in each queue fluctuates, growing and shrinking as the simulation progresses.

A computer running a simulation model can be connected to an LCD panel on an overhead projector so groups can analyze the process. The simulation time can be compressed so the patients and staff fly through the process and the queues grow and collapse dramatically. In contrast, the simulation can be slowed or even halted and advanced one step at a time, providing the opportunity for participants to examine and to question each step of the process. If a picture is worth a thousand words, then an animated picture must be worth 100,000 words. Participants can become involved in the animated process, and with their participation, the credibility of the simulation can be greatly enhanced. An instance of a simulation is shown in Exhibit 11.22. A patient has just arrived and is being registered by the nurse. Three patients are in the waiting room. One patient is in the examination room. The doctor is consulting with a patient in the office.

Segments of the routine output readily available from professional queueing simulation programs are presented in Exhibits 11.23 and 11.24. The statistics in Exhibit 11.23 reflect the last day of a simulation of 60 days. On this day, there were 47.94 minutes of overtime and ten patients were seen in the clinic. The doctor was "in use" 69.91 percent of the time, and the nurse was "in use" 25.00 percent of the time. Patients spent an average of 73.08 minutes in the waiting room.

Of more interest are the multiple replication summary statistics for the 60 days simulated presented in Exhibit 11.24. These statistics support the concerns of the staff working in the clinic. The overtime in minutes by day of simulation is shown in the lower segment of Exhibit 11.24. The mean of overtime in the upper segment of Exhibit 11.24 is computed over the 60 days of simulation, not the 21 days in which overtime occurred. Including only days with overtime, the average overtime is almost 70 minutes.

Although the content of the waiting room over time shown in Exhibit 11.25 is only for one day of the simulation, those data do

Exhibit 11.22 An Instance during the Clinic Simulation

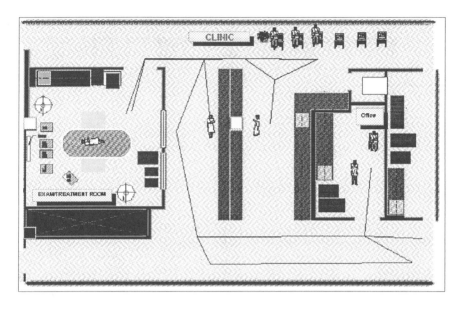

suggest a queue of patients beginning around noon. This concept is also supported by the fact that the doctor working in the clinic takes 30 minutes for lunch at noon. The queue decreases steadily after the doors are closed at 2:00 p.m. (6 hours into the simulation).

Given the model and the supporting data, the analyst then revises the clinic model as shown in Exhibit 11.26. An additional location is established as Office1 beside the Examination room and the full-time doctor, Doctor1, is located here to reduce travel. The part-time doctor is located in the original office. It is not necessary to redraw the layout to test the efficacy of a second doctor in the clinic.

In the revised model, Doctor1 works from 8:00 a.m. to noon with a 15-minute break. After an hour for lunch, Doctor1 returns to work until 5:00 p.m., or longer if necessary. A second doctor, Doctor2, comes to work at noon and works until 4:00 p.m., with a 15-minute break at 2:00 p.m. In this model, patients are accepted up until 3:00 p.m. The model assumes that the arrival rate during this extra hour will be the same as earlier in the day.

Results of simulation with the revised clinic model are presented in Exhibits 11.27 and 11.28. These results indicate that in the revised clinic operation, overtime would be reduced, patient throughput would increase, and patient time in the waiting room would be reduced.

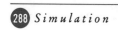

Exhibit 11.23 Segment of the Output from One Simulated Day:
Clinic

```
┌──────────────────────────────────────────────────────────────┐
│ ─                              D:\SIMULATE\CLINIC.RES          │
├──────────────────────────────────────────────────────────────┤
│ MedModel 1.11 Results for D:\SIMULATE\CLINIC.MOD [Clinic       │
│                                                                │
│ Date: Sep/05/1994    Time: 02:13:09 PM                         │
│                                                                │
│ Replication      :    60 of 60                                 │
│ Warmup Time      :     0 Hours    0.00 Minutes                 │
│ Simulation Time:       8 Hours   47.94 Minutes                 │
```

SINGLE CAPACITY LOCATIONS

Name	Scheduled Hours	Total Entries	Final contents	Avg Minutes Per Entry	Std Dev	Avg Minu Per
Recep	8	10	0	8.07	1.24	
Office	8	10	0	17.47	4.56	
Exam_rm	8	10	0	35.64	14.40	

MULTICAPACITY LOCATIONS

Name	Scheduled Hours	Capacity	Total Entries	Avg Minutes Per Entry	Avg Contents
Recept_Q	8	4	10	1.29	0.02
Waiting	8	6	10	73.08	1.38

RESOURCES

Name	Units	Scheduled Hours	Total Times Used	Avg Minutes Per Use	Avg Travel To Use	% In Use
Doctor	1	8	10	34.81	0.85	69.91
Nurse	1	8	20	6.60	0.09	25.00

The cost of these benefits is an additional high-cost employee
for four hours each day. The analyst and the quality improvement
team should consider improving other process variations such as those
suggested in the following section.

Exhibit 11.24 Segment of the Output of Simulation for 60 Days: Clinic

Continued

D:\SIMULATE\CLINIC.MRS

MULTIPLE REPLICATION SUMMARY

Statistics for:

	Reps	Mean	Median	Std Dev
Doctor - % In Use	60	67.3111	68.5514	14.2
Nurse - % In Use	60	24.5225	25.1711	5.45864
Patient - Total Exits	60	9.85	10	2.69227
Waiting - Avg Min/Entry	60	52.979	48.0608	38.3921
overtime - Current Value	60	23.0852	0	44.687

Confidence Intervals for:

	90%	95%	99%
Doctor - % In Use	64.1926 - 70.4296	63.556 - 71.0662	62.245
Nurse - % In Use	23.3237 - 25.7213	23.079 - 25.966	22.575
Patient - Total Exits	9.25874 - 10.4413	9.13804 - 10.562	8.8896
Waiting - Avg Min/Entry	44.5475 - 61.4104	42.8264 - 63.1315	39.283
overtime - Current Value	13.2713 - 32.899	11.2679 - 34.9024	7.1445

Data for: Sorted Data

Doctor - % In Use				
30.0479	39.8771	39.9021	45.7875	46.0
50.0604	51.3	51.8583	53.2271	53.3
54.1437	54.5271	55.2437	57.2437	5
60.112	60.5521	60.6187	61.7188	62.8
64.1792	65.9208	66.1292	66.6928	67.

Exhibit 11.24 Continued

D:\SIMULATE\CLINIC.MRR

Multiple Replication Data (by replication)

overtime - Current Value

0	0	120.63	0	0
0	0	0	0	0
98.14	0	0	6.46	0
48.57	0	55.46	0	22.62
0	0	74.87	0	50.42
124.86	80.48	21.12	0	0
0	0	0	0	17.88
0	18.63	58.87	0	0
216.63	0	25.62	74.45	137.85
0.01	0	0	0	0
2.37	0	0	111.23	0
0	0	0	0	17.94

Exhibit 11.25 Number of Patients in Waiting Room during One Simulated Day

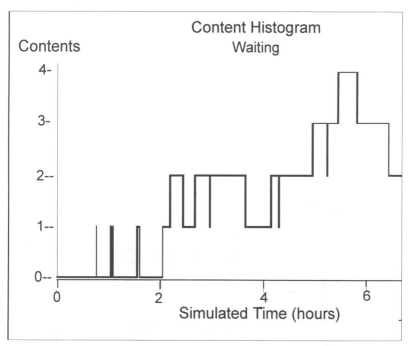

Model variations Although the focus of this chapter is on the use of simulation models for solving problems, there is little to be gained from simulating and improving unnecessary activities. As the data are collected and the models are constructed, especially the process charts and process diagrams, the analyst and the CQI committee should maintain a questioning attitude toward each step.

Early in the project, the analyst should involve the primary participants. As each process step is validated, the analyst should lead the participants through the same questioning approach using in developing the process charts and process diagrams in a typical CQI analysis. Questions to be asked of each step include the following:

- Can this step be eliminated?
- Can this step be simplified?
- Can this step be combined with another step?
- Can the work at this step be done better or cheaper by someone else?

Exhibit 11.26 Revised Clinic Model with an Additional Doctor

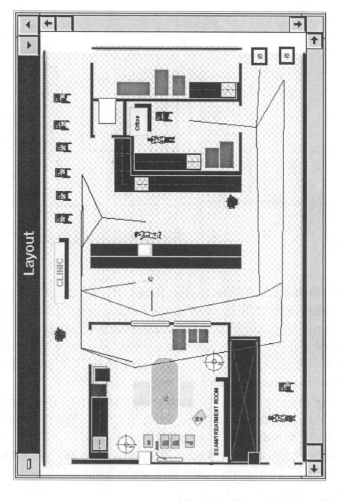

Exhibit 11.27 Segment of the Output from One Simulated Day: Revised Clinic Model

```
┌──┬─────────────────────────────────────────────────────┐
│ ─│              D:\SIMULATE\CLIN_REV.RES                │
├──┴─────────────────────────────────────────────────────┤
│ MedModel 1.11 Results for D:\SIMULATE\CLIN_REV.MOD [Clini│
│                                                         │
│ Date: Sep/05/1994    Time: 03:11:04 PM                  │
│                                                         │
│ Replication    :    60 of 60                            │
│ Warmup Time     :     0 Hours    0.00 Minutes           │
│ Simulation Time:     9 Hours    0.00 Minutes            │
│                                                         │
│                                                         │
│ SINGLE CAPACITY LOCATIONS                               │
```

SINGLE CAPACITY LOCATIONS

Name	Sche-duled Hours	Total Entries	Final con-tents	Avg Minutes Per Entry	Std Dev	Avg Minu Per
Recep	9	6	0	8.08	0.93	
Office2	9	3	0	22.54	4.91	
Exam_rm	9	6	0	29.63	13.99	
Office1	9	3	0	20.35	6.45	

MULTICAPACITY LOCATIONS

Name	Sche-duled Hours	Capa-city	Total Entries	Avg Minutes Per Entry	Avg Contents
Recept_Q	9	4	6	1.16	0.01
Waiting	9	4	6	6.03	0.07

RESOURCES

Name	Units	Sche-duled Hours	Total Times Used	Avg Minutes Per Use	Avg Travel To Use	% In Use
Doctor2	1	4	3	36.09	0.24	45.11
Doctor1	1	8	3	42.19	0.08	26.37

This questioning attitude can be intensified as the animation feature of professional queueing simulation programs is used to involve participants. Animation can create a new awareness of the process and can stimulate more questions than would be generated by examining a static process chart.

Another way to use animation to demonstrate characteristics of the

Exhibit 11.28 Segment of the Output of 60 Simulated Days: Revised Clinic Model

```
                           D:\SIMULATE\CLIN_REV.MRS

MULTIPLE REPLICATION SUMMARY

Statistics for:           Reps        Mean       Median      Std Dev
------------------------------------------------------------------------
Doctor1 - % In Use          60      51.0751        50.8      15.2973
Doctor2 - % In Use          60      62.9344     66.4792      17.8886
Nurse   - % In Use          60      28.6705      29.812      7.75746
OverTime - Current Value    60       6.1555           0      23.0522
Patient - Total Exits       60        11.8          12       3.38391
Waiting - Avg Min/Entry     60      32.3136     23.3471      25.5801


Confidence Intervals for:      90%                  95%               99%
------------------------------------------------------------------------
Doctor1 - % In Use     47.7156 - 54.4345    47.0298 - 55.1203     45.618
Doctor2 - % In Use     59.0058 - 66.863     58.2039 - 67.665      56.553
Nurse   - % In Use     26.9668 - 30.3741    26.619  - 30.7219     25.903
OverTime - Current Value 1.09292 - 11.2181   0.0594712 - 12.2515  -2.067
Patient - Total Exits  11.0568 - 12.5432    10.9051 - 12.6949     10.592
Waiting - Avg Min/Entry 26.6959 - 37.9313   25.5491 - 39.0781     23.188


Data for:              Sorted Data
------------------------------------------------------------------------
Doctor1 - % In Use      17.0979      25.7917     26.3708    26.8646    27.7
                        30.2229      31.9021     32.6521    33.3458    33.7
                        35.5187      38.35       38.4375    39.05      40.1
                        42.4937      43.0063     43.4458    44.1583    45.
```

D:\SIMULATE\CLIN_REV.MRR

Multiple Replication Data (by replication)

OverTime - Current Value

0	0	0	0	0	0
0	0	0	0	0	0
0	0	0	34.26	0	0
0	0	0	0	0	0
0	0	0	0	0	0
2.34	0	0	35.16	0	0
0	0	0	0	0	0
0	0	0	132.73	0	0
0	0	0	0	0	0
0	0	0	84.35	80.49	0
0	0	0	0	0	0

process is to increase the time scale so the icons move slowly across the screen. One of the facets of the clinic model is the wide variation in the time between arrivals. This aspect can be emphasized by having the clock run very slowly when the doctor and the nurse have nothing to do. Although the doctor and the nurse do experience overtime, they also have many hours when they have nothing to do, especially in the revised clinic model. Increasing the time scale of the revised clinic model after 3:00 p.m. can cause the participants to grow restless waiting for something to occur on the screen. This should stimulate them to ask for data about the amount of idle time in this model.

To answer such questions, the model can be revised to subtract the closing time from the time of the day the last patient left the clinic. On days when there was overtime, the result would be positive and equal to the amount of overtime. On days when there was no overtime, the result would be 0 or negative.

These data for the 60-day simulation period are shown in Exhibit 11.29. The last patient leaves the clinic, on the average, around one hour before closing time in the revised process. This information should lead to simulations with the part-time doctor for only three hours, two hours, and even one hour each day. Another approach would be to have the departure of the part-time doctor be a function of the number of patients in the waiting room. The model could examine the number of patients in the waiting room at 1:00, 2:00, and 3:00 p.m. Whenever there is one patient or no patients in the waiting room, the part-time doctor leaves the clinic.

Running the model slowly also can produce an awareness of the length of time between arrivals and the randomness of arrivals. Participants might want to have data about the referral source for each patient. A questioning attitude about how patients are referred can lead to ways to reduce the amount of randomness. Some questions that might be asked of referred patients include the following:

- Can the randomness of arrivals be reduced by scheduling some of the patients the prior day?
- Can patients be scheduled between a narrower range of hours (e.g., 10:00 a.m.–3:00 p.m.)?
- Can the clinic be called to schedule patients?

Application of the results The process changes suggested by answers to these and other questions can be incorporated into the model and examined. These results can lead to further questions and suggestions that can be analyzed. This process can continue until the committee becomes convinced that an optimum solution has been reached.

Exhibit 11.29 Operating Statistics after the Last Patient on the Sixtieth Day: Revised Clinic Model

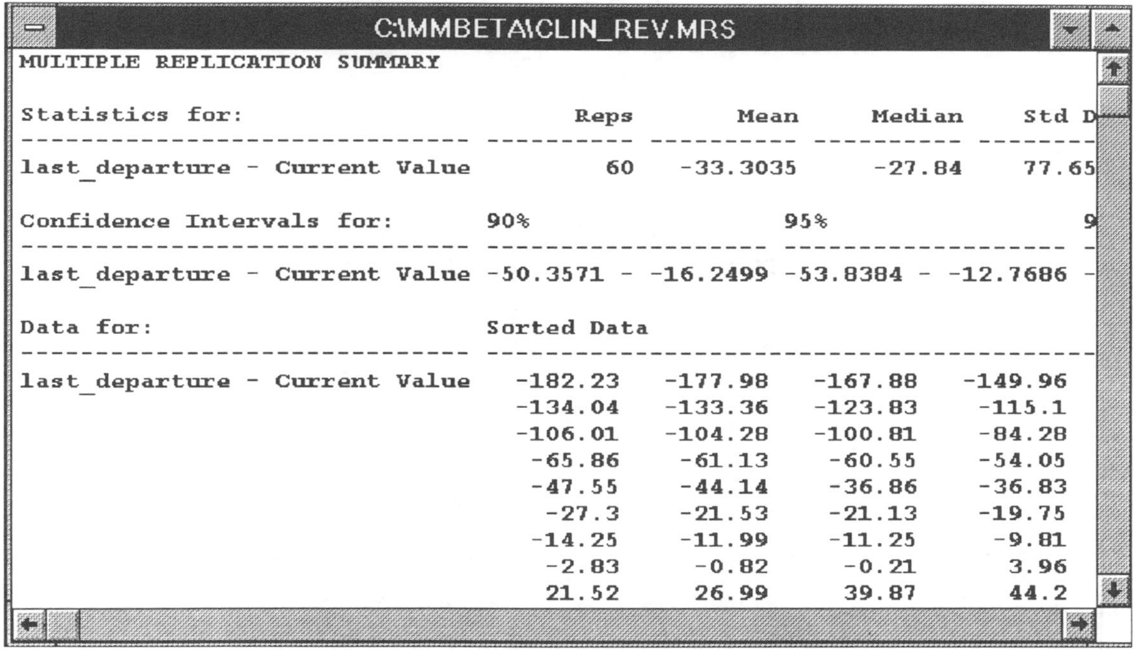

C:\MMBETA\CLIN_REV.MRS

MULTIPLE REPLICATION SUMMARY

Statistics for:

	Reps	Mean	Median	Std D
last_departure - Current Value	60	-33.3035	-27.84	77.65

Confidence Intervals for:

	90%	95%	9
last_departure - Current Value	-50.3571 - -16.2499	-53.8384 - -12.7686	-

Data for:

Sorted Data

last_departure - Current Value	-182.23	-177.98	-167.88	-149.96
	-134.04	-133.36	-123.83	-115.1
	-106.01	-104.28	-100.81	-84.28
	-65.86	-61.13	-60.55	-54.05
	-47.55	-44.14	-36.86	-36.83
	-27.3	-21.53	-21.13	-19.75
	-14.25	-11.99	-11.25	-9.81
	-2.83	-0.82	-0.21	3.96
	21.52	26.99	39.87	44.2

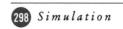

Armed with the initial model, a few of the intermediate models, and the optimum model, the committee can use a notebook computer and an LCD panel to make dramatic and effective presentations to those responsible for making the final decision.

Cases from the Literature

The previous section on case problems began with the spreadsheet simulation models and continued with queueing simulation models because of the potential for using the simplicity of basic spreadsheet models to illustrate simulation. This section reverses the order because of the chronology of development and of application.

Queueing Simulation Models

Queueing simulation programs for computers began in the early 1960s with GPSS by IBM (Greenberg 1972, 7). Beginning with the early works of Fetter and Thompson in the early 1960s, queueing simulation models have been reported in several areas of health care services. The range of applications is indicated in the following list of references:

- Nursing—Arthur and Ravindran 1981; Draeger 1992; Hancock, Martin, and Storer 1978; Hershey, Abernathy, and Baloff 1974; Zilm and Hollis 1983
- Clinic—Carlson, Hershey, and Kropp 1979; Iskander and Carter 1991; Keller and Laughman 1973; Wilt and Goddin 1989
- Laboratory—Dankbar, Shellum, and Bennett 1992; Klafehn and Connolly 1993
- Emergency—Graff and Radford 1990; Kumar and Kapur 1989; Pallin and Kittell 1992; Ritondo and Freedman 1993; Valenzuela et al. 1990; Wears and Winton 1993
- Surgery—Carter et al. 1992; Lowery 1992; Schmitz and Kwak 1972
- X-ray—Coffin et al. 1993
- Pharmacy—Mukherjee 1991

Two of these studies will be reviewed. Both these studies begin with the collection and organization of data, including the development of charts and diagrams illustrating the flow through the process.

Emergency Room (Kumar and Kapur 1989)

The emergency room (ER) at Georgetown University Hospital received an average of 71 patients a day. The manager was interested in developing an effective staff scheduling for meeting the uncertain workload patterns. Of special interest was the potential for 8-hour shifts, 12-hour shifts, and mixed 8- and 12-hour shifts.

The study began with collection of data. Flowcharts were developed to provide the analyst with a basic understanding of the process. Five levels of acuity were identified. Data were collected about the arrival date and time of 2,425 patients. The acuity level of the patients was collected by hour and day. Data were collected about the time to care for each of these patients, the particular route each took through the process, the resources each required at each step, and the ancillary services required. The current staffing schedule was identified.

The computer model was constructed, tested, and revised until the operating statistics produced by the model closely resembled those of the ER operating statistics. The model was run for 1,000 hours testing ten alternative staffing schedules. The optimal schedule was to be one in which nurse utilization was the highest, with the patient wait time and the patient queue length within acceptable ranges. The outputs of the simulations were grouped into 24-hour periods and transferred to a spreadsheet for further analysis.

A cost/benefit analysis of comparisons with the current schedule indicated that 12-hour shifts with nurses working 4-day weeks produced the optimum schedule.

Pharmacy (Mukherjee 1991)

This case involved the flow of orders into and through the 24-hour pharmacy operated by the University of Tennessee Hospital at Knoxville, Tennessee. One of the key features of this case is the different types of arrivals for service included in the model. The objective of the study was to examine the average time to process orders with different staffing schedules.

The data collection process began with flowcharts for the four major categories of orders into and through the pharmacy. The 24-hour pharmacy processed an average of 550 regular orders each day, which were received in groups arriving at the pharmacy each hour. Critical orders were received according to the exponential distribution with a average time between arrivals of 30 minutes. Telephoned or stat orders were received according to the exponential distribution with a mean that was a function of the time of day. Outdoor orders from the pharmacy serving patients and family were received according to the exponential distribution with a mean of 15 minutes during the 8 hours of the day this pharmacy was open. The model had to include a procedure for assigning priority to the critical orders and the telephone orders.

The model included information about the nature of the time required to process each order at each step, delays to obtain clarifications from doctors, delays to obtain information from literature surveys, etc. The model did not include data about breaks for employees.

The base staffing plan was 5-3-1 for 5 pharmacists on the first shift (7 a.m.–3 p.m.), 3 pharmacists on the second shift (3–11 p.m.), and 1 pharmacist on the third shift (11 p.m.–7 a.m.). After the simulation model was validated, comparisons were made to a 4-4-1 staffing schedule and a 4-3-1 schedule with a second pharmacist from 10 a.m.–6 p.m.

These changes in staffing would increase slightly the average time to process regular orders and would have no significant effect on the time to process other classes of orders.

Spreadsheet Simulation Models

Specialty programs for simulating risk analysis were in development by the mid-1980s (Morgan and Henrion 1990, 257). Their development apparently trailed very closely behind the evolution of microcomputers and of spreadsheet programs. As demonstrated in this chapter, by 1994, programs were available that took advantage of the power and the graphics capability of microcomputers.

Palisade Corporation, producers of the add-in simulation program @RISK, identified approximately 150 customers using their product in the health care industry (private correspondence, 1994). From registration cards, these customers have identified applications in health care in the following areas:

- Health risk assessment
- Financial management
- Employee benefits consulting
- Market research
- Capacity planning
- Budget projections
- Risk analysis in genetic counseling

In spite of this interest in their program, they were unable to identify literature references describing application of spreadsheet simulation modeling in health care. Uyeno, in an article in 1992, described the basic approach of simulation with spreadsheet add-in programs (Uyeno 1992, 418). Beginning with a brief review of the popularity of spreadsheet programs and the types of analyses conducted with them, Uyeno described the logic of including uncertainty into some of the analyses. After describing how risk analysis could be included with an add-in program in a net present value (NPV) project, Uyeno identified other application areas:

* Market planning
* Reliability analysis
* Simple project management
* Decision trees

Norton, in an article in 1994 focusing on new tools of managers, identified a study by Merck involving simulation (Norton 1994, 135). Although the details of the study are not included in the article, the model included thousands of formulas and incorporated Monte Carlo techniques to model uncertainty. The study reportedly helped the managers decide on an acquisition regardless of the direction of health care reform.

Simulation Software

One of the first commercially available computer simulation programs was the General Purpose System Simulator (GPSS) produced by IBM in the early 1960s to run on an IBM mainframe computer. As microcomputers have become more powerful, less expensive, and more pervasive, several companies have produced powerful programs for simulating processes. As with other programs for microcomputers, such as word processing, spreadsheets, and statistical analyses, simulation programs are becoming easier to use and much more powerful. Also, as with many of the other programs for microcomputers, simulation programs are taking advantage of the increasingly powerful graphics available on microcomputers.

A systematic approach to simulation involves several steps, including the collection and analyses of data and the development of process charts and process diagrams. The use of graphics also creates a need to capture, edit, and transfer graphical symbols. Several computer programs are available to facilitate these steps.

Each of the programs identified here include manuals and tutorials to guide users in the application. In addition, the companies provide technical assistance by telephone and through bulletin boards. Company addresses and telephone numbers are included in the list of all software in Appendix B.

Queueing Model Simulation

Most of the programs listed here take full advantage of the increasingly powerful graphics capability of microcomputers. This capability can facilitate the work of developing the model. Perhaps of even greater importance, the animation produced with these graphics can entice managers and TQM groups to become involved in the project. There is something about watching the movement of patients and staff and the ebb and flow of queues in their service areas that can capture the attention of managers.

Included with these programs are sample models that users can study and modify for their own use. Also included are options or supplemental programs for identifying theoretical distribution from sample data.

These companies maintain bulletin boards through which users can get answers to questions, obtain updates, and copy model programs. Users also access these bulletin boards and share their simulation models.

To stimulate interest in their product, these companies offer free demonstration disks. They also sell student versions of their programs at a greatly reduced rate. Generally, these student versions have the capability of the full program but restrict the size of the model.

- Arena from Systems Modeling Corp.
- GPSS/H from Wolverine Software Corporation
- MedModel from ProModel Corporation
- Micro Saint from Micro Analysis & Design
- SLAMSYSTEM from Pritsker Corporation

Spreadsheet Model Simulation

The two programs listed are add-in programs that bring simulation to spreadsheet models. These programs include a number of theoretical probability distributions (Crystal Ball, 12; @RISK, 35) that can easily be placed in the model in place of single-value variables. The programs also take advantage of the graphics of the spreadsheets to permit any of the theoretical distributions to be displayed. The output probability distributions are also displayed graphically.

Included with these programs are sample models that users can study and modify for their own use. These companies maintain bulletin boards through which users can get answers to questions, obtain updates, and copy model programs. Users also access these bulletin boards and share their simulation models.

- @RISK from Palisade Corporation
- Crystal Ball from Decisioneering, Inc.

Process Charts

Most process charts begin with penciled symbols and lines drawn on graph paper. These drafts can be quickly turned into professional charts with advanced computer graphics programs such as CorelDRAW and Arts & Letters. Listed here are several specialty charting programs that simplify the process and produce outstanding charts.

- ABC FlowCharter from Micrograx, Inc.
- Flow Charting from Patton & Patton Software Corporation
- Visio from Shapeware Corporation

Process Diagrams

Process diagrams begin with scaled drawings representing the layout of a service area such as an emergency department. Typically, the layout includes the walls, furniture, and equipment. Lines are drawn on the layout to show movement or flow through the service area. Scaled drawings can also be constructed with advanced graphics programs such as CorelDRAW and Arts & Letters and with advanced computer-aided design (CAD) programs such as AutoCAD and Design CAD. Listed here are a few specialty drafting programs that produce very acceptable diagrams for use in simulation projects.

- Floorplan Plus for Windows from ComputerEasy International, Inc.
- GammaCAD from Gamma Software
- Visio from Shapeware Corporation

Analyzing Distributions

One of the tasks in developing a simulation model is to select appropriate theoretical probability distributions for given sets of sample data. The major simulation programs include options or programs for fitting sample data and selecting appropriate distributions. This task can also be accomplished with such advanced statistical programs as SPSS and SAS. The program The Electronic Handbook of Probability (eHOP) provides a comprehensive computerized reference for 28 probability distributions. The programs listed here were developed specifically for use with simulation to facilitate the task of selecting appropriate distributions.

- eHOP from Crunch Software Corporation
- BestFit from Palisade Corporation
- UniFit from Averill M. Law & Associates

Graphics Capture

The use of graphics can enhance a queueing model simulation project by simplifying the development of the model and by attracting the attention of management and a TQM group. One problem is capturing graphics displayed in one program and putting them into another program. Listed here are two utility programs that aid the capture, edit, size, and placement of graphics. Many of the graphics in the exhibits in this chapter were captured with Grabit Pro.

- Grabit Pro from Software Excellence by Design, Inc.
- Hijaak from Inset Systems

Problems

11.1 Using the concepts of **certainty** and **uncertainty** as presented in the introduction and the section on spreadsheet models of this chapter:

Requirement: Identify the input variables in Problems 2.1 and 2.2 of Chapter 2 that are certain and those that are uncertain. How might the uncertainty be incorporated into the input variables? How might the output variable appear if uncertainty is included in the input variables?

11.2 Using the concepts of **certainty** and **uncertainty** as presented in the introduction and the section on spreadsheet models of this chapter:

Requirement: Identify the input variables in Problems 3.1 and 3.2 of Chapter 3 that are certain and those that are uncertain. How might the uncertainty be incorporated into the input variables? How might the output variable appear if uncertainty is included in the input variables?

11.3 Use *QuickQuant* to simulate Problem 7.1 of Chapter 7. Select different seed numbers as the choice for random number generation. Select 100 for the number of simulation trials. Save the output under an appropriate name.

Requirement: Compare the following output values from the simulation analysis to the corresponding values from queueing analysis for Problem 7.1.

- Mean number of customers in system
- Mean customer time spent in system
- Mean number of customers waiting
- Mean customer waiting time
- Server utilization factor

How would you explain the differences between the simulation results and the queueing results? Save the program under an appropriate name.

11.4 Use *QuickQuant* to simulate Problem 7.2 of Chapter 7. Follow the same procedure described in Problem 11.3.

Requirement: Compare the simulation results of Problem 7.2 with the results of the queueing analysis of Problem 7.2 in Chapter 7. How would you explain the differences between the simulation results and the queueing results?

11.5 Use *QuickQuant* to access the program created and saved in Problem 11.3 above. Run the program 10 times with 100 simulation trials for each run. At each run, examine only the first page of the log of the queueing simulation and store the output in a file named SIM100.TXT. Run the program 10 times with 500 simulation trials for each run. At each run, examine only the first page of the log of the queueing simulation and store the output in a file named SIM500.TXT. Using a spreadsheet program, import the mean number of customers in system into a table and compare the average value and the dispersion of the statistics for the runs of 100 simulation trials with the average value and the dispersion of the statistics for the runs with 500 simulation trials.

Requirement: Conduct the same analysis for these other statistics:
- Mean customer time spent in system
- Mean number of customers waiting
- Mean customer waiting time
- Server utilization factor

Why are replications necessary in simulation studies?

11.6 Verify the process using a second receptionist.

Requirement: Modify the second draft of the flowchart in Figure 11.5 to include a second receptionist. If one receptionist is busy and the other is idle when a call comes in, the call is routed to the idle receptionist. If both receptionists are idle when a call comes in, the call is routed to the receptionist who has been idle longest.

11.7 Use *QuickQuant* to access the program created and saved in Problem 11.3.

Requirement: Run the program one time with 500 simulation trials. At the end of the run, examine *each* page of the Log of the Queueing Simulation and store the output in a file named SIM500__2.TXT. Using a spreadsheet or statistical program, construct frequency charts and produce statistics of the distribution of the time between arrivals. Using a spreadsheet or a specialty program such as BestFit, test the fit of a theoretical exponential distribution to the sample data.

11.8 Arrange to tour a local health care clinic or hospital.

Requirement: Identify ten locations where patients may experience delays. Select one of these locations for further study and develop a flow diagram and flow process chart for this location. Identify the areas in which delays may occur. Review your charts with the supervisor of the area under study and revise the charts as necessary. Identify the data that would be required to:

a. describe those characteristics of the patients that affect the time required to provide service to the patients at the study location

b. describe the characteristics of the time between patient arrivals to the study location

c. describe the characteristics of the time to provide service to the patients

If the data are not currently being collected, describe a process for collecting sample data.

11.9 If a professional queueing simulation program is available:

Requirement: Collect sample data for the process charted in Problem 11.8 and build a simulation model of the process.

References

Arthur, J. L., and A. Ravindran. 1981. "A Multiple Nurse Scheduling Model." *AIIE Transactions* 13 (1): 55–60.

Bennett, A. C. 1974. *Methods Improvement in Hospitals*. Maspeth, NY: Preston Analearn.

Berwick, D. M., A. B. Godfrey, and J. Roessner. 1990. *Curing Health Care: New Strategies for Quality Improvement*. San Francisco: Jossey-Bass Publishers.

Carlson, R. C., J. C. Hershey, and D. H. Kropp. 1979. "Use of Optimization and Simulation Models to Analyze Outpatient Care Settings." *Decision Sciences* 10 (July): 412–33.

Carter, M., L. O'Brian-Pallas, J. Blake, L. McGillis, and S. Zhu. 1992. "Simulation, Scheduling, and Operating Rooms." *Proceedings of the 1992 Simulation in Health Care and Social Services*, 28–30.

Coffin, M., G. Lassiter, B. Killingsworth, and J. Kleckley. 1993. "A Simulation Model of an X-Ray Facility." *Proceedings of the 1993 SCS Western Simulation Multiconference on Simulation in the Health Sciences and Services*, 3–7.

Dankbar, G., J. Shellum, and K. Bennett. 1992. "The Use of Simulation to Evaluate Automated Equipment for a Clinical Processing Laboratory." *Proceedings of the 1992 Winter Simulation Conference*, 1065–70.

Draeger, M. 1992. "An Emergency Department Simulation Model Used to Evaluate Alternative Nurse Staffing and Patient Population Scenarios." *Proceedings of the 1992 Winter Simulation Conference*, 1057–64.

Gaucheer, E. J., and R. J. Coffey. 1993. *Total Quality in Healthcare: From Theory to Practice*. San Francisco: Jossey-Bass Publishers.

Graff, L., and M. Radford. 1990. "Formula for Emergency Physician Staffing." *American Journal of Emergency Medicine* 8 (3): 194–98.

Greenberg, S. 1972. *GPSS Primer*. New York: Wiley-Interscience.

Hancock, W. M., J. B. Martin, and R. H. Storer. 1978. "Simulation-Based Occupancy Recommendations for Adult Medical/Surgical Units Using Admissions Scheduling Systems." *Inquiry* 15 (1): 25–32.

Harrell, C. R., R. E. Bateman, T. J. Gogg, and J. R. A. Mott. 1992. *System Improvement Using Simulation*. 2nd Edition. Orem, UT: PROMODEL Corporation.

Hershey, J. C., W. J. Abernathy, and N. Baloff. 1974. "Comparison of Nurse Allocation Policies—A Monte Carlo Model." *Decision Sciences* 5 (January): 58–72.

Iskander, W., and D. Carter. 1991. "A Simulation Model for a Same Day Care Facility at a University Hospital." *Proceedings of the 1991 Winter Simulation Conference*, 846–53.

Keller, T. F., and D. J. Laughman. 1973. "An Application of Queueing Theory to a Congestion Problem in an Outpatient Clinic." *Decision Sciences* 4 (July): 379–94.

Klafehn, K., and M. Connolly. 1993. "The Simulation/Animation of a New Outpatient Hematology Laboratory." *Proceedings of the 1993 SCS Western Simulation Multiconference on Simulation in the Health Sciences and Services*, 12–15.

Kumar, A. P., and F. Kapur. 1989. "Discrete Simulation Application—Scheduling Staff for the Emergency Room." *Proceedings of the 1989 Winter Simulation Conference*, 1112–20.

Lowery, J. 1992. "Simulation of a Hospital's Surgical Suite and Critical Care Area." *Proceedings of the 1992 Winter Simulation Conference*, 1071–78.

Morgan, M. G., and M. Henrion. 1990. *Uncertainty: A Guide to Dealing with Uncertainty in Quantitative Risk and Policy Analysis*. Cambridge: Cambridge University Press.

Mukherjee, A. 1991. "A Simulation Model for Management of Operations in the Pharmacy of a Hospital." *Simulation* 56 (February): 91–103.

Norton, R. 1994. "A New Tool to Help Managers." *Fortune* (30 May): 135–40.

Pallin, A., and R. Kittell. 1992. "Mercy Hospital: Simulation Techniques for ER Processes." *Industrial Engineering* (February): 35–37.

Ritondo, M., and R. Freedman. 1993. "The Effects of Procedure Scheduling on Emergency Room Throughput: A Simulation Study." *Proceedings of the 1993 SCS Western Simulation Multiconference on Simulation in the Health Sciences and Services*, 8–11.

Schmitz, H. H., and N. K. Kwak. 1972. "Monte Carlo Simulation of Operating Room and Recovery Room Usage." *Operations Research* 20 (November–December): 1171–80.

Smalley, H. E., and J. R. Freeman. 1966. *Hospital Industrial Engineering: A Guide to the Improvement of Hospital Management Systems*. New York: Reinhold Publishing Corporation.

Uyeno, D. 1992. "Monte Carlo Simulation on Microcommputers." *Simulation* 58 (June): 418–22.

Valenzuela, T., J. T. Goldberg, R. T. Keeley, and E. A. Criss. 1990. "Computer Modeling of Emergency Medical System Performance." *Annals of Emergency Medicine* 19 (8): 91–94.

Wears, R., and C. Winton. 1993. "Simulation Modeling of Prehospital Trauma Care." *Proceedings of the 1993 Winter Simulation Conference*, 1216–24.

Wilt, A., and D. Goddin. 1989. "Health Care Case Study: Simulating Staffing Needs and Work Flow in an Outpatient Diagnostic Center." *Industrial Engineering* (May 21): 22–26.

Zilm, F., and R. Hollis. 1983. "An Application of Simulation Modeling to Surgical Intensive Care Bed Need Analysis." *Hospital and Health Services Administration* 28 (September–October): 82–101.

Additional Readings

Alessandra, A. J., T. E. Grasman, R. Paramesvaran, and V. Yauas. "Using Simulation in Hospital Planning." *Simulation* 30, no. 2 (1978): 62–67.

Arbitman, D. B. "A Primer on Patient Classification Systems and Their Relevance to Ambulatory Care." *Journal of Ambulatory Care Management* 9 (1986): 58–81.

Bulter, T., G. R. Reeves, K. R. Karwan, and J. R. Sweigart. "Assessing the Impact of Patient Care Policies Using Simulation Analysis." *Journal of the Society of Health Systems* 3, no. 3 (1992): 38–53.

Burr, J. T. "The Tools of Quality, Part I: Going with the Flow (Chart)." *Quality Progress* (June 1990): 64–67.

Cohen, M. A., J. C. Hershey, and E. N. Weiss. "Analysis of Capacity Decisions for Progressive Patient Care Hospital Facilities." *Health Services Research* 15 (1980): 145–60.

Davis, M. "How Long Should a Customer Wait for Service." *Decision Sciences* 22, no. 2 (1991): 421–34.

Fetter, R. B., and J. D. Thompson. "The Simulation of Hospital Systems." *Operations Research* 13 (1965): 689–711.

GOAL/QPC. *The Memory Jogger: A Pocket Guide of Tools for Continuous Improvement.* Methuen, MA: GOAL/QPC, 1988, 9–13.

Joint Commission on Accreditation of Healthcare Organizations. *A Pocket Guide to Quality Improvement Tools.* Oakbrook Terrace, IL: JCAHO, 16–17.

Keller, L., C. Harrell, and J. Leavy. "The Three Best Reasons Why Simulation Fails." *Industrial Engineering* (April 1991): 27–31.

Krall, A. "Moving Target: Clinical Cancer Center Simulation." *Proceedings of the 1994 Annual HIMSS Conference* 3 (1994): 41–53.

Levy, J. L., B. A. Watford, and V. T. Owen. "Simulation Analysis of an Outpatient Services Facility." *Journal of the Society for Health Systems* 1. no. 2 (1989): 35–49.

Lowery, J. "Multi-Hospital Validation of Critical Care Simulation Model." *Proceedings of the 1993 Winter Simulation Conference*, (1993): 1207–15.

Lowery, J., and J. Martin. "Design and Validation of a Critical Care Area." *Proceedings of the 1992 Winter Simulation Conference*, (1992): 1071–78.

Mahacheck, A. "An Introduction to Patient Flow Simulation for Health-Care Managers." *Journal of the Society for Health Systems* 3, no. 3 (1992): 73–81.

Melum, M. M., and M. K. Sinioris. *Total Quality Management: The Health Care Pioneers.* Chicago: American Hospital Publishing, Inc., 1992.

Omachonu, V. K., and J. E. Ross. *Principles of Total Quality.* Delray Beach, FL: St. Lucie, 249–50.

Scholtes, P. R. *The Team Handbook: How to Use Teams to Improve Quality.* Madison, WI: Joiner Associates, Inc., 1988: 2–18, 2–23.

Smith-Daniels, V., S. Schweikhart, and D. Smith-Daniels. "Capacity Management in Health Care Services: Review and Future Research Directions." *Decision Sciences* 19 (Fall 1988): 889–916.

Swartzman, G. "The Patient Arrival Process in Hospitals: Statistical Analysis." *Health Services Research* 5 (1970): 320–29.

Thompson, J. D., and R. B. Fettler. "Economics of Occupancy with Varying Mixes of Private and Other Patient Accommodations: A Simulation." *Health Services Research* 4 (1969): 42–52.

Whitt, W. "The Efficiency of One Long Run Versus Independent Replications in Steady-State Simulation." *Management Science* 37, no. 6 (1991): 645–65.

Whitworth, S. "From the Ground Up: Reengineering the Laundry Department." *Proceedings of the 1994 Annual HIMSS Conference.* (1994): 137–47.

APPENDIX A
Answers to Problems at End of Chapters

Answers are not included for discussion questions, graphs, and problems that do not have a single quantitative solution.

Chapter 2

2.1 Plan A—break-even at 667 tests.
Plan B—break-even at 2,174 tests.
Plan B becomes more profitable after 5,000 tests have been completed.

2.2 a. Break-even at 109 exams
b. Break-even at 150 exams
c. Price = $260

2.3 a. Break-even in year three
b. Total profits for five-year period—$153,774

2.4 a. Most optimistic: break-even at 65 home visits. Most pessimistic: break-even at 83 home visits.
b. With optimistic view, pick Option B.
With pessimistic view, pick Option A.

Chapter 3

3.1 a. Choose A (Profit = $27 million)
b. Regret for B = 30 – 26 = $4 million
c. Choose B—Maximin Value = $23 million

     d. Choose A—Maximax Value = $30 million

     e. Choose A—Exp. Profit = $25.7 million

     f. Exp. Profit with Perfect Information = $27.3 million

3.2 a. Optimist—Use minimin value: buy later.

     Pessimist—Use minimax value: buy now.

     b. Minimum Exp. Cost = $900: buy now.

     c. $p = 0.2857$

3.3 a. Choose B—Minimax value = 10

     b. Choose C—Minimum Exp. Cost = 9.5

     c. Exp. Cost with Perfect Information = 8.5

     d. Most we'd pay for the system = 1.0

3.4 a.

# Units Owned	0	No. of Units Demanded 1	2	3	4	5
0	0	−50	−100	−150	−200	−250
1	−20	80	30	−20	−70	−120
2	−40	60	160	110	60	10
3	−60	40	140	240	190	140
4	−80	20	120	220	320	270
5	−100	0	100	200	300	400

     b. Maximin—2 units

     c. Maximax—5 units

     d. Max. Exp. Profit—4 units

3.5 a. Max. Exp. Value—Choose Plan A

     b. Max. to pay for perfect information = 40

3.6 a. Risk Averse

     b. U($24 million) = 64

     c. Investment C—Exp. Utility = 75.3

Chapter 4

4.1 A is optimum; it is 1.4 more profitable than B.

4.2 b. Wait one year; if "worse"—must have surgery; if "same"—choose surgery; if "better"—never have surgery.
     Exp. Measure of Goodness = 8.28.

4.3 b. Hire 3 people; Exp. Cost = $150.30

     c. Break-even hourly overtime rate = $9.90

4.4 b. Use the consultant; if "good"—choose A; if "bad"—choose B.

     c. Max. fee I'd pay consultant = $48,000.

     d. Max. fee I'd pay for perfect information = $80,000.

Chapter 5

5.1 a. DRG-1—10 patients
   DRG-2—15 patients
   DRG-3—40 patients
   DRG-4—270 patients

   b. $136,000

   c. $3,000; no change

   d. Operating margin would increase to $190,000.

5.2 a. No home visits; 10 clinic cases; cost = $7,750

   b. 12 home visits; 10 clinic cases; 22 patients served

   c. 12 home visits; 10 clinic cases; 564 staff hours used (36 unused staff hours)

5.3 Pharmacy—15,000 square feet
   Radiology—25,000 square feet
   Laboratory—10,000 square feet
   Revenue—$840,000

Chapter 6

6.1

	Hos. A	Hos. B	Hos. C	Hos. D
Plant 1		6,000	3,000	5,000
Plant 2	4,000			5,000

Cost—$122,460

6.2 Multiple optimal solutions:

	D1	D2	D3
HC1	0	8	0
HC2	0	0	6
HC3	6	0	4
HC4	0	7	0
HC5	0	5	0

	D1	D2	D3
HC1	0	8	0
HC2	0	6	0
HC3	6	0	4
HC4	0	1	6
HC5	0	5	0

Cost—$187.50

6.3 Physician 1 to Committee B
Physician 2 to Committee A
Physician 3 to Committee D
Physician 4 to Committee C

6.4

	A	B	C
HC1	5	0	0
HC2	3	5	0
HC3	0	2	5
HC4	0	5	0

Cost = $400

6.5 Physician 1 to Clinic A
Physician 2 to Clinic C
Physician 3 to Clinic B
Physician 4 to Clinic D

Chapter 7

7.1 a. 0.5 patients
b. 10 minutes
c. 0.0125

7.2 a. 12 hours
b. 0.5 nurses
c. $4.00

7.3 a. 0.0016
b. Most I'd pay is the equivalent of $9.33 per hour.

7.4 a. 0.2831
b. 0.1365
c. 1.91

7.5 a. 0.0503
b. Not necessarily; it depends upon how people react to a busy signal compared with being put on hold.

7.6 Min. hourly cost of waiting time = $14.03

7.7 Optimal number of phlebotomists = 8; total cost = $129.50 per hour

Chapter 8

8.1 PERT Activity Report

No	Code	Name	Beg.	End.	Exp. t	ES	LS	EF	LF	Slack
1	1	Obtain CON	1	2	20.0	0.0	0.0	20.0	20.0	0.0
2	2	Cost Estima	2	3	4.0	20.0	20.0	24.0	24.0	0.0
3	3	Obtain Fund	3	4	16.0	24.0	24.0	40.0	40.0	0.0
4	4	Build New C	4	5	32.0	40.0	40.0	72.0	72.0	0.0
5	5	Hire Add'l	4	6	16.0	40.0	57.0	56.0	73.0	17.0
6	6	Install Equ	5	8	6.0	72.0	72.0	78.0	78.0	0.0
7	7	Publicity	4	8	12.0	40.0	66.0	52.0	78.0	26.0
8	8	Train Add.	6	7	4.0	56.0	73.0	60.0	77.0	17.0
9	9	Close Old C	7	8	1.0	72.0	77.0	73.0	78.0	5.0
10	D*1	Dummy--1	5	7	0.0	72.0	77.0	72.0	77.0	5.0

Where columns are headed: Activity (No, Code, Name), Events (Beg., End.), Planning Times (Exp. t, ES, LS, EF, LF, Slack).

Expected Project Duration: 78

The following critical path(s) apply.

```
1   2   3   4   6
```

PERT Network (Heavy arrows give critical activities. TEs and TLs appear below events.)

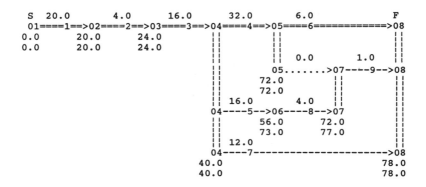

8.2 PERT Activity Report

```
     Activity              Events              Planning Times
    -----------------    ---------    ------------------------------------------
    No Code   Name       Beg. End.    Exp. t  ES    LS    EF    LF    Slack
    ---------------------------------------------------------------------------
    1  1      Pour Founda  1    2     5.0    0.0   0.0   5.0   5.0   0.0
    2  2      Build Walls  2    3     7.0    5.0   5.0  12.0  12.0   0.0
    3  3      Build Roof   3    4     5.0   12.0  12.0  17.0  17.0   0.0
    4  4      Install Plu  3    4     3.0   12.0  14.0  15.0  17.0   2.0
    5  5      Install Wir  3    4     4.0   12.0  13.0  16.0  17.0   1.0
    6  6      Plaster Wal  4    5     4.0   17.0  17.0  21.0  21.0   0.0
    7  7      Paint Walls  5    6     2.0   21.0  21.0  23.0  23.0   0.0
    8  8      Install Lt.  6    7     1.0   23.0  23.0  24.0  24.0   0.0
```

Expected Project Duration: 24

The following critical path(s) apply.

```
    1    2    3    6    7    8
```

PERT Network (Heavy arrows give critical activities. TEs and TLs appear below events.)

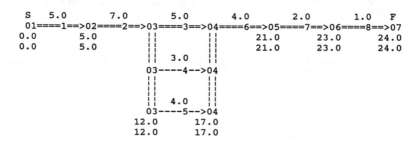

8.3 PERT Activity Report

Activity			Events		Planning Times					
No	Code	Name	Beg.	End.	Exp. t	ES	LS	EF	LF	Slack
1	1	Obtain CON	1	2	20.0	0.0	0.0	20.0	20.0	0.0
2	2	Relocate X-	2	3	2.0	20.0	20.0	22.0	22.0	0.0
3	3	Remodel Spa	3	5	16.0	22.0	22.0	38.0	38.0	0.0
4	4	Hire MRI Te	2	4	12.0	20.0	27.0	32.0	39.0	7.0
5	5	Order MRI	2	7	20.0	20.0	24.0	40.0	44.0	4.0
6	6	Install MRI	5	6	5.0	38.0	38.0	43.0	43.0	0.0
7	7	Train Perso	4	6	4.0	32.0	39.0	36.0	43.0	7.0
8	8	Schedule Pt	6	7	1.0	43.0	43.0	44.0	44.0	0.0
9	D*1	Dummy--1	2	5	0.0	20.0	38.0	20.0	38.0	18.0
10	D*2	Dummy--2	3	5	0.0	22.0	38.0	22.0	38.0	16.0

Expected Project Duration: 44

The following critical path(s) apply.

```
1   2   3   6   8
```

PERT Network (Heavy arrows give critical activities. TEs and TLs appear below events.)

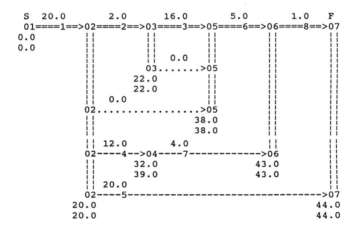

8.4 a. PERT Network (Heavy arrows give critical activities. TEs and TLs appear below events.)

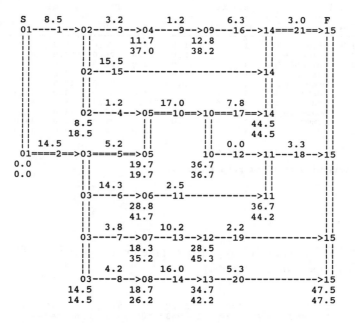

```
   S   8.5          3.2          1.2          6.3          3.0   F
   01----1-->02----3-->04----9-->09---16-->14===21==>15
   ||          ||          11.7         12.8         ||          ||
   ||          ||          37.0         38.2         ||          ||
   ||          || 15.5                                ||          ||
   ||          02---15--------------------->14        ||          ||
   ||          ||                                     ||          ||
   ||          ||  1.2        17.0         7.8  ||    ||          ||
   ||          02----4-->05===10==>10===17==>14 ||    ||          ||
   ||          8.5          ||          ||          44.5          ||
   ||         18.5          ||          ||          44.5          ||
   || 14.5           5.2    ||          ||   0.0         3.3  ||
   01====2==>03====5==>05        10---12-->11---18-->15
   0.0          ||          19.7         36.7         ||          ||
   0.0          ||          19.7         36.7         ||          ||
                || 14.3              2.5                ||          ||
                03----6-->06---11----------->11        ||
                ||          28.8                   36.7          ||
                ||          41.7                   44.2          ||
                ||  3.8        10.2         2.2  ||
                03----7-->07---13-->12---19----------->15
                ||          18.3         28.5         ||
                ||          35.2         45.3         ||
                ||  4.2        16.0         5.3  ||
                03----8-->08---14-->13---20----------->15
               14.5         18.7         34.7              47.5
               14.5         26.2         42.2              47.5
```

b. The following critical path(s) apply:

    2   5   10   17   21

Expected Project Duration: 47.5

c. .7364

8.5 a. PERT Network (Heavy arrows give critical activities. TEs and TLs appear below events.)

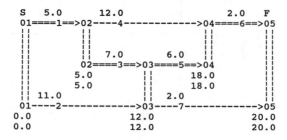

```
      S   5.0          12.0                    2.0   F
      01====1==>02----4------------->04====6==>05
      ||          ||                          ||          ||
      ||          ||  7.0          6.0  ||          ||
      ||          02====3==>03====5==>04 ||          ||
      ||          5.0          ||         18.0          ||
      ||          5.0          ||         18.0          ||
      || 11.0                  ||   2.0  ||
      01----2------------->03----7----------->05
      0.0                      12.0              20.0
      0.0                      12.0              20.0
```

b. The following critical path(s) apply:

 1   3   5   6

Expected Project Duration: 20

Total Cost = $882.

c. Crash 1 by 1; crash 5 by 1. Three paths become critical:

 1   4   6

 1   3   5   6

 2   5   6

Total Cost = $1,002.

Chapter 9

9.2 Day 11 exceeds the upper control limit at 2 sigma level.

9.3 No mean value exceeds the upper control limit at the 2 sigma level. Week 5 is below the lower control limit.

All range and standard deviation values fall within the control limits at the 2 sigma level.

9.4 Weeks 1 and 3 exceed the upper control limit at the 2 sigma level. For 9 of the 15 weeks, the mean wait time exceeds the standard of ten minutes.

9.5 Definite improvement in the second year.

Chapter 10

10.1 The manager should order 60 metal walkers. Orders will need to be placed every 3.6 months.

10.2 Order quantity—78

Reorder level—47

10.3 Optimum staffing level—16 home health aides

10.4 Order quantity—459

Reorder point—167

10.5 22 new persons should be recruited

APPENDIX B
Name and Address List of Software Vendors

ABC FlowCharter
Micrograx, Inc.
1303 E. Arapaho Road
Richardson, TX 75081
800/676-3110

Arena
Systems Modeling Corp.
The Park Building
504 Beaver Street
Sewickley, PA 15143
412/741-3727

@RISK
Palisade Corporation
31 Decker Road
Newfield, NY 14867
800/432-7475

BestFit
Palisade Corporation
31 Decker Road
Newfield, NY 14867
607/277-8000

CA-SuperProject
Computer Associates
1 Computer Associates Plaza
Islandia, NY 11788
800/642-7690

Crystal Ball
Decisioneering Inc.
1380 Lawrence St. #610
Denver, CO 80204
303/292-2291

DPL
ITP
Education Division
7625 Empire Drive
Florence, KY 41042
800/354-9706

eHOP
Crunch Software Corporation
7677 Oakport Street, Suite 470
Oakland, CA 94621
510/562-9900

Excel
Microsoft Corporation
One Microsoft Parkway
Redmond, WA 98052
800/420-4782

Floorplan Plus for Windows
ComputerEasy International Inc.
414 East Southern Avenue
Tempe, AZ 85282
602/829-9614

Flow Charting
Patton & Patton Software
   Corporation
485 Cochrane Circle
Morgan Hill, CA 95037
800/525-0082

GammaCAD
Gamma Software
P.O. Box 8191
Fort Collins, CO 80526
800/747-9960

GPSS/H
Wolverine Software Corporation
4115 Annandale Road
Annandale, VA 22003
703/750-3910

Grabit Pro
Software Excellence by Design, Inc.
14801 North 12th Street
Phoenix, AZ 85022
602/375-9928

Hijaak
Inset Systems
71 Commerce Drive
Brookfield, CT 06804-3405
203/740-2400

Lotus 1-2-3
Lotus Development Corporation
55 Cambridge Parkway
Cambridge, MA 02142
800/223-1662

MedModel
ProModel Corporation
Healthcare Systems Division
One Castle Hills
1100 NW Loop 410, Suite 700
San Antonio, TX 78213
210/366-8768

Micro Saint
Micro Analysis & Design
Simulation Software, Inc.
4900 Pearl East Circle
Suite 210E
Boulder, CO 80301
303/442-6947

Project
Microsoft Corporation
One Microsoft Parkway
Redmond, WA 98052
800/420-4782

QSB+
Quantitative Systems for Business
   Plus
Prentice-Hall, Inc.
Inglewood Cliffs, NJ 07632
800/223-1360

QuickQuant
Alamo Publishing
7083 Commerce Circle, Suite G
Pleasanton, CA 94588
510/463-3798

SAS
SAS Institute, Inc.
SAS Campus Drive
Box 8000
Cary, NC 27512
919/677-8200

SLAMSYSTEM
Pritsker Corporation
Suite 500
8910 Purdue Road
Indianapolis, IN 46268
317/879-1011

SPSS for Windows
SPSS Inc.
444 North Michigan Avenue
Chicago, IL 60611
800/521-2494

STORM
Storm Software, Inc.
24100 Chagrin Boulevard
Cleveland, OH 44122
216/464-1209

Time Line
Symantec Corporation
10201 Torre Avenue
Cupertino, CA 95011
800/628-4777

UniFit
Averill M. Law & Associates
P.O. Box 40996
Tucson, AZ 85717
602/795-6265

Visio
Shapeware Corporation
1601 Fifth Avenue
Suite 800
Seattle, WA 98101-1625
206/467–6723

INDEX

ABOUT THE AUTHORS

Charles J. Austin, Ph.D., is Professor in the Department of Health Administration and Policy in the College of Health Professions at the Medical University of South Carolina. He previously held the position of Professor and Chair of the Department of Health Services Administration at the University of Alabama at Birmingham. He has served in numerous academic leadership positions, including President of East Texas State University, Vice President for Academic Affairs at Georgia Southern College, and Dean of Graduate Studies at Trinity University.

Austin has served on the health administration faculties of the University of Colorado, Xavier University, Trinity University, University of Alabama at Birmingham, and the Medical University of South Carolina. His nonuniversity experience includes service as Chief of the Information Systems Division of the National Library of Medicine and systems analyst for the Procter and Gamble Company.

Austin has served as Chairman of the Board of Directors of the Association of University Programs in Health Administration, Chairman of the Editorial Board of *The Journal of Health Administration Education*, and Chairman of the Accrediting Commission on Education for Health Service Administration. He is a faculty associate of the American College of Healthcare Executives and a member of the Healthcare Information and Management Systems Society. He is the author or coauthor of five books and monographs and numerous articles published in professional and scholarly journals.

Austin holds a B.S. degree (summa cum laude) from Xavier University, an M.S. in health administration from the University of Colorado, and a Ph.D. from the University of Cincinnati.

Stuart B. Boxerman, D.Sc., is Associate Professor and Deputy Director of the Health Administration Program at Washington University School of Medicine, St. Louis, Missouri. He has over 20 years of experience teaching quantitative methods to health administration students. In addition, he has taught similar quantitative courses to engineering administration as well as graduate architecture students.

In addition to his academic experience, Boxerman has industrial experience as a radar systems analyst with a defense contractor, a power system planner with an electric utility, and director of information systems for an architectural firm. Throughout his health administration teaching career, Boxerman has worked with numerous hospitals on a variety of systems analysis, process improvement, and planning projects. Current research activities include projects in patient-focused care, care path development, process reengineering, and cost-benefit analysis.

Boxerman has been active in task forces and faculty forums sponsored by the Association of University Programs in Health Administration. These activities include the Quantitative Methods Task Force, the Information Management Faculty Forum, and the Curriculum Development Task Force for Information Management. He is a Diplomate of the American College of Healthcare Executives, and a member of the Operations Research Society of America, the Institute of Management Sciences, the Association for Health Services Research, and the Healthcare Information and Management Systems Society. He has been the author of numerous articles published in professional and scholarly journals.

Boxerman holds B.S. and M.S. degrees in electrical engineering and a D.Sc. in applied mathematics and computer science, all from Washington University, St. Louis.

Tee H. Hiett, Ph.D., is Professor in the Department of Health Services Administration in the School of Health Related Professions of the University of Alabama at Birmingham (UAB). He joined the faculty at UAB in 1972 after having served several years on the faculty of the School of Industrial and Systems Engineering at the Georgia Institute of Technology in Atlanta, Georgia. Over the years at UAB, he has developed courses and educational materials to teach graduate students in such subjects as quantitative methods, operations research, management science, engineering economy, mathematics, computers, information systems, and financial management.

Hiett's primary areas of interest include microcomputers in health systems and education and systems simulation with microcomputers. He has interest in international activities, having served in projects in the Republic of Panama, Guatemala, China, and Saudi Arabia.

From 1985 to 1991, Hiett served as Director of the Master of Science Program in Health Services Administration. During the school year of 1992–1993, he served as Acting Chair of the Department of Health Services Administration.

Hiett holds a B.S. degree from Auburn University and the M.S. and Ph.D. degrees from the School of Industrial and Systems Engineering at the Georgia Institute of Technology, where he specialized in health systems.